Memo

ROEDEAN

The First 100 Years

Compiled by Judy Moore

Consultant Editor: Ann Voigt

S.B. Publications

This book is dedicated to all Old Roedeanians,
but especially to Caroline McDowall.

First published in 1998 by S.B.Publications
c/o 19 Grove Road, Seaford, East Sussex, BN25 1TP.

© Copyright 1998 Roedean School.

ISBN 1 85770 152 6

Designed and typeset by JEM Lewes
Printed by Island Press
3 Cradle Hill Industrial Estate, Seaford, East Sussex BN25 3JE
Telephone: 01323 490222

CONTENTS

Front cover: Roedean School, 1998 (inset) 1927 pupils model the Roedean djibbah
Back cover: The Cloisters from a painting by 1920s pupil MVM Sanders

INTRODUCTION

ONE hundred years ago Roedean School began in the buildings it occupies today. For the thirteen years prior to 1898 the school, founded by the Misses Lawrence, and known as Wimbledon House School, was located in Sussex Square, Brighton.

To those who have no connection with the school, its name perhaps conjures up a preconceived image – Enid Blyton's *Malory Towers*, Muriel Spark's *The Prime of Miss Jean Brodie* or even *The Belles of St Trinians*. Another impression formed by many who have merely passed by is of a Colditz on the Cliff, an awesome and forbidding fortification. To Old Roedeanians, none of these is an accurate description.

Throughout the century the school has been home to thousands of girls from all over the world. They all have special memories of their years at Roedean, some of which are very vague after the passage of time, others as firmly fixed as if they had just left.

Today's girls are especially interested in what happened 'in the olden days'. I had not been at the school for very long when I realised that in order to answer the questions posed by present pupils, I would have to ask former pupils for the information. A questionnaire was sent to Old Roedeanians and this book is the result of that research.

I am grateful to many people for their help. Firstly I must thank all the Old Roedeanians who have contributed. Many have taken a great deal of time and effort to convey an accurate picture of life as they remember it. However, one must be mentioned by name. Caroline McDowall's story, a book within a book, encapsulates the texture of school life for one particularly imaginative girl in the middle of the twentieth century.

When, during World War Two, Roedean pupils were evacuated to Keswick, HMS Vernon occupied the school, and I am grateful to all of those Old Boys who so enthusiastically built up a picture of life at Roedean during the war.

Others who have given generous help include Lesley Morrill, Patricia Metham, Sally Packer, Sue Stanway, Caroline Quentin, Frances Hillier, Steve Knight, Lesley Raymond, Ian Stranack, Colin Bailey and Roy Foster. Finally, I must thank my husband Michael for his long suffering support during the entire undertaking.

Ann Voigt
Librarian, Roedean School

FOREWORD
by Lavender Patten

I EXPECT it is just as cold today, out on the playing fields of Roedean, as it was in 1955 when I first arrived at the age of ten. I can still see knees of varying degrees of pinkness as we battled up and down the pitch, waving our lacrosse sticks in the face of icy cold winds off the sea, encouraged by Miss Stenning, the games mistress, who had no problem in making herself heard over the natural elements. Nowadays I'm sure the girls wear tracksuits.

Roedean has been very successful over the years in keeping in tune with what parents want for their children, and what girls need and respond to. The facilities that the school now offers are a vast improvement on what many of us enjoyed – or sometimes endured! But throughout its first 100 years, Roedean has provided its pupils with a first-class education and the opportunity and encouragement to make whatever they wanted of their lives. I particularly appreciate the care and kindness of my house mistress, Miss Ratcliffe, and the enthusiastic teaching of many other staff.

This book is a real piece of social history; it will give some idea to the present generation of what life was like in the old days and bring back memories for us old girls. It is marvellous that so many people have responded with such enthusiasm to Ann Voigt's questionnaire, which started the ball rolling. Coming out in the school's centenary year, these memories of Roedean will make a splendid contribution to the celebrations.

Lavender Patten

Dorothy, Penelope and Millicent Lawrence, the joint founders of Roedean School.

Editor's Note

This book has been compiled entirely from information supplied in response to Ann Voigt's questionnaire (for the questions asked see Appendix C, page 173). It is not intended as an accurate history of Roedean, but rather a reflection of how the pupils of the last one hundred years saw life in a single sex boarding school, what they thought of the living conditions, the staff, the food, leisure activities, games and the enforced intimacy of house life.

A great deal of angst was caused by the problem of how best to identify, and date, the contributors without impeding the flow of the text. Should they be called by their maiden names, or married names? A list of contributors is given in Appendix B, page 170, but it was thought too awkward for readers to turn to the appendix to identify each Old Roedeanian. The solution chosen, whilst far from perfect, is to give the current name, followed by the maiden name and the dates between which the contributor was at school – for instance, Jane Hopkins (Meredith 1922-27). Thereafter, within the same chapter, the contributor is referred to as Jane or Jane Hopkins. The dates given are those supplied. In some instances they are a year or so out from those on the school's data base.   **JM**

INFLUENCE OF ROEDEAN

'My three years at Roedean were among the happiest of my life. I still have friends from school, and I have benefitted a great deal from what was taught me whilst there.' Marie Palmer (Francis 1924-26)

'The Roaring Twenties, that is the accepted image; a reckless, syncopated decade, in which the Bright Young People danced their promiscuous way down the primrose path which led them to world slump. If that conception is anywhere near the truth, I can only say that there were pockets of resistance; and one of those pockets was Roedean. No place on earth can have been more resistant to the spirit of whoopee than Roedean in the nineteen-twenties. The World, the Flesh and the Devil – unholy trinity – were kept at bay by a *cordon sanitaire* flung around the buildings by the Public School Code . . . To the west, on a clear day, we could see the Palace Pier glittering in the sunshine. But Brighton and Hove could not have been more inflexibly out of bounds had they been Sodom and Gomorrah. In any case, we did not have the bus fare.' Alison Adburgham (Haig 1925-29) in *Punch*

'Teenagers have many problems growing up . . . and nothing was available to students in the way of counselling services. The idea seemed to be that the subjection or repression of negative feelings was the way to build strength of character and self discipline – the stiff upper lip syndrome. This was probably the tenor of the times and certainly, those of us who survived, did achieve those goals. It was a harsh kind of life and not well suited to the creative or artistic temperament.' Iris Ingram (Clark 1929-31)

'I think the generation of 1920-30 schoolchildren benefitted from the tragedy of an older one. The staff were exceptional people, many of whom had not married because of the slaughter of men in the 1914-18 war. In those days, normally, married women did not work and if they had been able to marry we would have lost them.' Alison Leakey (Holmes 1932-36)

'I am grateful for the number of things we did other than academic lessons. Art was important, drawing, painting, pottery (including all the firing and glazing), not only gym but dancing as well, including country dancing from different countries. We all had to learn carpentry (which stood me in good stead later in life). There was a lot of acting and producing plays, and music, climaxing in the school orchestra. Whatever your bent you could find an outlet for it.

'An excellent thing about Roedean is that it did not spend so much time in trying to teach the "right answer" as it did in encouraging you to say what you thought was right and giving reasons for it.'

'There is only one thing that I am sorry Roedean left me with and that is my voice. I don't think the school itself was ultimately responsible but it certainly helped to develop it. I am afraid that it must be considered as a prime example of the pre-war, female, middle class, public school prefect's voice.'
Sonia Bicanic (Wild 1932-38)

'The legacy which my five years has given me are: a lasting foundation in the Anglican faith, a passionate love of science, the example of what a good school can be and with which I can compare all others, lasting friendships.'
Lavinia Greenwood (Malim 1933-38)

'I am very appreciative of my years at Roedean. They taught me firstly how to accept discipline, then gradually learn how to dispense it. Also, all that rotten food and dreadful weather and fresh air made me very tough and healthy.'
Gweneth Cannon (Feather 1931-36)

'The role of prefect was the best possible experience for management in one's future career.' Dilys Jordan (Dunn 1939- 44)

'None of us, I think, realised at the time how well and how broadly we were being educated by, probably, the last generation of teachers who were among the ablest of their peers, who taught because male-dominated professions were not open to them.' Anon (1930s)

'One memory which I always recall when visiting present-day girls' schools and hearing their cheerful chatter, is the fearful silence of Roedean. When the bell went for lesson change Miss Tanner emerged from her study, automatic files were formed and dead silence reigned. The same applied when filing up to bed. I cannot think what benefit was gained.'
Pauline Filipowska (Crommelin-Brown 1935-38)

'Roedean taught me to adapt and to hold fast to those values I treasured – and to make very good and enduring friendships.' Gay Sharpe (Clarke 1952-59)

8

HOUSE LIFE

'It was definitely a family unit.'
'The prefects furnished their studies like charming
sitting rooms and gave Sunday tea parties.'

TO the Lawrence sisters, school was an enlarged family, and their aim was to make the boarding houses as much like their pupils' homes as possible. Penelope, Dorothy and Millicent became housemistresses of, respectively, Three, One and Two, and Miss Hyde was housemistress of Four when Roedean opened in 1898. Each housemistress had her own bedroom, drawing room and study. The girls, too, had drawing rooms and preparation rooms and each girl had her own desk in the Junior or Senior Prep Room (JPR and SPR)). There were bedrooms, with from one to three beds, rather than dormitories, and studies for the prefects. In the 1920s the attics were opened to make extra bedrooms in each house, and what became known as Heaven was created. The houses were linked to School House by a long central corridor and by the back communication corridors, called the bunny runs. Work started in 1907 on Junior House, on a site to the east of the main school.

The house was home and the rest was school. 'It was definitely a family unit and there was a great sense of belonging,' said Ina Murray (Bidder 1927-33). 'The house was all important,' agreed Keturah Crawford (Robinson 1918-22) 'We chose who we wanted to room with and went about in cliques of about four to seven people, who could be various ages – some got left out, of course.'

The system of house life that Betty Kent (Bidder 1925-30) remembered, existed almost untouched until well into the Sixties. 'Each house had its own characteristics, depending no doubt on the housemistress and deputy housemistress, who were helped by a matron and a housekeeper,' she said. 'We knew everyone in the house very well, but we only knew girls from our form in other houses. In the house we did not remain in our year group at all but made our own set of friends. Once we left the School House and dropped back into house life it was very united.'

'House loyalties were very much *de rigueur,*' Helen Waterhouse (Thomas 1926-31) agreed. 'Contact with other houses came only during lessons and

9

through games, music and art clubs.'

'In Number Three House we considered ourselves normal,' Sally Miall (Leith 1935-36) wrote. 'People in Number One were known to be debutante material – brainless, idle and vain. We knew that they wore make-up in chapel and went to places like Juan-les-Pins for the summer. Number Two House was very sporty, too sporty we thought. On a cold rainy day the current joke was to say "Number Two is probably out practising at the nets". Number Four was a strange house, full of talented people, some of whom were foreign.'

The 'sets' that were formed among the girls in the upper school were described in detail by Sonia Bicanic (Wild 1932-38). 'You were formally asked: "Would you like to belong to our set?" The set I belonged to was quite large and included several generations. Janet was the oldest and best looking with the kind of creamy skin usually only to be found in novels. She was not specially good at anything but people liked to be with her. Her close friend was Clemency, very tall and spindly, and the best fast bowler in the school, which made her specially desirable in any set. The third member of the older trio was Daphne, who fitted in well with Janet and Clemency.

'My best friend from almost the moment I went to Number Three was Ali (Alison). Since she was Janet's sister we were very early on included in her set. I was very proud to belong so quickly; some people hovered as singles or pairs for a long time, and a few never were, or perhaps never wanted to be, included in any set. But I was always secretly anxious – was it me, Sonia, who had been asked to join the set or was it merely Sonia, Ali's best friend? I still remember the flush of inner pleasure when we were sitting in winter in some warm cupboard or linen room, probably a forbidden place, and playing truths, and one of the questions was "Who would you like to have a bath with?" Janet said "Sonia". Then for the first time I really believed that I was there as myself if Jan would like to have a bath with me.'

There were sets, and there were inner sets. Paula Haigh (Cannon 1934-38) remembered being on the edge of a set and 'left out of inner crowd activities'. She said: 'I was ambitious but always outclassed, very keen but very little use at sport, not sociable at all. I had no gossip, hence was only on the fringes of a gang of friends. One day, trying to get noticed, I deliberately side-stepped the official "Goodnight Miss Batho". I was gloating at missing it when, half undressed, I was summoned by a prefect and forced to go into the study and say "Goodnight Miss Batho". It was this same sense of seeking the limelight that made me fake a faint when I was in Chapel and try to give myself a temperature by drinking the contents of my hottie.'

House life was strict, but friendly. 'The housemistress kept a watchful eye on our health and behaviour, and sometimes read to us in her drawing room,'

Number Three House was home to a dynasty of McEwans from 1903 to 1972. Among the seven girls pictured sitting on a wall in 1905 are Bertha McEwan and her cousins Margaret and Ida McEwan. Bertha's sisters, Ethel and Elspeth, were also pupils. Bertha's daughters, Janet, Alison and Mary Hollington, Ethel's daughters, Audrey and Joyce Tyndale and Elspeth's daughters, Rosemary and Carol Sworder, followed their mothers, as did Ida's daughter, Joy Duncan. The third generation were Alison's daughters Frances, Jane and Sheila Carroll and Rosemary's daughters Janet and Kay Messer.

said Pauline Norman (Davenport 1928-33).

The prefects furnished their studies like charming sitting rooms and gave Sunday tea parties, inviting a mix of year groups and occasionally staff. They cut dainty sandwiches and ordered cakes from Brighton – Fullers' cakes, with frosted icing, were the best loved. The guests stuffed themselves from 4pm until it was time for the Sunday lecture at 5.30pm. If any food were left the prefects stood in their study doorways offering leftovers to the scum.

Girls could be at a distinct disadvantage if they were not the daughters of Old Roedeanians (ORs). 'In my house (Number Three) were the daughters of three sisters from the Lawrence era, plus some cousins,' said Pauline Filipowska (Crommelin-Brown 1935-38). 'They were all (nearly all) charming and delightful girls, about nine of them, and they were constantly promoted in the hierarchy and had an easy ride.

'In addition there were five of Miss Tanner's nieces, so those of us who were more ordinary landed up fairly low in the pecking order.'

11

In the Junior House there was a ticking list. 'You had to tick your name if you had a bowel movement, otherwise you got a rhubarb pill,' said Sheila Oberdieck (Miller 1935-43).

The war brought its disruptions. In 1939 Number One House was taken over by the Francis Holland School, which had been evacuated from London when war threatened, and the Number One girls were split between the three other houses. To her astonishment, Joan Cripps (Squires 1935-40) found they were 'just as amiable as Number One'. Sylvia Perry (Denis-Smith 1936-40), who had not got on with the housemistress in Number One, loved the upheaval, and went into Number Two where she had a much better time. Ruth Maclean (Gimson 1936-41) moved into Number Four, which she found far more agreeable than Number One.

When Roedean was evacuated to Keswick for the duration of the war, house life was less formal in many ways. There was greater freedom for girls to go out and about, and the houses, principally through lack of space, were on closer terms. A relaxation of the stringent house rules allowed more fun into the girls' lives and they took full advantage, enjoying all manner of frivolity that would have attracted serious censure in the pre-war years in Brighton.

In their free time girls knitted socks and balaclavas 'for the gallant Finns attacked by the brutal Russians,' Rosamund Huebener (Benson 1937-42) said. 'But, from 1941, we knitted for the gallant Russians attacked by the brutal Germans!'

Eve Bysouth (Dowson 1939-46) wrote, in her Christmas term, 1941, diary: 'After we had undressed into our pyjamas Vivian Lloyd's wireless was turned on and we put on bed jackets and danced about like the modern women who wobble their bottoms'.

In Keswick girls found themselves doing things that the carefully sheltered pre-war pupils would never have believed, such as Margaret Bashford's (Kay 1940-43) scavenging for coal on the railway bank for the fire in Miss Middleton's tiny bedroom.

Keswick's freedoms were sorely missed when the school returned to Brighton. It also became very wearing to new girls, said Joanna Burrows (Hamilton 1945-49), to hear the phrase 'when we were in Keswick' endlessly repeated. By the time Caroline McDowall (Gamlen 1955-60) was at Roedean, Keswick had moved into the misty world of school lore and legend. 'It was mentioned and referred to, a bit like the Middle Ages or the Lawrence sisters,' said Caroline.

The exclusivity of separate house life was quickly reinstated with a curfew at tea-time cutting off all social contact between girls in different houses. Carol Macdonald (Bennett 1945-48) had this to say of it: 'We knew our own house vertically, in both directions; other houses horizontally in our own years.'

'Your house was your focus until you were older, and very hierarchical,' said Sarah Curtis (Myers 1945-53), who was in Number Four. 'Each morning and evening there was bobbing, when you shook Miss Middleton's hand, saying "Good morning/good night Madam" whilst semi-curtseying.'

In the immediate post-war years rationing still had an iron hold and Nancy Gatzke (Vickerman 1946-48) remembered that there were fires only on Sunday afternoons in the GDR (Girls' Drawing Room) and on Wednesday evenings in the prep room because of coal shortages. Card playing and jacks were not permitted on Sundays, and if music were played on the wind-up gramophone it had to be classical. *The Times, The Daily Telegraph, The Daily Graphic* and *The Illustrated London News* were supplied to the GDRs and girls used to 'tig' (claim) photographs of the royal family by writing 'tigged by so and so', Ann Hulme (Prall 1945-50) explained.

'House curfews in the evenings prevented visits to friends in other houses, said Nicola Frith (1950-57). 'One had to go through the central heating conduit, which was dirty and very hot in winter. There was great consternation if one was caught in another house. The staff did not appear to know how we travelled.'

Nicola's contemporary, Susan Carlyle (Blatch 1951-54), was in Number One. 'The housemistress, Barbara Patterson, was very formal,' she said. 'We only saw her if we had done wrong.' Number Three, during the same period, was 'a very happy house with a real family atmosphere,' according to Jane Jervoise (Newnham 1953-57).

Stephanie Chapman (Watson 1952-57) said that relationships with the housemistress and staff were always extremely formal but this formality would be relaxed on occasions. 'When a friend's father died, she was surrounded by a very caring atmosphere and her friends, at the request of the staff, took it in turns to leave classes to comfort her.' she said. This contrasts with Carole Allsop's (1972-78) experience twenty years later. 'I was summoned with my sister one morning to Mrs Ellwood's study and told my mother was not expected to live much longer, then sent off to continue a normal school day,' Carole said. 'A week later the same thing happened, but this time the news was that my mother had died. I was fourteen and received no adult support or counsel from a single member of Roedean's staff. The only mention made was years later when I had broken a school rule and Mrs Davey said, in reprimanding tones, "What would your mother have thought?".'

Elizabeth Harvey (Frison 1974-77) confirmed the stiff-upper-lip attitude of the Seventies. She said: 'One of the worst things about school was the absence of any compassionate adult figures.'

The segregation of houses, and even of years within the same house, appeared to become more pronounced during the Fifties and Sixties. Diana Hinman (Hunter 1955-62) had two sisters in another house, and the only time they could meet, officially, was on Sundays after chapel. Ann Fernandez (Barnes 1957-65) had a sister, three years older, in her own house, but never spoke to her.

'We were not allowed to send sealed letters out of the school,' said Katharine Coleman (Mackenzie 1961-66). 'We had to post them, unsealed, with our initials pencilled on the back of the envelope, in the house postbox, and the housemistress would then check that we were not writing to anyone disapproved of (boys, of course, or the Press). When I was once particularly unhappy I wrote about it to my parents, but the housemistress refused to let me send it as she said it would upset them. On another occasion, during a postal strike, my mother drove all the way to school to deliver my birthday cake and presents, but was not allowed to see me. I saw her arrive and then drive away again. She had been told I was unavailable.'

Girls were not allowed to telephone their parents, ever, and they were not allowed to hold money. Katharine explained: 'At the beginning of term the housemistress logged in and "banked" our pocket money in a cash box. We had cheque books to pay for stationery and for chapel collections. Some of the cheques were reclaimed from our own monies, but most were just tagged on to our school bill (more groans from the anguished parents).'

Caroline Quentin (Druiff 1954-60) remembered that, towards the end of her schooldays, the parents of one of the girls in her year, in Number Two, gave a television to the house. 'We were allowed to watch it occasionally – I believe I saw Z Cars sometimes,' she said.

'The GDR was the meeting place for the Lower Fourth to Upper Fifth, so we mixed a certain amount,' said Susan Child (Locket 1955-61). 'Massive and furious games of Racing Demon round the large table are an abiding memory. Also the joy of using the gramophone – kept in the housemistress's study to be released at the weekend only. Two Way Family Favourites, on the radio, with Cliff Michelmore was Sunday morning's staple diet after compulsory letter writing.'

Baths were taken on a rota basis – Monday, Wednesday and Friday or Tuesday, Thursday and Saturday. Nobody bathed on Sunday. Katharine Coleman had the complicated job, as Head of House (Four), of working out the bath rota at the beginning of term.

'I think we had some six baths and well over seventy girls, who all needed a bath twice a week (maximum allowance). Each bath slot was allocated to two girls, so the first one had to hurry up to allow the second to fill the bath and jump in. It was difficult to ensure that people were not stuck having both their morning and evening bath on consecutive days. We had plenty of deodorant which we rolled about our persons, but we did stink terribly. Few of us in my early years there were lucky enough to have tampons, and the limited supplies of sanitary towels made having periods very unpleasant indeed.'

Katharine also remembered the twice weekly house readings, for the younger girls, after prep. 'We would be read seriously expurgated versions of the classics while we did our embroidery, fiddled with our knitting needles or quietly dozed. *Wuthering Heights* was a total puzzle, whole chapters being cut out as unsuitable (there might have been a kiss or an embrace to send us wild). Even *Pride and Prejudice* was lost on us as half the characters were cut out, and we could not understand why Lydia was in such disgrace.'

Bullying rarely occurred but Sarah Saunders-Davis (Osborn 1960-67) had to put up with a certain amount of teasing because, she said: 'I came from an old titled family – something of a rarity in my day, less so in my mother's. I used to dread writing my Sunday letter home in case anyone saw the address.'

'Our house life certainly changed when we started to use the new dining hall and discovered how much more informally other houses treated their inmates,' Katharine said. 'We stopped having to produce plays and other house events as the girls gently and firmly refused to devote their precious private time for them.'

The Seventies brought other benefits, one of which was a payphone that enabled girls to call home, and there was greater freedom to choose which television programmes to watch. Fiona Watson (1972-77) recalled avidly watching *Upstairs Downstairs* on Sundays, and the odd thriller on Saturday nights.

'My chief memories of House Two are of planning escapes (and getting caught); getting my drawers searched for cigarettes; having illicitly ordered pizzas removed just as we took the first bite; and finding Mrs Scott lying in wait for me – on my bed when I returned one night from visiting a friend,' said Zoe Green (1988-95).

Junior House life had mixed benefits, according to Sarah Saunders-Davis. 'I rather enjoyed the tiny cubicled dormitories and the walks to the main school for daily chapel. Miss Pike was a strict housemistress with a strong religious upbringing. Her scripture lessons were always excellent, particularly if we were daring enough to ask her to interpret certain words, like harlot, and the *Songs of Solomon*.'

'Not so pleasant were the communal bathrooms where five or six girls bathed and washed together. The ferocious matron insisted on "tops off" every morning – sheer purgatory to growing, sensitive girls. And changing our top navy knickers to grey (complete with a pocket for a hankie) was an after lunch ritual – a quaint old Roedean custom. Birthday girls were allowed a cake and a tea table with chosen friends. My mother always provided, via a bakery in Brighton, a huge confection of chocolate with fresh strawberries and cream.'

Sheila Oberdieck recalled some girls' thoughtless cruelty in her Junior House years. She remembered 'inquisitions' run by class leaders; the cold shouldering of refugee pupils from Nazi Germany; and how one small girl was ostracised for being seen to enjoy books.

Carolyn Phillippo (Williamson 1961-69) found Junior House staff remote and keen on discipline. 'Bullying was a major problem,' she said, 'particularly by the older year groups. It was not done to "tell" so you just had to survive.'

Ann Henley (1970-78) remembered the excitement of sweets at weekends and the fun of swinging on the cubicle bars. 'Main School was very much each house to itself and relationships with previous Junior House friends were distanced as a result of being separated into different houses, which was a shame.' she said. 'Lawrence House opened during my time and was a great idea. We all got quite fat there, however, as we could help ourselves freely to kitchen supplies.'

'Lawrence House was great,' Seema Sharma (Bahal 1983-85) agreed. 'We all lived on toast, and everyone was always behind the squash courts smoking, and hiding from the staff.'

Junior House in the 1920s.

16

Four senior girls from 1929 model the Roedean djibbah

SCHOOL UNIFORM

*'We were very proud of this peculiar and unique garment,
and there was quite a lot of grumbling when a well-designed and
comfortable tunic for gym and games was introduced.'*

MANY pre-war Roedean pupils admitted to fading memories of much of school life, but the one thing they all recalled clearly, and with great affection, was the djibbah – a uniform unique to Roedean.

'We wore the most sensible garments I think I have ever come across,' said Phyllis Bower (Hopkin Morgan 1917-21). 'They were called djibbahs – why, I don't know. The ordinary, everyday one was made of a rather thick, coarse serge, in navy blue, and it had a sort of yoke in a deep cream canvas, with RS embroidered in scarlet in the central point. The sleeves were not quite to the elbow, but almost, and underneath we wore a special sort of white blouse with a little bit of red embroidery around the neck. They were wonderful garments. They had to be made in a special place and they were considered to be terribly expensive in those days; I believe they were three guineas. But you kept the same one the whole time you were there, until it was skin tight and probably nearly up to your bottom. You were respected all the more by the shortness of your djibbah.

'They were very comfortable, very warm and they never slipped out of place. They must have been beautifully cut, because nobody ever looked untidy, not ever. You couldn't look untidy in a djibbah because it didn't move. There wasn't a single button in the whole thing.'

Girls had to have both summer and winter weight djibbahs, and many ORs remarked on the coarseness and 'hairiness' of the serge.

In the afternoon they changed into prettier djibbahs, made to order, and worn longer – midway between ankle and knee, Phyllis remembered. 'You could choose lovely colours and the insets, instead of having RS on them, had the most beautiful embroidery. They were made in a special place in London and you'd be sent a pattern book to choose your colour. Under them you would wear a silk blouse, which might be in some colour to tone with the embroidery. I had some very pretty djibbahs. My first was black velvet, with the inset embroidered with pansies, and with pale yellow sleeves. I had one blouse in mauve and two in yellow.'

Sylvia Lawrence, the designer of this remarkable garment, which became Roedean uniform in about 1905, was said to have been inspired by the dress of North African tribesmen. The purpose seems to have been to prevent girls from becoming figure conscious.

Girls vied with one another to have the most beautiful afternoon djibbah, Ruth Conolly (Warren 1921-26) remembered. They were the only opportunity girls had for individual expression as absolutely no clothes from home were allowed in the early years. In winter they were usually of velvet, and in summer of silk or shantung. The afternoon djibbahs had a long life, being 'inherited' by a younger girl as an older one left, and they were much treasured. Betty Kent (Bidder 1925-30) recalled a terrible family row when her mother threw away a black velvet djibbah of which Betty was the fifth, and very proud owner. 'It had been worn by three heads of house and I was considered lucky to own it,' she said.

'If a girl grew very tall, her housemistress might insist upon a new djibbah, but this was deeply resented,' Alison Adburgham (Haig 1925-29) wrote.

Sonia Bicanic (Wild 1932-38) had a favourite djibbah in deep purple velvet with a pink, wild silk yoke embroidered with dragons in dark pink, purple and green. 'Some people had herons or little houses with flowers or gnomes embroidered on them. Horses, dogs and fish swimming over green silk were also favourites,' she said. 'Most people thought a lot about how their afternoon djibbahs would look and some had them embroidered by mothers, aunts or grandmothers.'

The yoke could have either full or half embroidery. Gwen Hollington (Paxton 1932-37) had only half and longed for 'a full herbaceous border instead of one solitary heron'. Barbara Marshall (1935-38) had an afternoon djibbah in saxe blue velvet with a blue silk yoke embroidered with pink sweet peas.

'The shame of wearing a home-made djibbah was hard to bear,' said Nancy Kueffner (Hurst-Brown 1937-40), whose thrifty mother, a superb seamstress, made Nancy's djibbah. Another girl who felt uncomfortable was Sally Miall (Leith 1935-36), from Roedean South Africa, who always felt conspicuous because her South African version was navy, with a green yoke.

'We were very proud of this peculiar and unique garment, and there was quite a lot of grumbling when a well-designed and comfortable tunic for gym and games was introduced in about 1927,' said Betty Kent. Until then djibbahs were all purpose dress, used both for classes and for games.

Only one OR, Keturah Crawford (Robinson 1918-22) recalled wearing a cream, long-sleeved woollen top beneath the djibbah. Others were specific about a white or cream, long-sleeved, round necked blouse having a single button at the back of the neck. The blouse was short, ending just under the bust, with a drawstring, and so, said Ruth Maclean (Gimson 1936-41), 'was no use as a blouse on leaving school and facing wartime clothes rationing'.

During the djibbah era, which came to an end in the late Forties, the uniform also included a navy blue coat and skirt, white blouse and tie for Sunday wear, and for travelling to and from school; top coats and blazers; velour hats for winter, panama hats or boaters for summer; gym tunics fitted at the top and with inverted pleats at the sides (from the late Twenties); pleated shorts and Aertex shirts (from the middle Thirties); overalls and cloaks. The cloak was more than just a prosaic outer garment. 'We lived in them,' said Keturah Crawford. 'They were easier than top coats to fling on going out in the grounds, and we sat on them in the summer.' Girls snuggled into their cloaks in class during raw winters when piercing

Two 1920s versions of the coat and skirt: left, with a longer, belted coat; right, with a shorter, double breasted coat.

winds howled through the windows, they wore them over their top coats when it was very cold and used them as extra blankets on their beds.

'When I arrived in Junior House in 1937,' Vivien Allen (Hallett 1937-43) wrote, 'the uniform had been modernised. The round-necked navy tunics with a deep pleat at each side, but flat in front, which I think had formerly been worn for games, had just replaced the morning djibbah, but girls who still had djibbahs could wear them if they liked. Tunics had to be three inches off the ground when kneeling. By the time we reached the upper school we bitterly resented this because we thought it made us look childish. On the quiet we used to let our hems down a bit – they were sold with big hems to allow for growth. If caught at the next inspection we were made to take them up again, which we resented even more.

'For games we had just-above-the-knee pleated navy shorts, which were more like divided skirts, and beige Aertex blouses. After games you had to change down, which meant right down to your (presumably sweaty) vest, but it didn't go in the wash; it was hung over the back of your bedroom chair to air and put on again next day. You then changed into your afternoon djibbah. I have fond memories of a rust-coloured djibbah with salmon pink inset which had a square rigged ship in full sail embroidered on it.

'With morning tunics we wore thick brown wool stockings and with our

A girl's overall was an essential part of the uniform, both for work in the Studio, and here, in the carpentry shop. The photograph is dated 1949.

afternoon djibbahs, black ones, and there were knee-length socks for games. Soon after I arrived the uniform stockings were changed to beige lisle for all occasions, which we thought a great improvement.

'Underwear was awful and the bane of our lives. Does anyone else shudder at the memory of the mis-named liberty bodice? Navy bloomers, which had to be worn for a whole week, had white cotton linings underneath, which we were allowed to change only twice a week. I had been used to clean knickers, vest and socks every day and had to grit my teeth to force myself to put on dirty ones.

'Once the war and clothes rationing began, the school felt parents could not be forced to spend precious coupons on afternoon djibbahs. We still wore tunics in the mornings and those of us who had afternoon djibbahs often clung to them, but new girls could wear their own frocks in the afternoon.

'On Sundays we had hideous navy blue coats and skirts with a panama in summer and a navy velour po-hat in the winter. Cloaks were replaced with navy macs during the war. By about 1942 it became a mark of distinction to still wear one's cloak and afternoon djibbah as new girls did not have them.'

The uniform list was formidable and every item had to be marked with a Cash's name tape – even the hair bands and ribbons (navy, and of a prescribed width). Everything had to be exactly as laid down, with the exception of girls' pyjamas. Clothes lists were checked on arrival and departure each term. The uniform had to be laid out on the bed and counted and checked by a prefect, Sylvia Hatfield said. 'Luggage was sent well ahead by PLA (Passenger Luggage in Advance) and brought to our rooms on the first morning. We came back with a suitcase containing essentials for the first night, so spent the first and last days of term in our coats and skirts. We mended our own stockings but everything else seemed to be dealt with somewhere. We each had our own sheets, pillowcases, towels and table napkins. They were not sent home each holiday but returned at the end of our school life.'

In the mid-Thirties senior girls were permitted a regulation style silk dress for afternoon wear and for school dances. This was available in blue, green and yellow. A special version was ordered for the visit of Princess Alice, Countess of Athlone, on the school's fiftieth anniversary. Margaret Leakey (Holmes 1932-36) recalled the kindness of Emmeline Tanner on this occasion. Margaret's father had died, leaving her mother 'very hard up' and the Head told Margaret that her mother would not be billed for the special dress. 'I think Miss Tanner paid for it herself,' Margaret said.

The introduction of clothing coupons during the war years meant some relaxation of the strict uniform rules. The cloaks worn at Brighton gave way to heavy macs and pixie hoods at Keswick, said Dilys Jordan (Dunn 1939-44),

21

'and in wartime it was possible to have stockings re-footed as they required three coupons new'. Djibbahs were still worn by those who had them, but new girls went straight into gym tunics – or grym tunics as the Freudian gremlins in Nancy Gatzke's (Vickerman 1946-48) word processor described them.

'None of us minded wearing uniform. It was practical and comfortable and a great social leveller,' said Rosemary Read (Brett 1943-51). 'No matter how rich you were, money could not buy a more sophisticated tunic.'

Pupils of the Forties wore their own dresses after tea – 'very exciting when the New Look came in in 1949,' said Diana Kay (Johnson 1945-51).

Merry Rushton (Newth 1948-54) remembered the visits to Dickins and Jones to update the school wardrobe. 'We were given armchairs to sit on and a pretty woman who called us sweetie served us personally for many years. We loved our visits to her. In my day girls looked either like little girls, or like their mothers. There were no fashions in between. We felt more grown up and glamorous if we rolled our cardi sleeves up to just below our elbows – and were constantly being told to pull them down to our wrists again. One very pretty girl had darts put into her tunic; she looked wonderful but the rest of us looked shapeless.'

By the Fifties the uniform consisted of a tunic, round neck, short-sleeved cotton blouse for summer, long-sleeved Viyella blouse for winter, long brown wool socks for winter and short white socks for summer. Lisle stockings were still worn, although most girls had graduated to nylons. Shoes were brown and there was an afternoon woollen dress in light or dark blue, brown or red, and a striped summer dress in house colours. During the evenings and on Saturday afternoons senior girls wore home clothes – dresses, skirts and sweaters, but never trousers.

'The sheer loopiness of the uniform provided much entertainment over the years,' said Fiona Hodges (Ewart 1967-72). 'The tunic – waisted with a six gored skirt, and no attempt to fit across the bust, was nearly as restraining as any corset and its skirt could be briskly shortened to jail-bait length with a handy stapler. A totally useless headscarf had to be taken on every outing; it was not waterproof, could not be used as an emergency hanky and was only any good as a draught excluder.

'As few had the same sort of uniform at any one time (some had items handed on by their sisters' for example) we were quite varied to look at. There were hideous, itchy, box pleated culottes for sport, a boxy navy suit, Arthur Ransome type sports jerseys and a vastly gathered gingham dress for summer.

'In 1967 we wore uniform all day long and in the evening changed into a dress in sage blue, moss or cerise, looking suspiciously as if the 1951 Festival of Britain had been its original showplace. The best item was the cloak. It was versatile, warm and hid a multitude of sins.'

'Care was taken to ensure that we always looked well in our uniforms,' Katharine Coleman (Mackenzie 1961-66) said. 'Our housemistress used to police the hedges behind school on summer Sunday afternoons to catch girls sunbathing with their socks down.'

Navy blue knickers were still compulsory in the Sixties and Seventies and Deborah McKinlay (Hewitt 1968-77) said that junior girls had to lift their skirts as they came downstairs in the morning to show Matron that they were properly dressed.

The much hated boater and the long established Roedean coat and skirt were phased out in the Seventies and more practical skirts and shirts came in. Jeans made their appearance, for 'mufti', in this decade. A few years later girls were permitted to go into Brighton in their jeans – but not in short skirts. Sarah Bale (1984-92) and a jeans-clad group would set off for Brighton with short skirts in their bags, and change in the NCP car park.

Zoe Green (1988-95) wore chinos, a paisley shirt and penny loafers 'to be cool' when she was a junior, but by the time she was a senior, cool meant cords, boots or trainers, tight T-shirts and men's shirts.

Charlotte-Anne Nelson (1990-97) wrote about the altogether more relaxed attitude to uniform in the Nineties. Except in the top two years when 'home' clothes were worn, she said, the uniform was 'blue knife pleated skirt, striped shirt (red/white or blue/white), V-necked jumpers, school tracksuit (navy or sky blue), games skirt (blue) and an Aertex shirt'. The staff, she added, had an obsession for tucked-in school shirts and 'an ongoing battle was waged on this issue'.

PRE-WAR pupils were allowed no jewellery – except a wristwatch and a cross on a chain if permission were given – and no make-up. 'Unthinkable!' said Rosemary Naegele (Hurst 1938-40), who remembered a sub-prefect, returning from a Sunday afternoon outing with her parents, being sent from the supper table by the house head girl for wearing a faint smear of lipstick. Not many years later, at Keswick, girls were using talc as face powder, Vaseline for lip gloss and pencil to define their eyebrows. Some used clear nail varnish – the Peggy Sage make, which lasted for years.

By the end of the Forties, when annual dances were arranged for senior girls with the boys of Brighton College or Lancing College, girls were allowed a little powder and a hint of lipstick. Janet Garwood (Ing-Simmons 1947-51) recalled the first dance at Lancing College. 'A return invitation was not proffered at the time,' she said, 'the excuse being that there were not enough lavatories on the ground floor! There were at least a dozen!'

Elizabeth Thomas (Cawdry 1953-57) remembered being reprimanded by her housemistress for returning to school wearing lipstick after a day out with her parents. She was informed that this transgression delayed her promotion to sub-prefect.

Girls' hair had to be cut short, or plaited. Angela Pirie (Hunter 1922-30) recalled one girl being sent home for arriving with permed hair. In the very early years of the school pupils wore compulsory snoods to keep their hair from their faces. Later pupils wore hairnets for games on windy days.

In the Twenties a hairdresser came from Brighton once or twice a month to wash the girls' hair, and cut it if necessary. Bobs were popular then, Eton crops a few years later. There was no opportunity for styling in those days, hair just dried 'all over the place'. For a time, Pamela Thalben-Ball (1939-44) said, there was a fashion for girls to roll their hair around a ribbon to form a circle on the head 'a la Dame Emmeline Tanner'.

After the war, visits from 'crummy old visiting hairdressers' resumed. 'They used carbolic soap instead of shampoo, and ruined our hair,' said Gillian Grenfell (Manley 1946-50). 'Our hair was blasted by a very hot dryer, then we had to go to Matron's room and sit by her electric fire to ensure that it was really dry. By the time we got to our rooms it was bone dry and unmanageable!'

Even as late as the Sixties the girls' hair was washed only once a fortnight – 'unless our parents wrote to ask for a weekly wash', Katharine Coleman said. 'When I was in the Sixth Form, I was granted the privilege of using my own shampoo and washing my hair more frequently, but Matron had the only dryer and there was limited space in her little room for us all to get our hair dry. There were no power points in our rooms and we were not allowed our own dryers.'

Today, Roedean girls wash their hair daily if they want to and styles are no longer dictated. However the line is drawn on some of the more bizarre hair styles. Charlotte-Anne Nelson remembered the time when her best friend, who had beautiful long, blonde hair, dyed it bright green (the dye said aquamarine). 'Huge trouble ensued and, I believe, an addition was made to the school rules that prevents hair being dyed "unnatural colours",' Charlotte-Anne said.

MEAL TIMES

*'Garbage Pudding was a strange composite in which we swore we
could recognise the remnants of earlier puddings that week.'*

A N abiding memory for many, many ORs who were at school between the
wars is that they were always hungry. Another is Roedean rice pudding.
There are women in their eighties who can still, in their imaginations, taste the
warm, comforting creaminess of this much loved alternative second course.

From the very first, all meals were eaten in the separate houses. The staff
attached to the house, or the prefects, sat at the heads of the long tables at
lunch (dinner) time. Keturah Crawford (Robinson 1918-22) described the
scene: 'Prefects chose different girls to sit at their tables each term – a cross
section of ages – and presided at other meals, except tea, which was a buffet
with hunks of bread, marge or jam, and a tea urn.' Evelyn Condy (Finch
1918-23) remembered only one member of staff being present at supper
'whilst the others had a good dinner downstairs'.

'The food was adequate but dull. We had delicious wholemeal wartime
bread and marmalade,' Keturah said. 'The milk was horrible, supplied by a
local farmer who had no TT testing, so it was boiled and had lumps of skin
floating about in it.' Ruth Conolly (Warren 1921-26) thought the food was
'abominable'. 'No fresh vegetables, no fruit, tough cabbage leaves and no
variations through the year,' she said, 'but on Tuesdays we had good macaroni
cheese, and tea time every day was bread soaked in jam – no butter.'

'The dinners were quite good, but the supper was poor and tea after games
was bread and butter *or* bread and jam,' said Myra Cohen (Doniger 1922-28).
'On Wednesdays there were buns for tea, and on Sundays, cake.'

'Muck' was Erica Haxworth's (Silver 1924-30) favourite Sunday pudding.
This was chocolate blancmange covered with coconut.

Eluned Macmillan (Carey Evans 1929-39) remembered, especially, the suet
puddings – 'dead baby's arm' and spotted dick – and Barbara Harvey (Woods
1929-35) recalled the 'awful watery stews'.

Sonia Bicanic (Wild 1932-38) said there were special names for some of the
puddings, such as Carthaginian Brick for a rather hard sponge with jam on top,
Swimming Bath for a batter pudding with golden syrup in the middle, and

Garbage Pudding 'for a strange composite pudding in which we swore we could recognise the remnants of earlier puddings that week'.

'The food was so appallingly bad that it sticks in my memory to this day,' said Pauline Filipowska (Crommelin-Brown 1935-38). 'What we were given in Number Three House defies description. The best supper was jacket potato and cheese, which we had on Mondays.' Yet some found the food adequate, and there were fond memories of kidneys on toast for breakfast, of beans on toast and sardines on toast, and of cold salad on Sundays, when the servants had the day off.

Beryl Barns (James 1932-36) thought the food good, except for greens, which nobody ate on principle, she said. 'It was even better after a dietician was appointed and we were given barley sugar after lunch each day. Then Number Four House found that other houses had pudding at supper and they did not. They complained and got their pudding!'

Winsome Whitham (Butler 1930-36) said: 'We were not allowed any tuck, so five of us walked over to the next village and bought some warm doughnuts which Jane stuffed into her bosom, and she got all greasy before we got down the lane to eat them. It was worth it.'

In Betty Kent's (Bidder 1925-30) time there were eight girls to a table – a prefect, two or three subs and five or six scum (younger girls). 'This was organised at the beginning of term and again at half term. Each group moved

A house dining room in the 1920s

round the room to a different position each week. There was a staff member at each table at lunch. This was a fairly formal meal and you were expected to take your turn at making conversation with the mistress.'

The practice was called 'sitting up to' the mistress. 'Some staff were easy but conversation with Mrs FitzMaurice Kelly was terrifying,' Mary Marriott (Thompson 1937-40) said. If a French teacher were at a table, all present had to speak in French. 'Making polite conversation to staff was a wonderful training for social occasions in the years to come,' said Dilys Jordan (Dunn 1939-44).

'The housemistresses were present at breakfast but for tea and supper the prefects were in charge,' said Betty Kent. 'Breakfast was at 7.30am, lunch at 1.15pm, tea at 4pm and supper at 7.30pm. Good table manners were expected and we always used table napkins, kept in a bag for each table. We were not supposed to ask for anything, but could ask a neighbour if there were anything she required, and she was bound to say "No thank you; would you?" and see that what was needed was passed to you.'

Other than the prefects' Sunday teas, when younger pupils were invited to sandwiches and cakes, the only opportunity for girls to enjoy something out of the ordinary was when parents arrived to take them to tea, or when a cake or a box of fruit was sent for a birthday.

Keswick kippers remain a memory no wartime pupil will ever forget. Bridget Furneaux (Malden 1939-43) said she could still smell the kippers that were piled in boxes on the station platform when she passed on her way to class in the waiting room. Jenifer Fairpo (Fowler 1941-48) became skilled at taking a kipper to pieces, concealing it in its skin and not eating any.

'The war meant severe rationing and the introduction of the national loaf, a quite disgusting grey, on which we spread a concoction of mustard, pepper and salt when the minute butter and margarine rations had been eaten,' Dilys Jordan said. 'We were always hungry.'

Eve Bysouth's (Dowson 1939-46) Keswick diary tells of the arrival of a parcel from home, containing 'some carrots and turnips and a few apples'. Eve wrote: 'The food I put in my suitcase for safety . . . After lights out I passed round some of the carrots and turnips . . . June Lawrence came along to our room and I gave her some little carrots, she refused to take a big one.' The girls regarded raw vegetables as a treat almost on a level with buns and cakes.

Pamela Thalben-Ball (1939-44) thought Keswick food was 'shocking'. 'Soup was cold and congealed, vegetables were not properly washed (I found tadpole legs in my cabbage) and there was often newspaper in the boiled rabbit.' Pamela recalled the lunch time when a bottle of squash was placed on each table. 'An important visitor was coming. Our bottle contained a dark liquid. We sent it up to the staff member at the top of the table first. She put a little in her glass and filled it up with water, made a wry face and sent it back to us. Winnie Prieswerk and I realised it was cooking sherry. Naturally we finished it and I remember floating through the first class in a happy haze.'

Ann Hulme (Prall 1945-50) remembered the time she found a finger-shaped bandage in the pudding. 'I bore it triumphantly to the kitchen, hoping to be given something else; instead I received a lecture from the housekeeper about the starving in Africa!'

Keswick ORs spoke of salty kippers, sour porridge containing weevils and endless ill-cooked cabbage. 'We did not go hungry, but we *were* hungry,' Belinda McKinnel (Bleckly 1940-49) said. One starving girl remembered making scrambled, powdered egg in the bathroom on a little camping stove and, another time, returning from an outing with a round loaf fitted snugly into her panama – which she clutched to her chest to avoid detection.

'Once a week we had starvation breakfast (nothing cooked),' said Ann Portnoy (Levy 1944-47), 'and supper was sometimes a boiled potato floating in soup'.

'I was one of the fish and chip group who slipped out of school after supper in our dark cloaks, across Fitz Park, over the little river bridge and into the town's back streets,' Diana Poole (Wilson 1938-47) admitted. 'Two of us would go in and the rest of the gang waited outside. We ate the fish and chips walking back across the park. After a few weeks we were reported and Dame Emmeline summoned us. There were about thirty of us. I was demoted from being a sub-prefect for one term as I had proved myself "irresponsible".'

At Keswick, pupils were allowed sweets for the first time. They formed a queue outside the second housemistress's room to receive their weekly ration of two ounces of chocolate or four ounces of toffees or boiled sweets.

Back in Brighton the food was little better, ORs said. 'I particularly remember macaroni pudding, which I found singularly unpleasant,' said Jenifer Fairpo. Jill Sheppard (Robbins 1948-53) found meals 'terrible and monotonous'. She especially hated 'frogspawn' (tapioca with a blob of jam) and 'worms on toast' (tinned spaghetti).

After close on half a century Bernadette Warrington (Porter 1950-55) had a clear recollection of her first meal at Roedean. 'Supper in Number Two House, on September 20, 1950, consisted of one spoonful of baked beans and one of boiled potato, followed by a small square of very bitter marmalade tart (no custard).'

'The food was OK except for whale meat and Atlantic codfish,' said Janis Elliss-White (Cattley 1947-52). Gillian Van Gelder (Solomon 1946-51) hated the food and ate very little, but she appreciated the 'something else' list for religious reasons. 'Once I was caught putting corned beef into my hanky for later disposal and was told to report myself to the house mistress,' she said. 'I wanted to die!'

One consolation for girls returning from Keswick was the reappearance of Roedean rice pudding – 'delicious, creamy, wonderful,' said Janis. Another was the institution of a snack at 11am, when girls could have cocoa and a bun, or bread and dripping.

Cookery classes were very limited because of continued food rationing and at the end of one term, when the mistress was unable to attend, four girls were told they could cook and eat a full meal. The luxury of choosing what they wanted! The extravagance! 'We cooked the meal, and enjoyed it, only to get a telling off for eating all the food meant for the next three classes,' said Gillian Summersgill (Field 1945-48).

No 'private' food was allowed except for fruit and sweets, which were kept in a locked cupboard. 'After lunch the housemistress would unlock it and a small amount could be taken, but for immediate consumpton only,' said Lily-Claire Reitlinger (Brach 1943-51). 'Private jam for tea was permitted, again kept in a locked cupboard.' Girls found with illicit food stashed in their rooms faced severe punishment.

Sheila Vince (Martin 1954-59) kept a diary of her five years at Roedean and on re-reading it found that all the high spots were food-related. There were birthday teas and match teas, and the famous morning, when school inspectors were present, when coffee was on the menu for *one* day. 'Jaws dropped in amazement all round the dining room,' Sheila had written. In exchange for washing up after a prefects' study tea, she said, girls were allowed to eat the left-overs.

Fifties meals were sustaining but stodgy. There were sausages and mash, 'gorgeous' suet puddings, fish in batter, 'graveyard stew' with dumplings and lots of 'grey mince'. Ants Paradise was tinned apricots with ants floating in the syrup and Ganges River Muck was Caramello pudding. The girls always enjoyed treacle tart made with cornflakes, and cheese on toast, a short term option for morning break. Fried bread with marmalade was a breakfast many ORs remembered, some with pleasure, some with horror.

In the Sixties meals were still eaten separately in the house dining rooms. 'You were not allowed to visit other houses to eat with your friends,' Katharine Coleman (Mackenzie 1961-66) said. 'Breakfast was at about 7.30am. A handbell was rung and we trooped in to our set places at each table. It was pot luck whom you sat with, and you sat with the same group all year in House Four. The most junior sat at the far end and did the collecting of bowls and dishes for the table. Breakfast was cereal (occasionally porridge) and then a slice of bacon and fried bread/toast, a tinned tomato/kipper/haddock/boiled egg on Sundays and glorious sausages on Saturdays. The senior girl would be passed a tiny dish with a half ounce of salted butter and she would carefully draw her knife along the centre of the butter and then crosswise so that everyone on the table could have a tiny piece. There was plenty of white margarine for those whose butter had gone on the second bite.

'We were all so hungry by lunch time. I remember steel dishes containing huge, boiled, floury potatoes and the ghastly, sour, dark green, overboiled, chopped greens. We seldom had sight of peas, french beans, broccoli or any frozen vegetable. Carrots, swede and parsnips were mashed or chopped. We had a great deal of stew, occasionally a very small lamb chop, many rolled, boned, reheated and thinly sliced roast meats. The quality of the food at the time I was there was an absolute disgrace. We had fresh fruit rarely, possibly once a week. We never had salad except in summer. We had no fresh cold milk to drink and no fresh fruit juice. We had to eat everything on our plates.

'Tea was a simple affair of bread, butter and margarine, jam and occasionally cakes and/or biscuits. Plenty of tea, ready mixed with milk. The joy was we could sit with our friends from our own classes in the house rather than the formal mix of classes for other meals. Supper was a hot meal followed by some form of pudding.'

Princess Margaret opened the new dining hall in 1965 and catering at Roedean underwent a revolution. All the school ate together in the hall, while still retaining the traditions of staying together as houses, rotating tables and sitting up to mistresses. The staff ate separately unless allocated to a table. Fiona Hodges (Ewart 1967-72) said: 'Most of the food was edible enough although I remember with rising gorge a kidney stew that appeared at breakfast one morning, the sorbo rubber scrambled egg and the custard that was so solid that it remained standing in a block when the Middle Fourth serving up banged the china jug on the table and the jug shattered – but not the custard.'

Meals remained formal and an ability to converse with staff was essential. 'This could lead to desperate measures,' said Fiona. 'I've never had to discuss cannibalism at table since.'

By the Eighties the meals had improved substantially, a variety of hot foods and salads was available and there were few complaints. The Nineties brought even greater choice with the introduction of a canteen system. 'I always enjoyed school food,' Charlotte-Anne Nelson (1990-97) said. 'There seemed to be a huge variety of salads and main courses and lots of desserts. Tea was always particularly good with lots of cakes and cookies! The food became increasingly adventurous in my latter years, with some exotic dishes. There was always a very relaxed atmosphere over meals.'

HEADS

Penelope Lawrence (1885-1924)

'PL was a truly remarkable woman, an inspired educationalist, remembered with pride, admiration and affection by all who were there with her.'

JUST a handful of Old Roedeanians remember Penelope Lawrence (PL), the eldest of the three sisters (the two others were Dorothy and Millicent) who were joint heads of the school from its earliest days, as Wimbledon House School, in Sussex Square, Brighton.

The sisters were affectionately known as 'The Firm'. With the passage of years former pupils' memories have faded, but Penelope is the one invariably referred to by those ORs who recall the Lawrence era.

Iris Phillips (1916-19) commented poignantly that there was no contact between PL and the girls 'except when someone in your family was killed' and this happened distressingly often during the First World War as pupils' brothers, fathers and cousins fell in the battlefields. Emmie Hess (1916-20), Antonia Joll (Ramsden 1917-27) and Grace Briscoe (1918-25) all liked and admired PL but thought her remote. Grace said that PL spoke to her just once in seven years.

'PL interviewed everyone in their last term and urged girls not to become 'butterflies' but to have careers if possible,' said Keturah Crawford (Robinson 1918-22) 'She was a truly remarkable woman, an inspired educationalist, one in a million and remembered with pride, admiration and affection by all who were there with her.'

Myra Cohen (Doniger 1922-28) arrived late for her first term because of the Jewish New Year, and was received, with her mother, in PL's drawing room. 'Her first words were: "Myra must learn to plait her hair". I was quite frightened. She sat in her armchair and filled it completely. She was very fat and walked with two sticks when I knew her.'

Myra was the first from the Lawrence era to mention the famous PL phrase – 'Now go quickly and quietly to bed' – usually uttered ('or shrieked,' said Myra) in chorus with her by the girls. The phrase went down in school history and was continued by Emmeline Tanner and housemistresses for many years.

31

Emmeline Tanner (1924-47)

*'We were very proud of her when she became a Dame and
felt some reflected glory in her honour.'*

THE girls found Emmeline Tanner more approachable, although only rarely did they see an informal side to her. 'She knew us all by name' was a typical comment from her former pupils who thought her 'a wonderful, humane woman, very wise and kind, but strict'.

'We were slightly in awe of her, but she was always there when you wanted her,' said Marie Palmer (Francis 1924-26). The Headmistress, usually called The Tanner, was also known as Aunt Em because five of her nieces were at Roedean and their name for her was adopted by other girls.

When Betty Kent (Bidder 1925-30) went to Roedean, Miss Tanner had not long been headmistress. 'I think she went through some hard fights,' Betty said, the implication being that, although the Lawrences had retired, their awesome presence

Dame Emmeline with the portrait of herself that now hangs at the entrance to the library

was still felt. 'On official occasions PL and sometimes Uncle Paul (the Lawrence sisters' brother) would be present and expect, and receive, a great deal of attention. But Miss Tanner was a strong character and gradually won the admiration and affection of all the girls. We had great faith in her and she had no difficulty in showing us the difference between right and wrong. We were very proud when she became a Dame and felt some reflected glory in her honour. She was one of the finest, wisest and nicest women I have ever met.'

Sonia Bicanic (Wild 1932-38) considered Miss Tanner to be 'one of the great headmistresses.' Sonia's special memory of her was the fudge making episode. On Sundays there was cake for tea. 'Our favourite school cakes were without doubt Lyons' chocolate cup cakes – only to be beaten, in my opinion, by Fullers' walnut cake. However much we loved cup cakes, we loved fudge more, and so at Sunday teas, especially as there might be an extra cup cake to be filched from someone whose parents had come down at the last moment and so had not been counted out for cake, we would take the chocolate off the top of our cakes, secrete it in paper and then take the butter and sugar that we had been saving for several days in a similar way, to the labs, which were deserted on Sundays. There, over bunsen burners in porcelain dishes on tripods, we would make chocolate fudge, not often but once or twice a year. And there, one Sunday, Ali, Noel and I were making our delicious chocolate fudge when in sailed The Tanner, trailing behind her two prospective parents. "And these are the laboratories," she said in her majestic, level tones. "And here are some gels doing some experiments." I'm sure she couldn't really have thought that we were doing experiments, but we never heard anything more about it.'

Mary Cochrane (Wallace 1926-30) remembered the time that Miss Tanner, who taught scripture, caught her reading *The Seven Pillars of Wisdom* under cover of a Bible. 'She looked, and saw, and never said a thing.'

Former head girl Eluned Macmillan (Carey Evans 1929-39) called her a wonderful head, fair, firm, austere but never harsh. 'I had to report to her but was never tempted to be informal or chatty. She had the respect of everyone. I never heard a word of criticism about her from the girls or anyone else.'

Barbara Harvey (Woods 1929-35) said Miss Tanner was 'a wonderful woman, who knew every child in the school; she was a majestic and formidable presence, with a warm heart, although direct contact was rare'. Pauline Norman (Davenport 1928-33) remembered her as disconcertingly perceptive.

The Tanner sailed around like a galleon in billowing gown and mortarboard. 'She seemed to fill the whole corridor as she swept down it and we flattened ourselves against the wall as she passed,' was how one OR remembered her.

Jean Marwood (Sharp 1937-42) remembered her mainly for her erect stance, 'with bosom well forward' as she stood on the hall platform. 'She always had her hands linked in front and twiddled her thumbs,' Jean said. Miss Tanner reminded Margaret Shimmin (Greig 1946-60) of Margaret Rutherford.

Vivien Allen (Hallett 1937-43) considered one of the joys of Keswick 'was that one saw more of her and got to know her better than I think one would have done at Brighton, where she lived in her own separate house'.

'There was very little contact until one reached the exalted stage of prefect; then one valued the invitations to delicious Sunday afternoon tea,' said Joan Cripps (Squires 1935-40). Tatiana Macaire (Miller 1944-51) felt that the Head 'knew you from the first handshake'. 'You can talk to her like a man,' Sarah Curtis (Myers 1945-53) remembered her father saying of Miss Tanner.

Janet Tucker (Pinney 1946-53) called her 'quite marvellous'. Dame Emmeline, she said, 'thanked us by name when we held the school corridor door open; she remembered everything about us'. Nancy Gatze (Vickerman

1946-48) agreed. 'Sometimes if she saw me she would ask after my older sisters, who had been at Roedean quite a few years before,' she said.

Norah Horobin (1947-61)

*'I admired her enormously. She seemed very
direct, honest and appreciative of effort.'*

'WHEN Dame Emmeline was leaving she gave the school a pep talk on her successor's name. She was *not* to be called The Horror. A prefects' conference decided on The Robin, and worked hard at it. I don't know whether it stuck right down the school,' Carol Macdonald (Bennett 1945-48) explained. The lower three quarters of the school called her The Horror, Elizabeth Thomas (Cawdry 1953-57) estimated, and the upper quarter, The Robin.

Norah Horobin faced an impossible task when she succeeded the legendary Dame Emmeline. She was described as terrifying, stern, efficient, remote, sad, austere, formal and distant, but Janet Garwood (Ing-Simmons 1947-51) remembered thinking her very fair on the occasions that she was sent to the Headmistress. 'She looked tall and imposing; she was very straight-backed and had a short, grey, severe hair style,' she said. A pale cream coloured Pekinese, Ming, followed Miss Horobin wherever she went, Diana Clark (Bishop 1954-59) recalled. The Head, she said, 'was very neatly dressed, always wore a suit and had immaculate hair, with the waves never out of place. She wore red lipstick and had very large, babyish handwriting.'

Miss Horobin's chapel sermons were mentioned appreciatively by many ORs; they were 'excellent and memorable', said Merry Rushton (Newth 1948-54). Caroline McDowall (Gamlen 1955-60) said that her most enduring memory of school was the closing prayer and blessing of the solemn evensongs, 'when Miss Horobin bid us: "Go forth into the world in peace; be of good cheer; render to no man evil for evil; support the weak; comfort the afflicted . . . and finally, whatsoever things are true, whatsoever things are honest, whatsoever things are just, whatsoever things are pure, whatsoever things are lovely, whatsoever things are of good report, if there be any virtue, if there be any praise, think on these things."'

'Miss Horobin was a remote figure who struck awe in one if she passed by,' Merry said. 'Encouragement and valuing the individual did not seem to be part of her code. She was an elitist, perhaps.' Jill Sheppard (Robbins 1948-53) saw her differently. 'I admired her enormously. She seemed very direct, honest and appreciative of effort.'

Merry recalled the time when The Horror sent for the mother of a friend, who was about to take O-Levels. The mother, who lived abroad, duly arrived and Miss Horobin informed her that her daughter was unlikely to pass. 'To which the mother replied,' said Merry, '"Well, Miss Horobin, she wasn't mentally defective when we sent her to Roedean – what have you done to her?"'

Susan Carlyle (Blatch 1951-54) remembered the headmistress as 'always being away at conferences'. Stephanie Chapman (Watson 1952-57) said that on the day she left school and went to say goodbye to Miss Horobin, 'she had to ask me my name. Obviously I had made no more impact on her than she had on me.' A number of ORs revealed that in all their time at school they had not once spoken to Miss Horobin.

Girls who had never known Dame Emmeline had kinder recollections of Miss Horobin. Sarah Saunders-Davis (Osborn 1960-67) said that when Mrs Fort took over 'we found her a rather remote figure without the warmth of Miss Horobin'.

Jean Fort (1961-70)

'She was fiercely fair, and could be devastatingly, quietly cutting.'

KATHARINE Coleman (Mackenzie 1961-66) remembered Jean Fort for her immense height and grace, her sensibility and sensitivity, her sympathy and her support. 'She was fiercely fair, and could be devastatingly, quietly cutting when necessary. She was an excellent headmistress, and was responsible for weeding out those last vestiges of a past era.'

'She tried some informal contact – tea in her house, for example, but we thought that was rather "soft" behaviour by the Head,' said Eva Bull (Schwarz 1955-61).

Clare Holdsworth (Newnham 1956-61) was head girl for Mrs Fort's first term and found her very modern and open minded. Seniors were treated as

adults, she said, 'which came as quite a surprise'.

Jennifer Lebus (Harvey 1960-68) thought Mrs Fort very go-ahead. She introduced welcome uniform changes and relaxed some of the school's more stringent rules. 'The prefects had tea and toast-making facilities in their common room opposite her office, and she came in regularly to chat,' she said.

On one November 5, Jane Heathcote (Seigel 1961-63) had 'fireworks' (sparklers), in her bedroom, and she remembered the telling-off from the headmistress, who called her parents to the school to discuss the 'very serious' misdemeanour.

Mrs Fort was rather aloof, according to Elizabeth Chapman (1963-69). 'She seldom let down her guard.' Gail Maughan (Dawe 1968-72) saw Mrs Fort as a rather vague 'head-in-clouds' woman.

John Hunt (1971-84)

'He was impressive and intimidating – but he had a good sense of humour.'

'WE were always a little in awe of Mr Hunt,' Felicity Russell Heuter (Russell 1968-75) recalled. 'He invited the Sixth Form to a wine tasting at his house, which was nice, but perhaps too little, too late.' Gail Maughan wrote of his 'total inability to communicate with the girls'.

'Mr Hunt was quiet, but a good head,' Caroline Handler (Cohen 1970-76) said. 'He was withdrawn and detached'. Ann Henley (1970-78) called him 'extremely cold and aloof' and Carole Allsop (1972-78) described him as 'stiff and formal'.

Nicola Schrager Von Altishofen (Lovett-Standing 1971-78) recalled the time when Mr Hunt ordered her to plant hundreds of daffodil bulbs on the banks of the drive, for a long since forgotten misdemeanour, and the Head supervised the punishment personally.

Jessica Head (Gardiner 1971-78) said that Mr Hunt 'quickly moved on the terrifying old spinster teachers that we juniors had nightmares about'.

Mary Sgarlat (1974-75) thought Mr Hunt impressive and intimidating, 'until you got to know him – he had a good sense of humour'.

Ann Longley (1984-97)

'She was an excellent administrator and figurehead.'

ANN Longley was very easy to get on with, Nicola Bale (1981-87) said, and Sarah Watts (1986-94) considered her a great asset to the school – 'but she was hopeless at remembering names'. Sarah Bale (1984-92) agreed. 'She never knew anyone's name, even the Bale family who had all four girls at the school.' It may have been that, in her early years, grappling with the complexities of running a community the size of a small village left Mrs Longley little time to get to know every girl's name. Certainly by the Nineties the Head was known to address most girls by name.

'Mrs Longley was a very diplomatic lady,' Sona Shah (1988-90) wrote. 'Our meetings with her were always quite formal, unless we had a prefects' meeting in her house.' Zoe Green (1988-95) had the impression that Mrs Longley was 'more a business woman than an interactive head'.

'She was a little too keen on PR and had not enough contact with the girls, but in retrospect all heads are like that now,' Portia Da Gama Rose (1990-95) said, adding: 'She was an excellent administrator and figurehead.'

Acording to Charlotte-Anne Nelson (1990-97), 'Mrs Longley was always immensely clued up about our academic records and plans'.

THE STAFF

'We had the last generation of staff who dedicated their lives to the school.'
'As she entered the room we rose and without more
ado recited the verbs conjugated with être.'

THE amount of space allowed on Ann Voigt's questionnaire – one inch depth on an A4 sheet – for 'Memories of Teaching Staff: any characters?' was clearly too generous for some ORs who merely answered 'Yes' and 'Very many'. Most filled the space – often in ever smaller writing to cram it all in – and a few abandoned the form and covered page after page. One of these was Fiona Hodges (Ewart 1967-72), who wrote: 'We had quite a selection of people whose eccentricities and personalities etched themselves on teenage memories. I can recall one classics teacher with a swoopily, enthusiastic delivery and amazing Dame Edna glasses; a physics teacher who was a composer in his spare time; the senior Spanish teacher who had the sort of magisterial presence probably enjoyed by Torquemada, and who put people through the two year Spanish A Level course with a fervour and implacability which would not have disgraced the early Spanish missionaries (like them, she got results); the classics teacher who carried her small, yappy dog around with her books in a wicker basket; the art teacher who was a patient woman but who, if pushed too far, could throw the most spectacular, Oscar-level wobbly.

'There were the games staff, all impervious to any climatic variation; the English teacher who sounded by some trick of delivery exactly like Lady Constance de Coverlet (in *I'm Sorry I'll Read That Again*, listened to under the bedclothes); the needlework teacher who was said to be the only NUT member on the staff (an organisation of an apparent radicality which sat ill with this woman's demure exterior and gave her a faint aura of a double life).

'Other diversions included the Greek teacher who was a vegan and went green if you offered her coffee with milk. God knows how she managed to keep warm as she couldn't wear anything suitable, like woolly jerseys.'

Memories of individual staff members are mostly lost to the ORs who are now in their eighties and nineties, but Emmie Hess (1916-20) recalled that, for reasons not explained, she made up a bed each week, on a mattress outside the Chapel, for her 'cello teacher, Miss Theobald. Keturah Crawford (Robinson

1918-22) remembered being in awe of mathematician Marjorie Ford, 'but we liked her enormously. She read to the younger ones and seemed to care and understand us all'. Keturah added: 'Miss Nora O'Kelly taught maths to the dullard (me) for one term and was known to say: "I am not qualified to teach the mentally deficient", and Miss Child gave me a lifelong interest in history.'

Miss Child was 'able to quell unruly Fifth Formers with a look,' said a pupil from the Twenties. 'I was amazed to learn from my OR aunt that when Miss Child joined the staff she was hopeless at keeping order.' Rumour had it, said Josephine Bostock (Hall 1935-41), 'that The Infant (Miss Child) retired to bed to rest upon the Abdication because Dame Emmeline had denied the possibility'. According to Alison Carroll (Hollington 1933-37), Miss Child had steamed fish for lunch every day 'which upset her false teeth'.

By this time Miss Child was frail and elderly and, said Rosemary Naegele (Hurst 1938-40), was not permitted to go out alone when it was windy. 'She had an immense braid of chestnut hair wound round about her head and I could imagine it unravelling as she blew away over the cliff.'

Ella Lemaitre, the founding headmistresss of Roedean South Africa, cuts a dash at Brighton in the 1923 staff play.

'The staff,' wrote Alison Adburgham (Haig 1925-29), 'wore checked wool golf stockings in winter; lisle in summer or the new artificial silk, shiny and flesh-coloured. They wore loose jumpers and skirts with patent leather belts around the hips; in hot weather, sleeveless cotton frocks. They had slave bangles above the elbows, long earrings and long strings of wooden beads. They changed for dinner every evening into beaded georgette or crepe dresses, with fur-trimmed velvet bridge coats. No doubt, in their rooms, they smoked Turkish cigarettes in long holders, but they were never seen to smoke.'

Ella Lemaitre, the classics teacher, who later went on to found Roedean South Africa, was 'a charmer', said Ruth Conolly (Warren 1921-26) and, according to Helen Waterhouse (Thomas 1926-31), was 'alarming, eccentric, inspiring'.

Doris Humphry, who taught carpentry, and art teacher Dorothy Martin, each had a profound influence on the school. Miss Humphry started as a gardener in 1919, and took on the carpentry lessons five years later when the then teacher, a Mr Jay, from Brighton and Hove Grammar School, died. Classes were held in a shed close

39

In the studio, Dorothy Martin gives a lesson in throwing a pot. The tiles, which still line the walls, are the work of pupils from the 1920s and 1930s.

to the studio, on the site of the head's house. Miss Martin, known as DB, joined the classes and is said to have made 'a splendid Pembroke table'. The art teacher was expert at wool work, and she exhibited curtains in shaded wool in Paris. She was blind in one eye and used a magnifying glass for her needlework and paintings. 'Miss Martin was a wonderful artist and teacher,' Beryl Barns (James 1932-36) said.

Dorothy Batho was universally liked and admired by her pupils. 'When I was lucky enough to be with Miss Batho at lunch I enjoyed quick-firing conversations and arguments with her,' Alison Adburgham wrote, and Paula Haigh (Cannon, Pauline 1934-38) said: 'I was very fond of Deaconess Dorothy Batho – for me she was a noble and human person with high ideals I would like to emulate.'

'They were all characters,' said Betty Kent (Bidder 1925-30). 'Most were from Oxbridge or London, with four specialist gym and games mistresses and a number of music teachers. A few very specialist staff came down from London once a week. When I was working for my Newnham entrance exam, with two other girls, we had a maths master from Brighton College; the same may have been done in other subjects. The staff were of all ages, from one straight from Cambridge to others nearing the end of their careers, and they lived a life very like ours, ruled by the bell, as we were.'

Miss Mellanby, who taught English, left to join the prison service in 1935 – as Governor of Holloway some ORs believed. 'We understood she found the inmates there more stimulating to deal with,' said Sylvia Hatfield (Herford 1926-30). Others thought the posting was to run 'a girls' borstal at Aylesbury'. Irene Chaundler (Phoenix 1929-35) remembered Miss (later Dame) Mellanby as strict, but with an excellent sense of humour, and Joan Beaver (Spedding 1930-35) admitted: 'We still try to avoid the use of the word "got".'

Eluned Macmillan (Carey Evans 1933-39) had vivid memories of Elsie Fogerty. 'She was amazing and fascinating. She arrived from London in a taxi once a week and put us through our elocution paces. Her hats belonged in an Edwardian museum.' The 'great Elsie Fogerty' who, it was said at Roedean, trained Olivier, was the founder of the Central School of Speech Training and Dramatic Art.

'Miss Middleton told me at a reunion that she remembered everyone by their handwriting,' Beryl Barns said. Three decades later Miss Middleton was still teaching geography. 'She was my mother's housemistress,' said Sarah Saunders-Davis (Osborn 1960-67). 'Her description of the Trans-Siberian Railway was a credit to any travel agency. She was a total inspiration.'

Wildly imaginative Thirties pupils were convinced that French teacher Thyra Creyke Clark had been a spy in the First World War. 'She had one half closed eye,' said Gwen Hollington (Paxton 1932-37), 'and we claimed she had injured it while looking through a keyhole for the Secret Service.' Miss Clark's excellent European Civilisation class was remembered by Sarah Curtis (Myers 1945-53), as was her 'faintly Parisian raffishness'. She was 'too terribly civilised,' according to Carol Macdonald (Bennett 1945-48). 'Just as I imagine Edith Sitwell, with a voice to match.'

A later generation of Roedean girls suffered the same espionage fever at Keswick. Ann Hulme (Prall 1945-50) wrote: 'One girl, who shall be nameless, reported Tilda (Hilda Leigh) to the War Office for signalling to the Germans! It seems that Tilda was drying her hankies out of her window overnight.'

Mlle Lion was the character best remembered by Margaret Leakey (Holmes 1932-36). 'Her driving was erratic to say the least. I believe she once drove several times round the Quad because she could not remember how to put the brake on. I was told, by Monica Wingate, that a local garage would warn their customers "look out – the Lion is on the road".'

Monica Godfray, an Irishwoman, was an inspirational English teacher, Jean Marwood (Sharp 1937-42) said. 'She had an extraordinary laugh – a deep Ha Ha Ha, so the nickname of Minnie Ha Ha was inevitable when she read aloud.' Several ORs commented on Miss Godfray's curious way of pronouncing 'aren't I' as 'amn't I', and others remembered that she always wore purple. Rosemary Athay (1955-59), who thought that Miss Godfray taught English 'incredibly boringly', said she would not allow the girls to read *Rebecca* 'because it makes murder seem excusable' and hence was a most immoral book. 'Now, I think she may have been right,' Rosemary said. Merry Rushton (Newth 1948-54) recalled the time when she was sitting up to Minnie. 'When I had finished an animated anecdote she said: "Now, Meriel, tell that whole story again but without using your hands".'

Merry loved sitting up to Miss Ketteridge, who 'seemed to bring something of the outside world to conversations at lunch time'.

'Mlle Lavauden, who was Swiss, wore big cameos and entranced us with stories, in French, of operations,' Renee Wheeler (Lempriere 1935-40) recalled. Jean Marwood said she was 'quite exceptional' and Margaret Bashford (Kay 1940-43) remembered collecting mushrooms which, rumour had it, Mlle Lavauden stewed in her room.

Mrs FitzMaurice-Kelly was a brilliant teacher, all agreed, but terrifying. 'She was tall and thin with pale eyes that bored through you,' said Rosemary Naegele (Hurst 1938-40). 'As she entered the room we rose and without more ado recited the verbs conjugated with *être*. On completion we sat down and seized a pencil for the next ordeal – twenty verbs rattled off in machine gun style. Five errors and we had to stay in on Saturday afternoon. Mrs FitzMaurice-Kelly ate lunch in my house every day, finishing her meal with a banana that she peeled daintily with a knife and fork. I had nightmares about her for years, and I still can't speak French, but I know the verbs conjugated with *être*.'

Miss Tredgold, who left Roedean for the headship of Cheltenham Ladies' College, her old school, was an inspired teacher of mathematics, her former pupils agreed. Gwen Howe (Lawes 1949-52) retained clear memories of her as 'a tall, slim and austere lady, almost fearsome – I remember with respect and gratitude a brilliant and exceptionally dedicated teacher (did we really call her Topsy?). She often comes to mind when I am struggling with a crossword because legend had it that Miss Tredgold never came to breakfast without first having completed *The Times* crossword.'

Miss Lloyd Williams, housemistress of Number Two, always addressed her girls as 'my darlings'. 'Officially she taught chemistry, but she taught us many, many other things as well – travel, life, values; she was a wonderful woman to whom I am eternally indebted,' said Naomi Turner (Myers 1942-46). 'Unpredictable, and affectionate to those she liked,' was how Gillian Pemberton (Cameron 1944-48) remembered her. Carol Macdonald (Bennett 1945-48) said Lloydy Bill had tremendous personality, and a fierce temper. 'We used to say nicotine rather than blood flowed in her veins, but she was very likeable and absolutely fair minded.'

Miss Will, the biology mistress, was remembered for her repetition of 'the spitogyra is a long green filament . . .' and Miss Fyleman was remembered as the teacher whose green dress was eaten by a Highland cow while she was bathing in a tarn at Keswick.

'My life has been shaped by the caring influence and encouragement of Mary Middleton, my housemistress, and Barbara Russell,' Jillian Gordon (Albury 1939- 48) said.

Miss Middleton, who taught geography, was the housemistress of Number

Four in Katharine Coleman's (Mackenzie 1961-66) time. 'She was kindly, if very old fashioned in her rules and manners. Tiny, rather like a Mrs Tiggywinkle, she had a good sense of humour and ran a very tight ship. She had charisma and was liked,' Katharine said.

'Miss Woodcock became housemistress in Miss Middleton's wake. She taught English. Her original intention had been to run a finishing school in her beloved Austria where she had studied piano. Alas, thwarted by war, she was destined to work out her disappointments on our unsatisfactory souls. Everything became "too distressing . . ." which we gleefully mimicked.'

Joan Baron, who taught dancing, was a gifted choreographer and talented actor. 'On one final lesson she gave us worldly advice,' Elizabeth Hornby (Aston 1950-56) remembered. 'It was: "When you don't know what to do with your hands, don't do *anything* – they look perfectly normal by your sides".' Dilys Jordan (Dunn 1939-44) wrote: 'She was a great raconteur, and her stocky figure wasn't enhanced by the short red silk tunic she wore over black woollen tights.' It was rumoured, Diana Clark (Bishop 1954-59) said, that Miss Baron had 'a metal hip'.

Dilys remembered Joan Spearing as a keen fell walker with an inspiring and infectious love of English literature, and Miss Gulich, she said, 'took an immense delight in encouraging would-be actresses by inviting her theatrical friends to visit. A recital of poetry by Edith Evans and Peggy Ashcroft in 1940 was particularly memorable.'

Red-haired maths teacher Miss N O'Kelly 'threw things at you – compasses usually' both Lindy McKinnel (Bleckly 1940-49) and Frances Makower (1942-47) recalled.

Miss MacSweeney was remembered for her elderly cocker spaniel and her 'wee grey car'. Ann Hulme and Gillian Van Gelder (Solomon 1946-51) were among willing students permitted to take the dog, Berry, for walks. Another teacher's pet that Ann remembered was Pushkin, a splendid grey cat belonging to Miss Mortimer, the English teacher, a woman 'who blushed very deeply and easily'.

'Miss Butcher was one of the most unlikely teachers I've ever met,' Fiona Hodges said. 'Unpredictable, sharp-tongued (and sometimes bloody-minded), conscientious, interested in her pupils, a mine of information on 20th century affairs ("Well," snapped one colleague; "She's lived through most of them!") and opinionated about historical personalities in the way people are when they've lived with their subject long enough. Ruthless, demanding, acerbic, she marked your work comprehensively and with a thoroughness I wasn't to meet again until reading Ancient History at Oxford. She taught me the first rule of historical writing and research – read *round* your subject. She wouldn't let you accept something at face value. If you put forward one side of a question, she'd immediately produce the other.

'Miss Butcher's other asset (apart from the demonic teaching style which I've never dared emulate) was her appearance. She looked, and sometimes behaved, very like Elizabeth I in her later years. With her pale red hair, pale skin and beady brown eyes, she trotted about school in a White Knight tangle of handbag, cardigan, history books, papers and her glasses. Like Elizabeth, I suspect she took pains with her appearance, because she was in fact always dressed in colours and styles which became her and she had in particular a penchant for a nice court shoe, often in brown patent or brown glacé kid.

'Since, however, she had this pale skin, stretched tightly over a clearly defined bone structure, and since like many staff she was probably quite tired as term wore on, she could and often did look quite spectral. She was not called by any nickname other than the initials DWU, pronounced Dwoo. They stood for her initials, but composed an acronym – Death Warmed Up. My guess is that she knew her nickname full well and played up to it.'

'Miss Butcher had a marvellous, dry sense of humour and we somehow knew she was "on our side", said Merry Rushton. Stephanie Chapman (Watson 1952-57) felt differently about DWU. 'She disliked me and ruined history for me to this day,' Stephanie said. 'A memorable quote from her at an ORA reunion, when I greeted her with my sisters Miranda and Valerie was: "Ah yes, I always pwefewwed Valewie".'

Katharine Coleman had happy memories of 'dear DWU'. She was, Katharine said, 'a brilliant teacher of history, dearly loved a laugh, respected argument, and was a great joker. She could stand in front of a blackboard and start writing a sentence with her left hand, passing the chalk to her right hand and continuing in identical handwriting at impressive speed. She was discreetly kind and encouraging.

'Kindness and encouragement always came from Molly Gledhill as well,' Katharine added. 'She was one of the few members of staff with whom one felt relaxed and untroubled by being from a less wealthy home than most girls. She encouraged me in art and I loved her lessons. Molly suffered a terrible car accident while I was at the school and bravely bore the stares of all us stupid girls when she returned dreadfully scarred on her face.'

Stephanie considered that, for style, there was no one to touch Miss Braund 'who was always theatrical in appearance, elegant and could be relied upon for wit and a healthy disregard for absolutely toeing the line'.

Miss Gasston, second head of Number One, was 'always good for falling for a sob story and providing mugs of cocoa', Nicola Frith (1950-57) said.

Miss Ratcliffe was universally popular with all her students. 'Darling Rat,'

Jane Jervoise (Newnham 1953-57) called her. She was 'sweet and gentle', according to Elizabeth Thomas (Cawdry 1953-57) and Penny Taylor (Spathis 1958-62) remembered her 'with fondness and gratitude'.

Susan Child (Locket 1955-61) wrote: 'We had the last generation of staff who dedicated their lives to the school, and a few of these had lost fiancés, or not been married because of the war. Almost without exception they were excellent teachers and although relationships were formal, they were good, but none, in my view, qualified as a real character.'

Susan's contemporary, Mary Adams (Nock 1956-61), took a different view. 'There were some wonderful characters – like Miss Butcher with her wispy hair, wonderful vagueness and splendid knowledge, and Miss Hardisty who taught physics and used to play us Tom Lehrer records in her room. All the teachers were dedicated and devoted, and had great stores of information to impart.'

Miss Boyd, the maths teacher, stands out in Fiona Hodges' memory. 'In those days Miss Boyd was a commanding sort of woman. She had dark hair, dark eyes and a sonorous voice. She had classroom behaviour completely taped and could appear soundlessly at your elbow, often when you were using your slide-rule for levering something open, or doodling. We were not an attractive group to teach, being unmotivated and unenthusiastic (all the wizard keen people were in Div I and we bozos were in the no-man's-land of Div II). One grey morning in the Lent term, in what is now a jolly computer room, she looked at us silently as we failed yet again to grasp the trigonometry, or log problem we were trying to solve (after a week's slog on her part) and she said to us resignedly: "When I look at you, Upper Five, I am reminded of the hymn *New Every Morning*".

'I duly failed maths O Level. You had to have maths to apply for university, or else a science. I didn't have this either. There was nothing for it but a re-take. All through the Michaelmas term Miss Boyd taught me all over again and she never once said "I told you so" or "if only you had listened". Eventually I did pass and could safely apply for university.

'Later I discovered that music had been one of her great interests before she took up teaching – a salutary reminder never to judge a book by its cover.'

The new generation of post-war staff was recalled by Ann Fernandez (Barnes 1957-65). 'Miss Weaver, who was a breath of fresh air in her analysis of history; Mrs Hopper who could sing any voice range except soprano; Miss Gledhill who made me realise I was narrow-minded'. Ann also remembered the matron of Junior House, Miss Harms. 'What a temper! Was it for her that the phrase "to keep out of harm's way" was coined?'

'Smelzer, the chemistry teacher and The Pick, my Latin teacher and the assistant housemistress, were both so enthusiastic on their subjects that we positively excelled in them,' Frances Taylor (Gordon-Smith 1958- 62) said.

Sarah Saunders-Davis remembered Mrs Baxter 'peering over the rim of her glasses during biology lessons, with us trying to contain our giggles during the human anatomy studies. She was brilliant at dissecting rabbits, which she did with the precision of a surgeon, much to our ghoulish delight.'

'Don't put your bosoms on the table, dears,' Miss Pickering used to tell the girls, according to June Chadwick (Burke 1961-69). The Pick was a very patient woman, said Carolyn Phillippo (Williamson 1961-69), and Sheila Sorby (Eastcott 1964-72) remembered the cod Latin verse her pupils chanted:

Pickibus sittibus on deskeorum
Deskibus collapsibus
Pickibus on florum.

Miss Pickering's dog, a delicate white whippet called Ajax, after the Greek hero, was known as Vim throughout the school.

Mrs Cassaniga, the French teacher from Corsica, favoured 'the zut-alors volatile style of French teaching', Fiona Hodges remembered.

'Dear Stooge' was fondly remembered by Amanda Stokes-Roberts (1967-73), and by Gail Maughan (Dane 1968-72), who said: 'She ruled by fear but had a heart of gold'.

'Miss Plumpton! What a character!' Ann Henley (1970-78) wrote. 'She was head of languages and very strict, but underneath she cared a great deal about her students.' Anne also recalled Miss Smith, the Latin teacher, who went everywhere with her Pekinese in a basket, and Miss Gledhill, the art teacher, who flew into dreadful rages 'when her earrings jingled in sympathy'.

Carole Allsop (1972-78) thought Miss Plumpton 'very driven' and Dr Diffy 'sweet and vague', while Frances Graham (1982-89) remembered Mr Christie as 'the most diplomatic man on earth'.

More recent ORs mostly confined themselves to describing teachers as stern, theatrical, friendly, odd – whether because, as Susan Child said, there were no real characters left, because they were being diplomatic or because they feared a pi-jaw from a prefect is difficult to assess.

Chemistry teacher Mr England was best remembered by ORs for setting himself on fire during an experiment and, said Anitha Sudheesh (1993-95), 'as a one-man comedy show'.

Sarah Bale (1984-92) had fond memories of matron Miss Sertig, who taught the girls to knit in her room, and told them ghost stories about when she lived in Jamaica.

The 'fiercely Welsh' Miss Doughty, who kept toy dragons in the chemistry labs, and Dr Grassie 'the most intelligent teacher of all', were two who stayed in a Nineties pupil's memory, and Anitha remembered Dr Bailin 'who moved so elegantly and effortlessly in saris and ghagra cholis'.

For Charlotte-Anne Nelson (1990-97), the school's most unusual teacher was Dr Birch. 'A convert to Buddhism, she was also a vegan, a former Communist and a feminist, and she was in all sorts of other politically correct minorities,' Charlotte-Anne said. 'She was, however, the kindest of people, always with a coffee cup in hand, defying the no-jeans dress code, surrounded by an aura of immense calm.' Zoe Green (1988-95) remembered Dr Birch 'drifting along in a haze of sandalwood' and propping her bare feet on the desk during lessons.

Staff nicknames

'Miss Tanner once told the school that we were being unimaginative in our names for teachers; this, I felt, was a dangerous thing to tell children.' Cynthia Marsh (Moodie 1934-37)

Miss Atkinson	Flatty Atty
Miss Ball	The Pill
Miss Joyce Baron	Hercules (Hurky)
Miss Batho	The Bath Mat
Miss Boselli	Vogue or The Beauty
Miss Margaret Boyd	The Boyd
Miss Braund	Maggie B
Mrs Bremner	The Nose
Miss Brown	Whiney B
Miss Butcher	DWU (Death Warmed Up)
Miss Cameron	Smelzer
Miss Child	The Infant
Miss Thyra Creyke-Clark	TCC or Crikey
Mrs Crossley-Holland	The Egg
Miss Cumberland	Cucumber
Miss Cursue	The Curse
Mrs Fitz-Maurice Kelly	Fitzy
Miss Fyleman	The Hebrew Prophet
Miss Gasston	Gassy
Miss Monica Godfray	Minnie Ha Ha
Miss M Gulich	Mabs
Miss Norah Horobin	The Robin or The Horror

Miss Hyde	The Hydro
Miss Lilian Hyde	The Lily Bug
Miss Ketteridge	The Ket
Miss Penelope Lawrence	PL
Mlle Therese Lavauden	The Lav or Love-a-duck
Miss Hilda Leigh	Tilda
Mlle Lion	Lioness or The Lion
Miss D S Lloyd-William	Lloydy Bill
Miss C P MacSwiney	Pat Mac
Miss D B Martin	DB
Miss McCullough	The Mess
Miss N McCullough (her sister)	The Muck
Miss Mercer	The Melon or Melons
Miss Middleton	Tiddles or Tiddle Pom
Miss O'Callaghan	O'C or Stonehenge
Miss N O'Kelly	Nokey
Miss B M Patterson	The P or Ma P
Miss Pickering	The Pick
Miss Plumpton	Plummy
Miss Ramsden	The Ram
Miss B M Ratcliffe	Ratty or The Rat
Miss Robinson	Bobby Rob
Miss Smith	Spit
Miss Joan Spearing	The Spur
Miss Stenning	Aunt M
Miss Sturgis	Stooge
Miss Tanner	The Tanner or Aunt Em
Miss Joan Tredgold	Topsy
Miss DB Will	The Will
Mrs Wilson	The Willy
Miss Nina Woodcock	The Peahen

PRESUMED INNOCENT

'I remember the whole emotional thing of keen ons and keenites. I adored a prefect in secret, went weak at the knees when she passed.'

AN anecdote from Merry Rushton (Newth 1948-54), a great niece of Emmeline Tanner, throws light on the sexual innocence and ignorance of Roedean girls in the middle years of the century.

'After a summer half term at home I said to our gang of seven: "Girls, come to the music wing, I've something to tell you",' Merry wrote. 'The practice rooms were the place for all our intimate chats. "I hardly know how to tell you this – but Mummy and Daddy do it for fun!" The stunned expression on all of their faces, and the silence which followed, is remembered by every single one of us to this day. After a few seconds one recovered enough to say "Well, mine certainly don't" quickly followed by the others – "Nor do mine"; "Or mine"; "Or mine". Then a kind girl said: "Look, girls, I don't think this ought to make any difference to our friendship with Merry". After a moment's consideration they all, one by one, generously agreed. Many times after that my parents sat in the gallery of the Chapel happily ignorant of the fact that at least seven pairs of adolescent eyes were boring into them. My mother had said something like "it's a very happy thing to do", but we all thought you only "did it" once to have a baby.'

Vivien Allen (Hallett 1937-43) said that Roedean had had a reputation for being a 'hotbed of lesbians', which Miss Tanner did her best to dispel. '*The Well of Loneliness*, strictly banned, had been, it was whispered, written by an OR,' Vivien said. 'My parents sent me *Gone With the Wind* for my birthday . . . my present was whipped away from me as "unsuitable" and not returned till the last day of term.'

The fad for being keen on older girls was more innocent heroine worship – what in other schools was called a crush – than lesbianism, which was a word few, if any, Roedean pupils would then have understood. It amounted merely to 'watching them excel at games, and putting our Saturday night chocolate digestives in their rooms,' said Isobel Bernstein (Forsell 1935-41).

'We younger girls used to be keen on some of the seniors,' Jeanne Reeves (1940-44) explained. 'My "passion" was Gill Weatherill. It was really funny. If they smiled at us we were so delighted, and we used to try and get one of their discarded pieces of clothing when they left, and treasure them.' Sarah Curtis (Myers 1945-53) said: 'Being keen on an older girl was totally innocent but it was officially discouraged for reasons I now understand.'

Ann Portnoy (Levy 1944-47) thought it demeaning 'giving part of one's sweet ration, cleaning their sports tack, running errands'.

'I remember the whole emotional thing of keen ons and keenites,' Gilllian Van Gelder (Solomon 1946-51) wrote. 'Some of the older girls probably took advantage but mainly I think it was innocent. I adored a prefect in secret, went weak at the knees when she passed but never told her or anyone else. I was pestered by contemporaries to reveal my keen on. Occasional staff worries brought pronouncements that "younger girls must not make beds for older girls". Luckily I didn't understand the sexual implications at the time or I would have been convinced I was a lesbian.'

'Oooh! I do love "Her" so much! I feel so goofy about "Her", "She's" SO sweet!!!' Eve Bysouth (Dowson 1939-46) wrote in her 1941 school diary. Eve, and two of her friends, were keen on Rose Benson, the "Her" and "She" in the diary. Towards Christmas, Eve wrote: 'I got some of my raisins and tied them up in a piece of green material and wrote a note saying – "Dear Rose, Here are a few raisins, I hope you will like them. Tons of love From EVE". I wrapped the whole thing up in a piece of brown paper, with "To Rose" on the outside. Roysia put some chocolate in an envelope and put "To Rose, from Roysia" on the outside . . . Roysia and I were sitting in our room when Eve Rigby came in, she said, "Roysia and Eve, come here", we followed her outside the door and she said, "Will you go to Rose, in her room," she seemed rather cross. Then Roysia and I went to room 202, and Roysia knocked, we heard a "Come in," and so we went in and I shut the door behind me. There was Rose standing in the middle of the room, She said, "Oh, sit down, you can sit on that bed," we both sat down on a bed just by the door, then "She" said, "Look here, you really can't go on giving me things," "She" then went to a chest of drawers, like the one we have in our room that has three little drawers down one side and three down the other side with one thin draw across the middle and nothing below that draw, and you put your legs there, if you are writing etc. Well "She" went to a small draw on the left hand and took out the two parcels and came over to us. "She" said "You really must take these back". "Oh no, it is quite all right, you must keep them," Roysia said, all I said was "Do keep them,". Roysia spoke quite a bit. Then Rose said, "You really must promise me, not to give me anything more." We went out then, and went to a bathroom and locked ourselves in, and talked it over. Roysia said that she thought Rose looked most annoyed about something. It may have been because "She" had to thank us, or "She" may not like us giving "Her" things, or "She" may have been annoyed because I was "keen" on "Her", or "She" may be so because Ann was hurt that I was not "keen" on her, because lots of people have thought that I am "keen" on Ann and it may have got to Ann, that I was.'

'There were wonderful friendships and a lot of heartaches as we were all meant to be keen on someone,' said Angela Pain (Packham 1954-58). 'I smile now to think that Lynda Chalker (Bates) came across from Number Four to Number Two to put a bar of chocolate on *my* bed.'

Susan Child (Locket 1955-61) said: 'Within a day or two (of arriving at school) the Upper Fifth hauled us in to the GDR one at a time and asked who we were going to be keen on. It was in fact decided for us and we were then told that we should turn down this girl's bed each evening, which entailed creeping into her room without being seen. A sweet could be left on the pillow. Later the older girl duly presented the younger with a photograph.'

During her first winter at Roedean, Jean Marwood (Sharp 1937-42), who had spent some years in Barbados, felt the cold badly. 'One bitter morning, when the water in the jug in my bedroom was frozen solid, I decided to take all my clothes down to the boiler room to dress in delicious warmth,' she said. 'When I was starkers the man whose job it was to stoke the boiler came in. He complained to Miss Patterson, the housemistress, and I was accused of a terrible crime. I was so sexually innocent at the time that I never really understood what all the fuss was about.'

Sylvia Perry (Denis-Smith 1936-40) remembered the advice given to her by Dame Emmeline when she left school. It was: 'Always keep your legs crossed when alone with a man.' 'Unfortunately,' Sylvia said, 'she omitted to say why!'

Girls could ask to share rooms with particular friends, 'and we actually put into the request box "Please may Gay Clarke sleep with Priscilla Willmott next term". So innocent!' said Gay Sharpe (Clarke 1952-59).

Susan Ryan (Plummer 1954-57) remembered that on the day before she left she was nearly expelled by Tiddles for saying goodbye after lights out in another house. 'Because of my good record she overlooked "this shocking behaviour".'

'We had no sex education so just lived on dirty stories, not knowing what was true or false,' Yvonne Hulsen (Madsen 1953-56) recalled.

Rosemary Athay (1955-59) remembered one Hallowe'en: 'We had been told that if you lit a candle at midnight and looked in the mirror you saw behind your shoulder the face of the man you were to marry. I was volunteered to go down to the kitchen to get a box of matches. We had candles from someone's birthday cake. I was caught in the act by The P. Of course she demanded an explanation for the matches, let alone my presence in the kitchen. I was quite unable to admit to the truth (sex was completely incompatible with The P, even in such dilute form) and so she was convinced that I was bent on arson. I was never able to disabuse her.'

Merry Rushton was amazed when she visited Roedean in 1959 to see boys walking in the school corridor, and she asked Miss Ketteridge what was afoot. 'She replied: "My dear Meriel, if we didn't let them in through the front door, they'd only come in at the back!" I could hardly believe the speed of such a change and, with all the prudery of a newly-wed, was deeply shocked,' Merry said.

Vivien Allen said that the censorship of letters had the predictable result of making girls devious and sly. 'Letters to boy friends were smuggled out and banned magazines were hidden and devoured by torchlight after lights out. I was caught with a copy of *Lilliput* under my mattress – Lloydy Bill called it "a mucky little magazine" as she tore it up. Recently I found that short stories from wartime *Lilliput* were being set for study by GCE candidates!'

Mary Lisa Owen (Davies 1956-63) remembered the time 'when boys from Christ's Hospital arrived for a debate, tinks rang and we went into our rooms, closed the curtains and sat on our beds. When the boys were safely in the school hall we opened the curtains and it was back to normal!'

'Older brothers were particularly popular and a target for "ogling" from the SPR windows,' Sarah Saunders-Davis (Osborn 1960-67) said. 'A good deal of chatting could ensue if one had sucked up to the sister.' But ogling visiting boys was frowned upon, Fiona Hodges (Ewart 1967-72) said. 'And anything more murky had apocalyptic consequences, not to mention faster transmission than any computer-driven system.'

Pranks, dares and midnight feasts

ROEDEAN girls had read their Girls Crystals and their Angela Brazils, and knew what was expected of boarding school pupils in the way of midnight feasts, practical jokes and pranks. But of the few ORs who owned up (and some of those requested anonymity, fearful, perhaps, of retribution even after all these years), just a handful succeeded in anything of a spectacular nature; others were doomed to failure, perpetrators being frequently caught in the act.

'I was extremely tiresome,' a Twenties student admitted. 'With my friend Mary Turner I climbed every tower and we scratched our initials on the cupola of Number One roof. We even went over the Downs to Ovingdean at night to buy sweets – strictly forbidden on all counts, but luckily were never caught.'

Iris Ingram (Clark 1929-31) said: 'Sunday afternoon, when the weather was inclement, was the only leisure time when we were not monitored. We would sit in the prep room by the fire and burn holes in the wood above the fireplace with a hot poker. Of course, we were caught. I owned up to it and lost a term's pocket money (for repair). But those were fun times.'

A Thirties pupil said: 'My set, aged 15, lurking and larking behind the bank on the drive approach, threw a stone that broke the windscreen of a father's car. It was a Sunday. The whole school was summoned to the hall. Auntie Em, solemn on the platform, stone in hand, said: "Gels, who did this disgraceful, thoughtless deed? Please come to my study after this meeting." They did. I was seen to blush, and was questioned. I established my alibi. I was quite a naughty girl, but not in sympathy with this act, and was lucky not to be there.'

The human side of Monica Godfray was discovered by Sylvia Perry (Denis-Smith 1936-40), who recalled: 'After Sunday Chapel three or four or us decided to climb the tower over the front entrance – reached by devious means. Having achieved my object, and on descent, I spoke animatedly to those already landed, and did not notice their silence, so was horrified when I landed to find myself looking up at a severe and forbidding Minnie Ha Ha. I believe she was a woman of much humour. After a reprimand there was no

School House, a photograph from the 1920s,
showing the much climbed towers.

other punishment nor did she report us to higher authority.'

Sonia Bicanic (Wild 1932-38) was an earlier climber. She said: 'One of the most strictly forbidden things was to go up the school towers. Ali, Noel and I did it at least twice. The only reason that we could do it was because of our various brands of nonconformist background. I do not mean that this made us more intrepid or defiant of authority, but simply that there were certain times when everybody had to be in Chapel, except nonconformists, Catholics and Jews. We timed our tower climbing to coincide with these gatherings, the more so since the staff were all Church of England, and we had to go through the end of the staff wing. It was an exciting escapade and probably marginally dangerous. One had to go through an attic in the top back corner of Number Three bedroom corridor, through the staff bedroom floor via another small enclosed place into the bottom of the tower. There was always the danger of an unsuspected nonconformist or Catholic among the staff. Going up the tower was OK until the very end when there was a nasty twist to get out on to the balcony, and then we crouched down behind the parapet looking at the tiny Lowry-like creatures walking about below and feeling very proud that we'd done it, and very nervous because it was a rather rickety balcony, and even more nervous because the whole trip had to be done again in reverse with more fears of pouncing mistresses.'

Among the other roof walkers were Lorna Doveton (Scutt 1932-37) and Vivien Allen. 'There was a tradition in Number Two House that new girls had to climb up in some way on to the roof, which was, of course, against the rules, but we all did it so as not to lose face,' Lorna said. Vivien remembered climbing the tower and exploring the attics 'and finding Lloydy Bill sitting on the bath waiting for us when we emerged through the trap door coming down'.

When she was bored, Jill Sheppard (Robbins (1948-53) amused herself in the service passages under the houses, entering from Number Four's locker room. 'You could go from one end of school to the other through the tunnels,' said Jill, who may well have encountered another Jill bent on exploring the subterranean tunnels – Jill Fraser (Fox 1953-58), who said it was a great game, and considered very daring.

Tatiana Macaire (Miller 1944-51) remembered an attempt to frighten the staff with 'a skeleton made from old wire and loo paper that we put in the staff bathroom'. She said: 'We were, of course, caught, punished and had to pay for the toilet rolls – but it was worth it!'

Janet Garwood (Ing-Simmons 1947-51) recalled midnight feasts with sweets or biscuits smuggled in to school in packets of sanitary towels sent from home. Did Tiddles really know, but turn a blind eye, she wondered. Jane Jervoise's (Newnham 1953-57) midnight feasts consisted of tins of peaches mixed with chocolate biscuits and condensed milk.

'When about to leave you had to rebel in some way,' Janet said. 'A group of us took our alarm clocks and hid them behind the books in the library – all set to go off together. They were found before this happened and we had to own up and get our clocks back.'

Sarah Saunders-Davis's memories of pranks included: 'Throwing a banana skin to a friend out of the SPR window just as Mrs Fort and Miss Sturgis emerged from the front door – a sense of humour failure and a summons to the study for instant retribution; placing a dead sardine in the same friend's pencil case after a biology lesson resulting in screams and tears of fright when the slippery customer was felt during the geography lesson that followed; trying on Miss Sturgis's frocks on her day out and giving a passable imitation of her walk and mannerisms.'

In the Fifties three pranks were perpetrated *on* Roedean. 'One evening after lights out Lancing College (we believe) raided Number Four House,' said Cherry Edgerton-Bird (1953-59). 'The boys climbed up the fire escape. However the noise alerted the matron and she sounded the alarm. The boys were not caught, but seen. Great excitement.'

Sarah Gibbons (Miller Logan 1956-58) remembered the 'invasion' by the students of colleges in Brighton in October 1957, when Miss Patterson, head of Number One, was said to have leaned out of a window to repel a young man on a ladder, saying 'Go back you stupid boy'.

Mary Lisa Owen (Davies 1956-63) recalled the excitement of the Brighton Rag in November 1958. 'This,' she said, 'brought hundreds of young men to the school and into the grounds at about 11pm, much to our sheer joy. They shouted, clashed things together, played bugles, climbed fire escapes. We waved and shouted back. They ran along the terrace and the staff rushed from room to room telling us to return to our beds. There was noise, lights and excitement until the blue lights appeared. The press made much of it the next day and we heard many stories, some possibly true and many probably false, of the encounters between the excited girls, the students and staff.'

'One Hallowe'en in House One we tied each doorknob with string to the next door knob,' Elizabeth Chapman (1963-69) said. 'This was carried out with huge organisation after lights out. At the last door the string was pulled through the keyhole. Unfortunately the housemistress was disturbed and we heard her walk along cutting each string. Next day the form below had to clear it all up. We assumed she never knew who did it.'

'Many happy hours were spent practising the "black arts" – like witchcraft, levitation, ouija board,' Lynn Glyn (Weksler 1965-71) admitted. 'My own daughter also tried this at Roedean and turned JH into an hysterical mass.'

Nicola Schrager von Altishofen (Lovett-Standing 1971-78) and her friends elevated the practical joke to a higher level. She wrote: 'On the last day (or within the final week) we suspended a For Sale sign between the bell towers – (a) we faced expulsion for going up to the towers; (b) the sheets used had been "liberated" from the laundry; (c) we inadvertently reversed the "S" in Sale (after all that education!); (d) when asked at lunch to own up, the entire year raised their hands with only two exceptions. That is what Roedean was all about.'

Frances Graham (1982-89) owned up to a more serious misdemeanour. 'One day I went to Brighton and had to walk back – I had bought a bottle of vodka and didn't have enough money for the bus ticket. The whole Sixth in House Four was done for drinking. It got me suspended and was Mrs Bitt's biggest nightmare in her first year.'

Sarah Bale (1984-92) remembered the shambles when boys from Wellington were invited to a dance in the school dining room. 'We danced on the tables and broke them, and the floor was covered in beer and ruined,' she said. Daring Sarah also owned up to 'sneaking out through a door in a room on the top floor into San, down the stairs and through the hall into the music wing where we put a chair out of the window and got down to the front path. We were dressed in going out clothes under our dressing gowns. If we were caught we could pretend someone was ill. We went into Brighton and dumped our gowns in the bushes. Coming back we did the reverse and were never caught.

'You always did something as a Six Two when you left,' Sarah said. 'My sister's year ordered a strippagram. He came in as a traffic warden during Assembly in the Hall. He stripped and had a rose in his G-string. A reporter was there from *The Sun*. All the Six Two were called out to be disciplined and Mrs Lewis, the deputy, took the film from the photographer. One teacher was crying.'

Zoe Green (1989-95) was once locked out of Number Two after a late night excursion to Number Three. She said: 'After trying the library (too scary) and staff room (too cold) I ended up sleeping under a pile of coats in the staff toilet. I was awoken by a screaming cleaning lady at 6am the next morning. She was convinced she'd discovered a body.'

THE SAN

*'Common ailments like strep throat and 'flu were treated by aspirin,
inhalations, gargles, hot water bottles and "onion" medicines.'*

ROEDEAN'S sanatorium, always called the San, was built in 1908 as three
interconnecting cottages, each of which could be isolated. A new wing,
with twenty single bedrooms and four bathrooms, was added in 1911. In the
early Sixties the wing was converted for use by Sixth Formers as a place
where they could have more freedom, and learn to be self sufficient. In the
Seventies the San became Lawrence House, a semi-autonomous home for
senior girls who were free to cook their own meals, to entertain friends and to
come and go as they chose.

Just a handful of Old Roedeanians remembered the school's first, and worst,
health crisis, when Spanish 'flu swept across Europe and North America in
1919, killing millions of people. The San was overwhelmed and sick girls
were nursed in the houses. But youth, allied to the Lawrences' determinedly
healthy lifestyle, was on their side and all the patients pulled through.
Although, at the height of the pandemic, only a few girls remained unaffected,
the school stayed open and fit girls were taken on daily walks to Rottingdean.

The Sanatorium – the San – now Lawrence House

Primarily the San was built to isolate girls suffering from such common childhood complaints as chicken pox, measles and whooping cough. Everyday complaints were dealt with in-house by the matrons, but pupils with games injuries, persistent coughs, and the kind of 'flu then called a 'nervous cold' went to the San. The young patients were transported in the San cart, described as 'an ancient horse-drawn vehicle' – allegedly a pensioned-off hansom cab – and put to bed. The horse, called Dolly (or was it Daisy?), lived in a stable in the grounds; the driver was one of the gardeners.

Pauline Norman (Davenport 1928-33) was never ill enough for the San, but she remembered the spectacle of the 'gloomy little cab, drawn by the equally gloomy horse' being backed right into the house porch 'where the patient, swathed in eiderdowns, was smuggled in secretly, to avert unseemly panic'. The wheels rumbled on the terrace, she said, and there was great speculation as to who was being borne away, and why.

Compared with house life, the San routine was very relaxed. The food was better (consistently, right up until the San closed, ORs insisted), there was a plentiful supply of books and jigsaw puzzles, and girls tended to enjoy their enforced convalescence. There were separate San books for different diseases, Ann Hutchings (Carter 1938-40) recalled – measles books, mumps books and so on, presumably so that infection was not spread.

Ruth Hadfield (Timpson 1917-23) remembered spending a couple of weeks there with seven friends, all with whooping cough, and having 'a wonderful time'. Grace Briscoe (1918-25) thought that being in the San was an excellent opportunity to make contact with other age groups, and with girls from different houses.

Erica Haxworth (Silver 1924-30) claimed responsibility for giving chicken pox to most of the school in the winter of 1929. Unaware that she had the virus, Erica went around obtaining a signature from every girl to welcome Emmeline Tanner home from a visit to Roedean South Africa. Helen Waterhouse (Thomas 1926-31) remembered the epidemic well. 'It was brought back,' she said, 'by Erica Silver, the head girl, from a home weekend, which would not have been allowed to anyone with a less important (OR) mother!'

Illnesses too serious for the San were treated in local hospitals. Alison Adburgham (Haig 1925-29) went to a Hove nursing home for an ear operation and was returned to convalesce in the San, from where she walked daily to lessons in school.

Eluned Macmillan (Carey Evans 1929-39) hated the San, and everything about it from the 'smelly old cab and tottery old horse' to the 'stern and unpleasant' sister and the smell of disinfectant. For Barbara Harvey (Woods 1929-35), though, the San was a real treat. 'We were pampered, given hot water bottles and palatable food,' she recalled. Irene Chaundler (Phoenix 1929-35) also enjoyed her only visit, when her neck 'was put out' while bowling at cricket. 'As far as I remember one always got a Friar's Balsam inhalant as a matter of course. I enjoyed having a few days off and lots to read.'

Sylvia Perry (Denis-Smith 1936-40) said: 'Common ailments like strep throat and 'flu were treated by aspirin, inhalations, gargles, hot water bottles and "onion" medicines.'

The San Cart was retired in about 1936; Vivien Allen (Hallett 1937-43) remembered seeing it lying behind the San when she arrived at the school.

A year or two after the war there was a nationwide polio scare, and a Roedean girl fell ill. Massive precautions were taken, the new penicillin tablets were handed out, and Frances Makower (1942-47) remembered that all the food tasted of Dettol, and that temperatures were taken two or three times a day. The victim was Elaine Hardie (Cameron 1944-51), who remembered being isolated immediately in the San, and then removed to local fever hospital. Gillian Pemberton (Cameron 1944-48), Elaine's sister, and some of her friends, spent three weeks' quarantine in the San. Elizabeth Griffin (Blyth 1944-49) was there at the same time, with jaundice, and she too was put into quarantine. Elaine, she heard, was in an iron lung.

'No one else caught it, luckily,' Elaine said. 'They prayed for me in Chapel and I recovered.'

Transport to the San post war, Rosalie Ball (1942-48) recalled, was 'an ancient Rolls', or 'a World War One ambulance' according to Gillian Grenfell (Manley 1946-50); the vehicle, possibly an old Rolls ambulance, was driven by the head groundsman.

There was an outbreak of scarlet fever in the Lent term of 1947 and Number One House was made into an isolation ward, with a *cordon sanitaire*. Rosemary Clark (Adcock 1945-51) remembered being allowed to listen to Dick Barton on the wireless 'providing we had used our potties!' A diary Julia Oakley (Harding 1946-50) kept recorded the virulent passage of the illness. 'Jan 26th: Heaps of people ill. Feb 2nd: No house dancing. Feb 9th: Everyone ill, very cold. Feb 16th: No organ, no games, no marks. The P got Scarlet Fever. The Tanner made speech about Scarlet. Very deep snow. Feb 23rd: Everyone having swabs taken; kept moving rooms as sick bay could not cope. Letter from ill friend had to be baked before I received it. March 2nd: Phoebe, Morn, Pen and Dickie back from leper colony.'

Joanna Burrows (Hamilton 1945-49), arriving from Roedean South Africa, was smitten by the cold and developed chilblains. She remembered how 'lovely and warm' the San was, the extra milk she was given there, and the ultra violet treatment.

Sarah Curtis (Myers 1945-53) recalled the 'two terrifying, iron-grey ladies' who ran the San. 'I had a strep throat in the first term back at Brighton, aged nine, and remember lying alone for hours, or so it seemed, silently weeping.'

Favourite treatments for a wide range of symptoms seemed to be 'the dreaded enema, painting with gentian violet, and brown tinted glasses for pink eye', Ann Hulme (Prall 1946-50) said.

Merry Rushton (Newth 1948-54) wrote: 'Going to the San – very dramatic in the San bus – could be exciting and a break from the noise and hurly burly of school life. It was lovely writing and, better still, receiving sentimental letters – "Darling, we're all missing you so much – get well soon . . . Nothing much has changed here in the ghastly routine . . . " and then a whole lot of news. We were terrified of Sister who wore a uniform like that of a nurse in the the First World War, but we loved Bluey, the little nurse who was kind and warm, and smiled a lot. I enjoyed the hours of quiet, uninterrupted reading that a spell in the San afforded. But I remember being terrified at nights if I had a room on the ground floor. The bedrooms seemed huge compared with the ones in our houses, and I was certain someone would climb in the window. An awful memory is of a girl being waved off to the San. "Goodbye darling, good luck," and everyone deciding while she was away that she had got too big for her boots and that a spell in Coventry would do her good. She returned expecting smiles and a welcome and was greeted instead with icy hostility. Is there any species more cruel than a teenage girl?'

The huge importance of games, and of house loyalty, was highlighted by an anecdote from Nicola Frith (1950-57). Nicola was sent to the Royal Sussex County Hospital in Brighton to have a verruca dealt with by Dr Hall Smith. 'The housemistress gave me a letter for him. Years later he told me that she had instructed him to give me a strong local anaesthetic as I had to play in a house cricket match that afternoon! I played with a large hole in the sole of my foot and survived by merely hitting boundaries.'

Stephanie Chapman's (Watson 1952-57) first spell in the San was because a netball post fell on her head during a gale. 'I had a wonderful black eye. I was kept under supervision for possible concussion and was visited daily by the housemistress. My only other time in the San was during a mumps epidemic. Later, when there was a 'flu epidemic there were far too many of us struck down to be accommodated in the San, so we were nursed by our housemistresses, Tiddle and Peahen, and matron, Ponder. Our care was scrupulous, with frequent bulletins sent to our parents on postcards.'

Cherry Edgerton-Bird's (1953-59) one and only incarceration in the San was a tragedy, as far as she was concerned. 'It was the day we had our dance with Lancing College boys. I was so excited. We had been allowed to go in to

Brighton to have our hair done and I started to feel ill.' There was no dance for Cherry, who ended up in the San with 'flu.

Mary-Grace Browning (Feachem 1955-62) spent almost an entire term in the San with impetigo, and was very, very bored. She filled time with games of solitaire, jigsaws, and studying Latin.

Pamela Mainwaring (Watson 1956-63) hated being in the San – once for a burst ear drum, another time for a foot injury. 'It felt like being banished,' she said, but she remembered the little beaded crochet covers over the water jugs, and listening to *Workers Playtime* on the wireless, as radio used to be called. Mary Lisa Owen (Davies 1956-63) explained that selected programmes from the Home Service were piped into the bedrooms via loudspeakers. The San, she said, was considered to be a haven of good food and fun, particularly with Bluey 'who was always cheerful'.

'We were all a bit afraid of Sister Mallett, but we liked Bluey enormously – she used to call us "sweetie pie",' Susan Child (Locket 1955-61) said. 'The San was spacious and quiet, and it was a great relief to get there when really ill. The sitting room was cosy, with lots of books, and cards, and you really felt cared for. I remember Hong Kong 'flu when the epidemic was so bad that Lower had to be turned into an extension of the San. Aspirin gargle – I wonder how much went out of the window?'

Frances Taylor (Gordon-Smith 1958-62) and a group of her friends wanted so much to be sent to the San – 'very luxurious, television, radio, good food and kind Bluey' – that they rubbed their wrists with stiff bristled hairbrushes to raise a rash. 'After a week it became very boring so we then "felt better" and returned to the house.'

All illnesses and complaints were dealt with initially by the house matron, Katharine Coleman (Mackenzie 1961-66) said. 'She issued aspirin gargle for all complaints, be they sprained knees or headaches. Some lucky ones got spoonfuls of malt (Radio Malt), and for the most part we were a very healthy crowd. I did experience a very painful ear infection, for which I got a dose of aspirin gargle. When my ear drum burst matron did get a doctor to have a look and prescribe some antibiotic. My parents were notified but would not have considered complaining. I have been deaf in that ear ever since.'

Penny Taylor (Spathis 1958-62) had good and bad memories of the San – the bad being kept in there with an acute ear infection for much of her first term; the good of living there when she was in the Sixth Form, and enjoying a small measure of freedom.

Sarah Saunders-Davis (Osborn 1960-67) had the same experiences. 'I spent many a long week cooped up with dear Bluey. Mumps, measles, chicken pox and a particularly vicious strep throat came my way in quick succession during the Junior House years. I had to miss being an angel in the nativity play, and other treats. Two school doctors visited us regularly. They were Dr Beynon, a grey haired lady who wore her hair in a bun, and Dr White, who always seemed over eager to sound our chests. Part of the San was used as a Sixth Form house where I spent a very happy term.'

Felicity Russell Heuter (Russell 1968-75) was in the San with a sprained ankle and there she was taught to play pontoon, for matches. 'My mum was shocked,' she said. Felicity, too, was shocked when she heard afterwards that a fellow patient had had typhoid.

The San became Lawrence House in 1972 and health facilities, properly called the Medical Centre, but still referred to as the San, moved into the main school. The new San, Sarah Bale (1984-92) was intrigued to discover, could be entered through doors in some rooms in main school, 'like secret doors'.

Portia Da Gama Rose (1990-95) remembered 'the daunting Sister Mingay' who, she said, 'had some seventh sense which detected when we were fooling and just wanted to spend the day in bed!'

'San was run with an iron rod by the universally feared Sister Mingay (who was, in fact, soft at heart),' said Charlotte-Anne Nelson (1990-97). 'She had a reputation (probably unjustified) for either not believing you or just handing out a paracetemol regardless of the ailment. When 'flu epidemics swept the school, most people jumped on the bandwagon even if they were fine!'

THE WEATHER

'On windy days girls bowled along the terrace in their cloaks,
their arms held wide, trying to become airborne.'

THE weather is probably the only thing not to have changed in the century that Roedean has occupied its clifftop – and Roedean weather is unique, often unrelated to the weather in Brighton, just down the road, or inland, behind the Downs. On its chalk eyrie the school is buffeted by the prevailing south westerly winds that gather and intensify over the Atlantic and, seemingly, bowl up-Channel to make landfall on this particular spot on the Sussex coast. The winds range from a howling gale that rattles the windows, lifts the tiles and threatens to sweep unsuspecting girls off their feet, to a welcome summer zephyr – welcome because the salt laden gusts kill off all but the hardiest of plants and, on scorching summer days, there is barely a leaf for shade.

Snow is rare on the coast; for it to settle is even rarer, so the occasional snowfalls always caused great excitement at school. A billowing sea mist is more prevalent, and can spoil summer days on the coast when, a mile inland, the sun shines brightly.

Roedean weather has produced tough, hardy women – women so impervious to anything the elements can throw at them that the devastating hurricane of October 16, 1987, was barely mentioned by ORs. 'Wow' was all Frances Graham (1982-89) had to say, while Sarah Watts (1986-94) said she spent the night of the hurricane in Junior House happily 'swinging along the dorm on curtain rails until the early hours'. To Roedean girls, the Great Storm, as it became known, was probably little more than a stiff breeze.

The blustery conditions had their advantages; girls became very, *very* good at playing tennis, and other games, in high winds Jennifer Joel (Tyler 1947-51) said, and they revelled in the discomfort of visiting teams.

The panoramic views of Downs and sea have had a profound effect on many of the women who passed through Roedean; the ever-changing seascape, the white horses in rough weather, the lights of passing ships at night, moonlight on a calm, flat sea and glorious sunsets are memories that have remained sharp over the years.

'Memories of hot summer days come first, then cold, windy winters, but the air was wonderfully invigorating,' Keturah Crawford (Robinson 1918-22) said. Grace Edelsten (Briscoe 1918-25) remembered the spectacular views of the sea, and loved all the weather conditions 'especially the strong wind'.

Long ago, before the original windows were replaced, towels, discarded curtains and thick layers of old sheets – storm rags, they were called – were wadded against windows on the seaward side during storms to mop up the water that seeped in through every crack and crevice. In the most vicious of gales the old leaded windows sometimes blew in.

Ruth Conolly (Warren 1921-26) remembered one spectacular thunderstorm when the cricket pavilion was struck and forked lightning flashed over the sea all night. 'Prayers of thanksgiving for our preservation were offered by PL next morning,' she said.

The cricket pavilion, damaged by lightning, 1924

'It certainly could blow,' Angela Pirie (Hunter 1922-30) said. 'And it could also be unbearably hot.' But up on the cliffs conditions could change in a moment from a lovely sunny day to cold, damp greyness when a sea mist rolled up and enveloped the school. Iris Ingram (Clark 1929-31) enjoyed all the weather changes – 'December winds seemed almost to blow us off the cliff road into the sea, but I can feel the warm water of bathing in the sea in the summer even now. I remember occasional snowflakes when we would hide ourselves under the huge woollen capes after games, summer sunsets and the sound of bat against cricket ball. Being close to the sea gave me great comfort since it was just about my only link with my Nova Scotia home.'

In bright, clear air after rain, sometimes it was possible to see the Isle of Wight, seventy miles away, shimmering like a mirage on the sea, and one or two ORs claimed to have seen the Normandy coast of France, even further away.

Erica Haxworth (Silver 1924-30) remembered beautiful summer days when prefects' study teas were taken *al fresco*, and girls sat out on the lawns eating cakes ordered from Brighton. There were days when the shimmering sea gave back brilliantly blinding reflections of the sun, when Brighton's piers seemed to swim in a haze in the summer heat, and there were long, languorous days

64

when girls sunbathed in lush grass on the Continental Shelf – the terrace above the games pitches. Officially, sunbathing was discouraged – girls were warned that their complexions would be ruined.

Tatiana Macaire (Miller 1944-51) wrote: 'I can remember one ordinary spring afternoon, standing in goal on the flats, the second pitch, so looking out over the wall to the sea, sparkling blue, with the sun bright on the grass, and thinking maybe I'd always remember this day with its total feeling of well being – and that was fifty years ago, so maybe I did. You learnt to accept and enjoy extremes of weather, to survive.'

Then there were days, Sylvia Hatfield (Herford 1926-30) remembered, when it was too dangerous to walk outside for fear of being blown over. Eluned Macmillan (Carey Evans 1929-39) recalled the time when a small girl was blown down from the upper terrace to the drive. 'She was wearing her cloak and it just filled with wind and carried her away.' Miraculously, the child was unhurt.

Out of school hours, if girls were not playing games, they were expected to be outside, and groups of girls would link arms in windy weather and parade up and down the terrace in their cloaks. The rule was that they had to keep in groups of five; if one were hurt, two went for help and two stayed. On windy days Ruth Cousins (Gauntlett 1935-42) and her friends enjoyed bowling along the terrace in their cloaks, their arms held wide, trying to become airborne. Mary Marriott (Thompson 1937-40) said: 'I remember it being given out in Prayers that as the wind was so strong would small people going outside please hold on to someone larger!' Rosamund Huebener (Benson 1937-42) remembered orders being given that frail little Miss Child was not to walk from one building to another in high winds, 'unless flanked by two robust girls'.

It could also be very hot on the south coast, and many ORs remembered buckets of ice being placed around the Hall when they sat for their School Certificates.

'Winter was usually what is known as bracing – wet and windy,' said Rosemary Watts (Stephens 1933-37), 'and summers were unbroken sunshine, with glorious afternoons playing or watching cricket.'

'We were spoilt with sea views,' said Margaret Jackson (Harris 1935-39), who remembered 'endless summer days in Spiders and other special and secret places'. 'The sea was a constant joy, particularly in a storm,' Rosamund Huebener wrote. 'The views of the sea were magnificent,' said Jillian Gordon (Albury 1939-48).

On stormy nights girls were lulled to sleep (or kept awake) by the crashing of waves breaking over rocks and the roar of the withdrawing shingle. On balmy nights there was the gentle lap of waves on the shore. In her first letter home, Julia Oakley (Harding 1946-50) wrote: 'I love it here. I can hear the sea at night.' Julia's lifelong love of the sea, wind and gales started at Roedean.

In the first winter of World War Two there was heavy snow and Ruth Maclean (Gimson 1936-41) remembered 'borrowing' tin trays from the kitchen and sledging on the Downs.

A summer treat was being taken down through the old tunnel to explore the rock pools on the shore. Merry Rushton (Newth 1948-54) remembered lines of girls dodging spray along the Undercliff Walk – 'having braved the steep, pitch-dark tunnel to get there. So many steps, feeling each with one's heel, and shouts of "landing!" for the levelled out bits. So many shouts above and below that one never knew when one was going to arrive at a landing.' Merry recalled stormy seas 'and some of the loveliest sunsets I have ever seen'. She remembered lying in the grass in hot sun, and the banks of cowslips alongside the drive.

There were vivid storms to enjoy from the safety and security of school, crashing rolls of thunder and forked lightning illuminating the seascape. The view was especially good from Heaven, said Gwen Howe (Lawes 1949-52), whose room-mate 'used to dive under the bedclothes and not be seen again until it was all over – in case lightning struck her metal curlers!' After a big storm, or a fierce gale, the window panes were encrusted with salt whipped up from the sea.

Nicola Frith (1950-57) wrote of the wonderful contrasts in the weather, the ever changing seascapes and the lovely sunsets. Josephine Breyfogle (King 1953-55) loved the views of the sea and Downs, 'so open and different from what I was used to' and Kristin Hollis (Stephenson 1953-60) recalled 'wonderful summer days with golden wheat in the surrounding fields, blue skies and seas, and freezing winters with snow on the sea's edge and icicles in the bedrooms'.

'I was always staring out to sea when the cricket ball came my way,' Angela Jefferies (Blunt 1954-57) said. 'It was an unforgettable experience being perched on the cliff at Roedean exposed to healthy winds and sea air, and seeing the wonderful sunsets and beautiful seascapes.'

'Summer days were glorious, and the wind and the sea were exhilarating,' Angela Pain (Packham 1954-58) wrote.

'A sea-facing classroom was a particular treat. A window seat (near the radiator) allowed glimpses of shipping on the horizon, as did the SPR's lovely bow-shaped windows,' said Sarah Saunders-Davis (Osborn 1960-67). 'The Marina was only just under construction when I left. The summers were usually gorgeous – sunbathing on conti, house cricket and rounders on a summer evening. Winter gales could be very severe. Occasional snow blizzards allowed us to toboggan down the slopes below the terraces, and ice skate on the flats. Our long cloaks were ideal protection.'

Elizabeth Chapman (1963-69) remembered a freak snowstorm (probably in 1967) when cars were abandoned on the coast road, stranded strangers were put up at Roedean overnight and forty or so girls tramped in to Brighton to buy bread the next morning. There was snow cover for the whole of Lent term 1963, Carolyn

Skating on the flats during a spell of wintry weather

Phillippo (Williamson 1961-69) recalled. 'We were allowed to wear *trousers* for games, which consisted of tobogganing down the field in front of the school, often on tea trays. There were two broken arms sustained that term.'

Felicity Russell Heuter (Russell 1968-75) enjoyed sunbathing, topless, on the roof of Lawrence House. 'There were lots of us,' she said, 'and several helicopters . . . '

Roedean gave Nicola Schrager Von Altishofen (Lovett-Standing 1971-78) an abiding love of the sea 'especially on appalling days' and a love of windy weather. Mary Anne Sgarlat (1974-75) thought the weather was great, 'even the bad weather. I grew up in Boston, by the ocean, so was in heaven – the wind, the lovely summer days, the glorious views that are emblazoned in my memory.'

FABRIC OF THE SCHOOL

'Having experienced university, Roedean was the height of luxury.'

FEW of the women who were at school in the early years remember any form of heating, other than an occasional open fire, possibly because the inadequacy of Roedean's 'erratic and cranky' coal-fired heating system, with its cumbersome iron radiators, fought a losing battle against draughty windows and winter winds whistling along the corridors. And of those who did remember the radiators, the recollections were more often of being warned not to sit on them, for fear of getting piles, than for any warmth they produced.

Coal shortages during and after the First World War meant the system was barely operative and the girls shivered under layers of clothing, and suffered from chilblains. Keturah Crawford (Robinson 1918-1922) wrote of 'the threadbare carpets in the school corridors that billowed up in the wind, which rattled all the windows and howled around in the winter.' Sally Miall (Leith 1935-36) had a vague recollection of underfloor heating somewhere in one of the corridors. 'You could pause there for a few seconds and enjoy an upcurrent of warmth,' she said. Sally, head girl from Roedean South Africa, found Roedean 'terribly windy, wet and cold to someone from a dry, sunny climate'.

Antonia Joll (Ramsden 1917-27) remembered 'an extra week's holiday one summer when they installed electric lights!' Until then the school had been lit by gas.

The bedrooms were spartan, furnished with washstands, chests of drawers or dressing tables, iron beds 'with saggy mattresses', chamber pots under the beds – 'why did we need them when there were five lavatories on each floor?' Rosemary Watts (Stephens 1933-37) wondered, – and rugs on what some remembered as linoleum others as polished plank floors. On bitter nights, Pauline Norman (Davenport 1928-33) said, girls added the floor rugs to their bed covers for extra warmth. On the washstands were metal jugs and bowls for girls to wash themselves in their bedrooms, using cold water. Only five items were allowed on the chests of drawers.

The windows had to be open at night, Evelyn Condy (Finch 1918-23) said. 'My bed was under the window and sometimes there was snow on the covers in the morning.' Tatiana Macaire (Miller 1944-51) had the same experience more than twenty years later. 'I woke up, under the open window, with an inch of snow on my eiderdown,' she said.

The bathrooms were primitive, Evelyn recalled, and girls were allowed only three inches of water – up to a black line drawn round the bath. Other ORs remembered the line being at four, or five inches according to when they were at school.

Prefects' studies were much cosier, with furniture and rugs from home. 'We made very comfortable small homes for ourselves,' said Diana Poole (Wilson 1938-47).

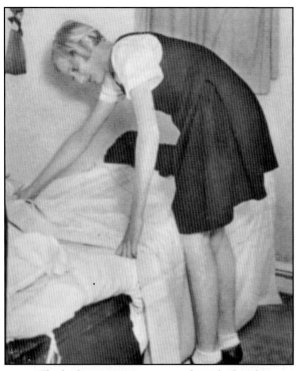

The bedrooms were spartan, furnished with iron beds having 'saggy mattresses'.

Some pupils from the Twenties remembered there being radiators in all the bedrooms (made ineffective by the gaping ventilators behind them) and coal fires in the prep rooms and housemistresses' drawing rooms. The boiler, Eppie Bartlett (Rutherford 1927-32) thought, was underneath Classroom 15. The heating system deteriorated the higher up the building you were, Beryl Barns (James 1932-36) said. 'It was almost non-existent on the top floor, likewise the hot water. One descended floor by floor as one progressed in seniority.'

Eluned Macmillan (Carey Evans 1929-39) remembered the frozen water in the bedroom jugs on winter mornings, and rain beating through the windows, but she always felt well at Roedean, she said – 'all that fresh air!'

Number Four had good carpeting, and the whole house was very well kept 'because we were the show house,' Pauline Norman said. Did she mean that only Number Four was shown to parents of prospective pupils?

Jean Borradaile (Gilmour 1932-38) claimed that girls caught cockroaches, for dissection in biology classes, in the long school corridor, and 'the catches were good,' she said. This was the corridor down which the wind 'howled like a banshee' on winter days, as Edith Hafenrichter (Burbeck 1931-37) described it, and where the linoleum rose with the wind making girls feel airborne.

When the school returned from the north at the end of the war it was to a building pitted and damaged by the Navy, to bleak, cold bedrooms and unseemly graffiti in the lavatories and the tunnel. Parents were instructed to supply girls with their own cutlery as the Navy had made off with the school's stock.

Ann Hulme (Prall 1945-50) remembered the 'threadbare carpets' on the landings and the dark green bathrooms in the Forties.

'Spartan' was the word most often used by ORs to describe conditions in the years after the war but, interestingly, few had complaints. 'We expected nothing else' was a phrase used almost as often. Pupil power was unknown in those days, the girls had no say in how their bedrooms were arranged, how often they should take a bath, whether windows should be open or closed. Rules were laid down and the girls accepted them without question.

Towards the end of the Fifties girls were allowed to personalise their rooms with pictures, postcards and ornaments, and portable radios. In the Sixties the old iron bedsteads and lumpy horsehair mattresses were replaced with modern divans. At the same time a scheme to modernise and replace the bathrooms began, and rattling, leaky windows – original from the time the school was built – were also replaced. The Eighties brought carpeting to the bedrooms, new central heating, the installation of showers – and an end to picturesque descriptions of bleak, icy, austere conditions. Girls who came afterwards moaned about insignificant inconveniences (the date when the central heating was switched on, sticking wardrobe doors), unaware of the pioneering, we-can-take-anything spirit of their tough predecessors.

Lawrence House was a revelation to senior girls, far removed, Ann Henley (1970-78) said, from the howling winds, draughty windows, threadbare carpets and cold plank floors of Main School.

'Having experienced university, Roedean was the height of luxury, although we never appreciated it,' Portia Da Gama Rose (1990-95) admitted. 'House Four was definitely the best decorated house, House Three the worst!'

GAMES

'We were not allowed to shower or take a bath after games . . . the locker room where we kept our games clothes stank appallingly.'

FROM the time that the Lawrence sisters opened their boarding school for girls in Kemp Town, Brighton, in 1885, physical education was high on the agenda. The prospectus stated: 'Special pains will be taken to guard against overwork, and from two to three hours daily will be allotted to out-door exercise and games. Opportunities will be given for Swimming, Riding, Dancing, and Gymnastics.'

Although the 'two to three hours' proved over ambitious, some form of physical exercise did form a large part of early pupils' working day. Girls walked, swam in the sea, rode and ran. Members of the Atalanta Club, formed in 1892, ran twice a week after breakfast to Ovingdean or Bevendean, and in the club's first year thirteen members took the train to Lewes and ran back.

The founders' sister, Christabel, launched Excelsior in 1892 as a junior cricket club and soon extended its scope to include other team games, and gymnastics. From her mother, who left Roedean in 1904, Ruth Maclean (Gimson 1936-41) heard that when the girls walked to the hockey field, in what is now East Brighton Park, they tied tape around their waists so that they could pull up their long skirts in order to run. 'However local residents were so shocked by the girls showing their ankles that they used to draw their curtains as they passed!' Ruth said.

Cricket fixtures against other schools began before the turn of the century, the Fathers' Match started in 1900 and lacrosse was introduced in 1902. Hockey was played until 1922 and later came netball, tip and run (a form of cricket), rounders and stoolball. All were called games, never sport.

Iris Phillips (1916-19) remembered the first eleven playing cricket against wounded soldiers who were recuperating in Brighton during World War One, but not which team won. Every afternoon in the summer Iris and her friends swam in the sea. To reach the beach, girls used the extraordinary tunnel cut through the chalk cliff from school to shore. It was unlit, three feet wide and had 144 steps, at the bottom of which was a small sheltered platform and a boathouse excavated in the base of the cliff. Until the Undercliff Walk linking Black Rock to Rottingdean was built, Roedean girls enjoyed a very private beach. 'Climbing back up was rather an effort,' Antonia Joll (Ramsden 1917-27) said.

The school's first swimming pool was built in 1907. It was out of use during the Great War, and for a year or two afterwards, because there was no coal to heat the water. The pool re-opened in 1921 but it was never popular with the girls. Joan Bowman (Read-Smith 1921-26) called it 'antique' and others described it as absolutely freezing, 'often with a film of dead insects and leaves on it'. Ruth Conolly (Warren 1921-26) remembered the pool being used for shooting practice.

The 'lovely teas' after home or away matches stayed in the memories of both Myra Cohen (Doniger 1922-28) and Winifred Hargreaves (Wade 1923-28); the teas were an important consideration for girls who were always hungry. Iris Ingram (Clark 1929-31) was useless at cricket, but learned to score just so that she could 'partake in match teas'. Even as late as the Seventies, Elizabeth Harvey (Frison 1974-77) saw match teas as a great fringe benefit. 'My years at Roedean had a pervading theme of wondering when my next decent meal would be,' she said.

Margaret Watson (Wheatley 1924-27) remembered rowing lessons, with Miss Lilian Hyde, on the sea, and Ruth Conolly remembered the weekly Scout

The cricket First Eleven, 1923, with coach Mr Bailey. Captain, L Brown.

runs over the Downs – 'a blissful liberation from being enclosed'.

'The school was divided by age into Excel for the under sixteens and Over-excel for older girls,' Betty Kent (Bidder 1925-30) explained. 'However good a girl might be, she was not allowed to play in the older group, although she could move from Excel straight into the first team when she reached the right age. Colours were awarded in both groups. Some people would win Excel colours but never achieve School colours.

'The games staff graded the whole school into sets, and school games were played on Tuesdays and Fridays, with matches against other schools on Saturdays. There could be as many as five school teams playing at home or away. I managed to achieve the second eleven at lax, so often went to a match on Saturday and travelled quite long distances to play suitable schools. If you were not playing you were expected to watch any matches at home. The important ones were those against Wycombe Abbey and Queen Anne's Caversham.' In later years the list of 'suitable schools' grew to include Benenden, Battle Abbey and Priorsfield.

Games were compulsory, and dreaded by girls who were not sporty. Edith Hafenrichter (Burbeck 1931-37) said that in her day senior girls were, instead, allowed to walk on the Downs in largish groups, with a mistress or prefect in charge.

Lorna Doveton (Scutt 1932-37) remembered the misery of practising lacrosse and cricket before prayers 'and coming in with a bright red face, and ears aching so that I could hardly work for the first period'. Nancy Spain, Lorna said, was a hard taskmaster at cricket practice.

Barbara Marshall (1935-38) recalled cup running. She explained: 'If our house had won a lacrosse or cricket match, the captain had to run along sixty bumping chairs while clutching the silver trophy, in order to get it safely on to the dining room dresser.'

In Keswick girls swam in chilly Derwentwater once the temperature of the lake had risen to 60°F. 'Rumour had it that Miss Tanner was rowed out into the middle of Derwentwater to dip in a thermometer,' Jenifer Fairpo (Fowler 1941-48) said. 'The bathing place was rather muddy and changing arrangements primitive. Those who could swim did; those who couldn't splashed about.'

Cricket and lacrosse were played 'in deep mud on Fitz Park', where there was a footpath running diagonally across the pitch. Gymnastics classes took place in the church hall where, Diana Poole (Wilson 1938-47) said, 'there were only four forms, four mats, a vaulting box, a vaulting horse and two springboards. The PE teacher, Miss Campbell Thomson, worked wonders with us on so little equipment.'

Post war, back in Brighton, it was 'endless games, without cease' according to Sarah Curtis (Myers 1945-53). 'Matches were intensely played and watching was compulsory. "Esprit de corps Number Four" was a better slogan than "A1 Number One", I thought. I became school cricket scorer to escape the game and get some of the glamour.' Carol Macdonald (Bennett 1945-48) hated games – 'a daily penance on an endless series of windswept pitches' – but she enjoyed stoolball, 'a kind of Sussex rounders', played against Brighton Girls' Club.

'I played sport as often as possible,' said Margaret Shimmin (Greig 1946-50). 'I played all sports as seldom as possible,' said Ruth Misa (Spielman 1945-49). Merry Rushton (Newth 1948-54) also loathed games. 'The best lacrosse and cricket teams played on pitches nearest the school, the least good furthest away. As I was bad and not interested in games, my team's pitch was always so far away that we were virtually next door to St Dunstan's! By the time we got there and got our team ribbons sorted out it was almost time to come back again.

'A vivid memory is of wearing a short tunic for lacrosse in mid-winter, and the wind like a whetted knife slashing across my thighs. I remember fighting back tears of pain and sheer misery.'

Caroline Quentin (Druiff 1954-60) tied a hot water bottle round her waist under her voluminous games sweater to keep warm while playing lacrosse on the icy, exposed clifftop. Sarah Watts (1986-94) always wondered why it was that girls were forced to take off their jumpers in the depths of winter to play lax 'when mistresses got to stand around in layers and layers of clothing and anoraks'.

Rosemary Athay (1955-59) remembered the occasional arrival of a flasher, known as 'Dirty Dick', outside the netting when the girls were playing cricket, and the subsequent confrontation with him by the mistress in charge.

Groundsmen had to be out of sight when girls were playing on the pitches, Merry said.

To Angela Pain (Packham 1954-58) deep fielding meant 'making daisy chains'. 'I was demoted to rounders and occasional stoolball. Lacrosse was more fun – exhilarating in the wind, but I was in a very lowly game.'

'We had to play some sort of games every day unless we had an excuse, signed by the housemistress for illness, or for having a period,' said Clare Holdsworth (Newnham 1956-61). 'If our periods seemed to be going on for too long we were made to see the doctor.' Katharine Coleman (Mackenzie 1961-66), on the same subject, said: 'If we suffered heavy and painful periods, games could be murder; we were seldom treated with sympathy. Colds were not considered sufficient excuse unless one ran a high temperature.'

'I faked a signature in order to get out of gym, at which I was no good,' said

74

An al fresco gym lesson in the cloisters, c1929.

Sheila Oberdieck (Miller 1935-43). 'I was better at forging!'

Katharine said: 'We were not allowed to shower or take a bath after games in any circumstances. If we got muddy, we could wipe our knees and do our best to clean up in a washbasin. The locker room where we kept our games clothes stank appallingly.'

Hockey was re-introduced in the Sixties, but was considered by some to be 'very inferior'. Sandra Ruddock (Watson 1979-84) remembered a hockey game against a team of local journalists, when newspapermen from the *Evening Argus* dressed up as St Trinian's girls. Which team won? Sandra did not say.

Fencing was an option in the Sixth Form. Jacqueline Rokotnitz Zhislin (Sawyer-Kammer 1953-57) took it up to avoid other games, found she was rather good at it and fenced for the school. 'There was great excitement when we had a match against Lancing College and were the envy of the whole school, going to see all those boys!' Jacqueline said. Mary-Grace Browning (Feachem 1956-62) was another who fenced to avoid team games.

The small, cold swimming pool – open air for many years after its roof blew off – was still in use when Carolyn Phillippo (Williamson 1961-69) arrived at Roedean. 'I loved swimming and went whenever allowed,' she said. 'If you dived in you got used to the temperature quickly.' After the new heated and covered pool was built, complaints about the water temperature ceased, although Elizabeth Harvey (Frison 1974-77) did detest the 'freezing, horrid walk to the pool in winter'. 'Swimming was great,' said Felicity Russell Heuter (Russell 1968-75), who described herself as 'a B- or C-team kid whom no one wanted in their team'. Felicity and Gail Maughan (Dawe 1968-72) both remembered a 'good gag' on Sports Day 1970, 'when some wit filled the old outdoor pool with potassium permanganate and the water turned bright purple'. Junior House girls were very impressed.

The new pool brought new opportunities, not least swimming matches for the first time against boys' schools. 'The boys were handicapped by starting a few seconds later,' Ann Henley (1970-78) said.

In the Nineties, 'games' became 'sport' and the options available would astonish, but also delight the Lawrence sisters who pioneered active physical exercise for girls at a time when walking, croquet and tennis were considered more than adequate.

Between them, Adaora Nwandu (1988-96), Sona Shah (1988-90), Zoe Green (1988-95), Portia Da Gama Rose (1990-95), Beatrice Arnell (1990-95), Michelle Chan (1992-96) and Anitha Sudheesh (1993-95) listed basketball, netball, rounders, tennis, swimming, fencing, yoga, bowling, karate, squash, cross country running, aerobics, lacrosse, hockey, athletics, wall climbing, badminton, multigym, trampolining, indoor hockey and archery among their sporting activities. 'When I arrived, sport was every day and compulsory,' Zoe said. 'My friends and I would go to any lengths to miss it, including standing on the seats in locked toilet cubicles, having three-week periods and pretending we couldn't use tampons because our parents wanted us to be virgins when we married.'

The Keswick Hotel, with the River Greta in the foreground.

KESWICK

'The windswept Downs of Sussex gave way to the beautiful, wooded, welcoming mountains ... the rigid discipline of Brighton was replaced by a less formal way of life. At last we began to feel like real people.'

WHEN war seemed inevitable in 1938, air raid shelters were dug between the Chapel and the Science Block, and the old tunnel to the beach was fitted out as a shelter for Number Four House. A year of fragile peace ended with the declaration of war on September 3, 1939. Sussex had been nominated as a reception area and the Francis Holland School, at Clarence Gate, London, was evacuated to Roedean where its pupils occupied Number One House.

Senior girls and some staff returned early for the autumn term in 1939 to help screen the school's 3,020 windows and paint white guide lines to the air raid shelters. Jean Marwood (Sharp 1937-42) remembered putting up plywood at the windows each evening, and the bathrooms had 'purple-coloured paint on the windows and orange-coloured bulbs in the lights – the principles of physics apparently said that purple plus orange equals black'.

Mary Marriott (Thompson 1937-40) was one of the Sixth Formers who went to the Royal Pavilion in Brighton to help fill in Ration Books. 'All the treasures had been removed for safety,' she said, 'but the ceilings were still a riot of colour with golden dragons looking down on us.'

A searchlight was placed near the cricket pavilion and staff were trained in ARP duties by Brighton Fire Brigade. It was the period of the 'phoney' war, an uneasy breathing space before the collapse of France.

'In the summer term of 1940 I remember lying with some friends, all of us with our ears to the ground, listening to the thump of guns in northern France,' Vivien Allen (Hallett 1937-43) wrote. 'At night, those of us whose rooms looked out to sea would twitch the blackout aside after lights out to see the flashes from across the Channel.'

Vivien described the procedure for air raid practice: 'You left your cloak and thick white games sweater by your bed at night and when the sirens sounded you put them on and went "as quickly as possible without running" to your allotted place'.

British troops were evacuated from Dunkirk in May 1940 and Roedean girls watched, on a day of absolute calm, as laden hospital ships sailed in to Newhaven Harbour. 'We could see big white ships with red crosses on the sides coming across the Channel from France,' Mary Marriott remembered. 'An emergency request for hundreds of bags to be ready in a few hours' time was sent to the school as they wanted to give each wounded soldier a shoe bag to put his personal belongings in. The whole school set to work sewing white drawstring bags, and produced more than 300 in no time at all.'

Dunkirk made the position of Roedean – on an exposed cliff top just seventy miles from the enemy across the Channel – untenable, and the decision was taken to evacuate.

On June 20 the school received a cable from the National Council of Education of Canada offering to take fifty Roedean girls at Edgehill School in Nova Scotia; within a week a party had been assembled and the girls sailed from Liverpool in the *Duchess of Atholl*, accompanied by Miss Briggs and Miss Marshall. Rosemary Naegele (Hurst 1938-40) was among them. She wrote: 'Our ship crossed the Atlantic alone, without a convoy and went far to the north to the coast of Labrador, past many icebergs, before sailing up the spectacular St Lawrence to Montreal. After a night there we started the long journey to Nova Scotia, by train and boat across the Bay of Fundy, and down to the province by train to Windsor, where the train chugged down the middle of the main street. Edgehill was a forbidding looking frame building, white, with peeling paint.'

Edgehill girls enjoyed the comfortable Canadian homes, the glorious food and the generous hospitality, and they became adept at winter sports – but they worried about their families, they felt guilty about the plentiful food, knowing that rations at home were so short, and they found the curriculum limited. There were no science, geography, art or cookery classes, no dancing or gym.

At school leaving age some of the Edgehill girls went to Canadian and American universities, others remained in Canada for the duration, but most returned to England to join the forces in the autumn of 1944, and special flights were arranged for them. A handful of younger girls returned at the same time to rejoin Roedean, now in Keswick. Their route was more circuitous, on neutral, civilian ships to Portugal where they awaited flights to an unknown destination in Britain.

When the Edgehill party left England, in 1940, the Upper Fifth and Sixth Forms moved to Oxford to avoid interruptions during the examination period. 'We slept and had breakfast in a convent, but took our exams and ate other meals at Lady Margaret Hall,' Sylvia Perry (Denis-Smith 1936-40) said. 'We were fascinated by the old world charm of Oxford and did very little revision.'

Back in Brighton, the term finished early and a search was mounted to find a suitable home for the school, away from enemy action. By the beginning of July, Hilda Leigh had scouted the Lake District for Roedean and discovered the Keswick Hotel, built by the Cockermouth, Keswick and Penrith Railway Company in the 1860s as a resort hotel. This, and a second hotel, the Millfield, offered the space needed and, more importantly, safety.

The decision was taken and the massive task of transporting equipment and arranging accommodation for 260 girls and all the staff was swiftly completed. School opened on September 5. The four senior houses occupied the Keswick Hotel and Junior House was spread between the Millfield Hotel and the Shu-le-Crow guest house.

For classrooms, the school used a gym and rooms behind the Methodist Church, the local art gallery and the waiting room and first floor rooms of Keswick Station. Cookery classes were held in the guest house and a science laboratory was located in the glass conservatory that linked the station to the Keswick Hotel. A studio was created in the hotel garage and, although bitterly cold in the winter, was soon bright and pleasant once art mistress Miss Martin had decorated it and covered the walls with colourful art work. There was no San, and when the sick room could not cope girls went to the small cottage hospital nearby. Nor was there a chapel and girls had the choice of the Methodist Church in Keswick or the Anglican parish church at Crosthwaite.

The first term at Keswick lasted fourteen weeks, to make up for the short summer term, and by Christmas 'everyone was very cross and tired', Susan Gatti (Booth 1940-45) said. But after the rigid restrictions of Brighton, the girls revelled in a new freedom. 'It was fun, and crazy – not really like school,' Ruth Misa (Spielman 1945-49) said.

Vivien Allen wrote: 'I loved the relative freedom and the beauty of the fells, but one friend said she couldn't stand all those mountains breathing down her neck, and left early. We had been so penned in at Brighton that walks and bicycle rides were a great joy. I remember one beautiful Saturday in May bicycling all round Bassenthwaite and meeting no other traffic. The only person we saw was a man ploughing with a team of horses, and seagulls following him. It reminded me of Masefield's *Everlasting Mercy* – "With holy white birds flying after".'

'Living in a large hotel and having lessons in the station waiting room was a novelty,' Ruth Maclean (Gimson 1936-41) said. 'Skating on the lake and walking and cycling in the fells made it the happiest year of my schooldays.'

'All its shortcomings were more than compensated for by my being allowed to go anywhere alone with my sketch book, a quite extraordinary change from the Brighton rules,' Isobel Bernstein (Forsell 1935-41) said.

The shortcomings included mice (and sometimes a practice piano) in the bedrooms, crowded accommodation (squashed luxury, one OR called it), bitter cold when jugs of water froze in the bedrooms and flannels became 'hard and crisp', frozen pipes (but the plumber was dishy and the subject of scandalous rumours) and chilblains.

In the hard winter of 1944/45 there were twenty seven degrees of frost, and eighteen inch long icicles hung at the windows. Bedroom ceilings collapsed at the Keswick Hotel and the bedrooms were so cold, Ann Portnoy (Levy 1944-47) remembered, 'that we rolled ourselves in blankets and then got into bed.' In class the girls wore mittens to keep their fingers from turning blue.

'We walked each morning to the Methodist Chapel for Prayers and Fitz Park became our sports field. We had bicycles and made use of them to see the Lake District. The situation at Keswick was more informal and we enjoyed a different school life there,' Audrey Kenyon (Hinchcliffe 1937-41) said.

'School at Keswick was more flexible because an hotel and a railway station are built differently from a school,' Rosamund Huebener (Bensen 1937-42) wrote. 'We were usually four to a bedroom instead of the two or three at

Brighton. The house identity was blurred and the whole school (except Junior) ate together. Staff were somehow less distant, because they were also scattered about the building. We walked daily through the town and were not cut off as in Brighton.'

Diana Poole (Wilson 1938-47) remembered long dining tables of ten or twelve with a member of staff at the head of each. 'We sat in houses, and there was a complete change of seating plan about two or three times a term. The hotel owners, the very portly Mr and Mrs Wivell, always stood and surveyed us all rather sternly.'

There was little heating in the Keswick Hotel – until then just a summer resort hotel – and at bath time girls were allowed only three inches of water, and ten minutes to wash. Incredibly, cold showers were introduced, Pamela Thalben-Ball (1939-44) recalled. 'After the first one I was excused as I remained blue for half a day!' Pamela also remembered snow in the Lake District in June. It was so cold in Miss Martin's art class, Margaret Bashford (Kay 1940-43) said, that to keep warm girls would all get up and dance the Sir Roger de Coverley.

Jillian Gordon (Albury 1939-48) was one of the girls who returned from

The railway station showing the waiting rooms where classes were held.

Canada in October 1944. She loathed Keswick – 'the food, the Wivells, the isolation – it was one of the worst years of my life. I was teased mercilessly for my Canadian accent and I had free elocution lessons to get rid of it.'

The classrooms in the station waiting room had 'frequent strange visitors – a marvellous distraction from a tedious lesson,' Jean Peacey (Thirlby 1937-45) thought. Ann Portnoy explained that there was nowhere for the public to wait for the noon train to Carlisle 'so they sat at the back of our class whilst we were being taught German (in World War Two!)'.

The conservatory science lab was more of a glass-roofed corridor linking the station to the hotel. 'I can hear now the indignant, high-pitched Scottish voice of Miss Will squeaking "Well, really and truly" as her botany lesson was interrupted yet again by a dripping wooden crate of kippers being carried through to the hotel kitchen,' Margaret Williamson (Blench 1944-46) wrote. Margaret Bashford remembered the biology class's frogs escaping into the large potted palms, and Miss Lloyd Williams trying to explain the mysteries of chemistry while snow dripped through the glass roof.

Susan Tolfree (Kelly 1937-41) took her School Certificate in 1940 in the stationmaster's office and the waiting room; Margaret took hers in the local museum 'among locks of Wordsworth's hair, strange maps and old prints'.

Six Roedean girls were taught physics with six boys from Keswick School. Jean Marwood, one of the girls, said the boys did the practical experiments, leaving the girls to make the analytical deductions and write up the results. 'Very sexist, but it didn't bother us in those days,' she said.

The sick bay was presided over by Mrs Wilson – The Willy – formerly matron of Number Four. Dilys Jordan (Dunn 1939-44) and another girl spent one Easter there with mumps. 'The Willy was so kind and the Wivells served us special food – but we couldn't eat the pigeon (supposed to be a delicacy) and it wouldn't go down the loo!'

If life was sometimes difficult in the cramped accommodation for girls and staff, it must have been equally fraught for the hoteliers, but the Wivells, who owned both the hotels, made great efforts to house and feed their guests as well as circumstances allowed. For the duration of the war they were honorary staff and entered into the spirit of school activities. In her 1941 diary, Eve Bysouth (Dowson 1939-46) wrote: 'To-night it was Hallowe'en's night, and at supper, after we had just sat down, the lights were turned out and through the dining room door came Mrs Wivell and three maids all draped in white sheets and long pointed hats with another sheet over the hats and face. They came dancing in shaking rattles and holding a large bowl with minced potato in it. They doled out the potato to everyone and told them to eat it carefully. They then danced round the room again and went out. Some people found charms and others found silver threepenny bits wrapped up in paper, in the potato. When the "witches" had come in everyone shrieked and hooted with laughter and stamped on the ground. I found two threepenny bits but Roysia found nothing.'

Dilys remembered 'a wonderful little man called William who spent his entire time stoking the foul-smelling anthracite stoves in the Keswick class rooms'; and she recalled the younger girls' loo roll rolling contests on the long, linoleum-covered top floor corridor at the hotel. 'War time loo paper was shiny, and scarce,' she said, and inevitably there was trouble when contestants were caught.

'Keswick seemed to be perpetually shrouded in mist,' Dilys said. 'The rain seemed to isolate us from the rest of the country. I found it unutterably depressing to be so hemmed in by mist-shrouded mountains. So rare was good weather that we were usually given a day's holiday when it came.'

She remembered playing games among the sheep in the park, the Sunday trek to church and seeing the salmon leap in the river. There were rehearsals for the colour play in the museum and piano practice in houses in the town.

'There were hilarious comments from soldiers arriving at the station on their way to commando training on seeing schoolgirls hard at work in the waiting rooms, and even more astonishing, the sight of nubile young women drilling as Rangers outside the station – one or two never did learn to co-ordinate legs and arms when marching!' Dilys added.

Jeanne Reeves (Stranack 1940-44) said: 'In the Rangers we had a man to teach us mechanics, which I enjoyed and it was very useful in later life. He showed us how to strip a car engine and put it back, and explained what the parts did.'

Roedean was welcomed into the community, not least for the prosperity it brought the town, and many enduring friendships were made, but there were inevitable small rivalries and animosities, and Janet Bailey (Ross 1942-47) recalled Keswick children's taunts of 'Rodie rat poison!' as columns of girls walked to lessons or to chapel.

Junior House in the Millfield Hotel was about ten minutes' walk from the Keswick Hotel. After the 8am breakfast girls had to walk to the Methodist Chapel for Prayers, and lessons were held in prefabricated huts in the garden and at Shu-le-Crow. Some of the girls slept in the guest house and others were lodged in private houses in the town. Ann Hulme (Prall 1945-50) slept out at 51 Blencathra Street for one term. 'The handbell was rung out of the window at Millfield, and woe betide you if you were late for breakfast,' she said.

The dormitories in Millfield were named after local mountains, and the classrooms after current war leaders – Churchill, Roosevelt, De Gaulle and

Stalin. Belinda McKinnel (Bleckly 1940-49) remembered passing time outside in the garden, playing ball against the wall, hopscotch, skipping and keeping caterpillars and snails as 'pets'.

Diana Kay (Johnson 1945-51) was desperately homesick and hated Junior House life at Keswick. 'We had a matron called Wallie who could make life hell. One poor girl ran away and her punishment was to be kept in a dark sick room for over a week, with no books or anything. She ran away again and stayed away in the end.'

Because of the difficulty of travelling in war time, few parents visited their daughters at Keswick. Jeanne Reeves remembered the time when she had chicken pox and her parents splurged their saved petrol coupons and travelled all the way from Malvern, in an Austin 7. 'My father was 6ft 6in, and how he got behind the wheel and squashed in his legs I don't know, it was a labour of love,' Jeanne said. 'Great excitement seeing them, and then The Muck said I couldn't go out with them as I still had one scab on my back. Naturally, I was very disappointed, but she was called out and my father got his penknife and removed the scab, and when The Muck returned he said "I think Jeanne's scab seems to have gone now", and The Muck looked, and was amazed. A friend and I were allowed out for a meal – a great treat.'

At the start of each term a special school train from London picked up girls en route. Jeanne joined the train at Stafford, with her brother, whose prep school, Windlesham House, had evacuated to Ambleside; he travelled as far as Penrith. 'I remember being miserable when it was time to say goodbye and had to hide in the loo in case the other girls saw me crying,' she said. 'It was a long journey and we had to have two engines up Shap Fell.'

In the winter of 1944/45 Derwentwater froze over and girls sent for their skates. Janet Bailey (Ross 1942-47) recalled that the girls back from Canada were very much envied for their *white* boots.

For the war effort, girls collected rose hips for syrup, and sphagnum moss, to be made into bandages. They knitted sea boot socks and balaclavas in oiled wool for sailors and organised sales of work to raise money for good causes – the Russian Army's horses, the Red Cross and Keswick Cottage Hospital.

Despite difficulties caused by the war, Roedean continued to arrange regular lectures and concerts given by visiting notables. Vivien Allen remembered, in particular, a song recital by a young woman with a glorious voice. 'Miss Monk said, "Remember that name – Kathleen Ferrier". She was then just a bank cashier in Carlisle.'

The traditional Saturday evening dances continued, pupils performed in plays and concerts for local people, and occasionally they went to the cinema.

There was a daily morning service in the Methodist Chapel and on Sundays

*The walk across Fitz Park – in Keswick Roedean's ironclad
rule of never being seen outside school without a hat was relaxed.*

an 11am service at St Kentigern, the parish church at Crosthwaite, or the high
Anglican St John's Church. Evensong on Sunday evenings was taken by Dame
Emmeline in the hotel lounge. Some of the girls joined Crosthwaite's depleted
team of bell ringers, others sang in the choir, and memories remain of fellow
choristers – Tom Wilson, who drew caricatures during lessons, prayers and
sermons, Billy Thompson, the joking policeman, Percy McKane, the printer,
with his terrific nasal bass and Mr Fleming, the decorator, with his one flat
lock of hair plastered round the front of his bald head, and his large ruby ring.

On VE Day in May 1945 the girls celebrated victory on top of Latrigg,
behind the hotel. 'We climbed to the top of the mountain and lit a huge bonfire
in the evening. There was singing and dancing, and we ran home in the dark,
very late,' Gillian Pemberton (Cameron 1944-48) said.

Mary Driver (1939-45), who spent most of her Roedean schooldays in
Keswick, said: 'I cannot speak highly enough of what was done to help us in
difficult circumstances by all the staff.'

The return to Brighton was accomplished amazingly smoothly, Mathilde
Edward (1944-50) remembered. But it was to a Roedean very different from
that of 1939. In the bleak post-war years shortages and rationing continued and

no longer were there some fifteen men working on the estate, and seventy five resident domestics.

IN September 1990 women who had been at Keswick as schoolgirls held a two day reunion in the Keswick Hotel on the fiftieth anniversary of Roedean's evacuation. It was organised by Pamela Allen (Day-Winter 1936-42) who said, of her schooldays: 'For those of us who had been in Brighton it was a wonderful feeling of release to be surrounded by the ever-changing views of the fells, and to enjoy the freedom of movement between classrooms, the town, our outings and our expeditions'.

Old Roedeanians attended from all over the world. 'Some of us were trendy in culottes, some sensible in tweeds, but we were all agreed that at our age our clothes should not actually hurt,' ran an account in the *OR Magazine*. 'Had anyone fallen ill we need not have worried – six of us were doctors. We also mustered two diplomats, a musician or two, a deacon, a lawyer, a journalist, a recently retired headmistress, a ditto head of BBC Children's Radio, a number of businesswomen and plenty of straight up and down housewives. But for two days all that was of no consequence; we were a happy group of old friends and a high old giggly time we had of it.'

Pamela devised a programme that included walks and talks, a dinner and a service in Crosthwaite Church. Ann Longley, the then headmistress, arrived from Brighton for the dinner and another guest was Brigadier Anne Field, who before her retirement was head of the WRAC, and ADC to the Queen. To the ORs she was Anne Hodgson of Keswick High School and a member of the Crosthwaite church choir. Also present was Carol Sarsfield Hall, who had the distinction of being Roedean's only day girl at Keswick.

Excerpts from memories of Keswick written by some of the ORs during the reunion follow.

'Fifty years on the truth can be told. It was a remarkably hot day, incredible in the heart of the fells and velvet green hills that usually held mist and rolling clouds like a fur collar around Keswick. Our close group of four friends were all preparing mock exams and were on a fairly loose rein between revising. We were also sub-prefects so we could go off on cycle rides. Jane Goldsmith, Joyce Pinney, Maureen Miller and I headed towards the lake and without much ado we hired a boat, a skiff, to row out to a further island.

'By the time we had manoeuvred oars and rudder almost to the middle of the lake we were falling about with laughter and a sense of freedom that a year at Keswick had blessed us with after the isolation of the old gaunt school high up on the flats of Brighton.

'We grounded the boat on a pebbly strand and decided to sunbathe in the remarkable heat. In those days there was no teenage culture, no Ambre Solaire, no search for the ideal shade of brown tan. It was war time and life was honed down to bare essentials. We decided to do the same with ourselves in the blazing sun. So off came all the clothes and in we went into rippling clear unpolluted water. There were no tourists in those days, no coach tours, wind surfers, sail boats or launches. Derwentwater was its pristine, innocent, original essence, a lake of clean water.

'Consider then our consternation when another skiff glided silently and swiftly round the curve of the island. It was Miss Godfray – Minnie Ha Ha of the waters! And we were skinny-dipping with nowhere to hide.

'Taken in tow we were, dripping hair, hastily dragged on shorts clinging to our wet bodies. We were rushed up to the hotel by this irate staff member, straight in to see Miss Middleton. All I can remember was her hawklike, speechless stare, and a rapid transfer to Dame Emmeline Tanner's study where her august frame, in its ruched and pleated bodice with many tiny buttons, seemed to tower over us.

'I can't really remember the admonitions we must surely have received, but I do remember all four of us were un-sub-prefected in front of the school next day, like so many hens being de-beaked.' Anon

'Dressed in my very ill-fitting uniform – nearly all secondhand, or made rather badly from ex-naval blankets, and bought to allow for lots of growth – I say goodbye to my parents, and we set off on the long journey north . . . Finally we arrive at Keswick Station. It has been raining heavily, but the rain has stopped and the sun has come out. Every leaf sparkles, the air has a sharp freshness and the view of the mountains which surround us is intoxicatingly beautiful. It is one of the most magical moments of my life.

'Memories of Millfield . . . the hard yellow field peas, the almost uneatable pies that we used to hide in the napkin bags, the bread dipped in tepid bacon fat, the lumpy porridge.' Susan Crosfield (Martin 1945-50)

'Grey skies, grey stone houses, the smell of smoke from the trains, Grace walking up and down the platform ringing the bell between forties. Trying to get chocolate out of the machines on the platform – they soon ran out. Being hungry – kedgeree and rabbit and damson jam on semolina. A bun and an orange to sustain one on long Saturday walks up hills. Seeing Dean Inge, which meant nothing at the time, but whose prayers and sayings I rather like now.' Anon

'There was a letter box outside the station with a stamp machine above it. Every time we passed on the way to lessons in the station rooms we lifted the flap of the stamp machine – once a girl had found a stamp there. There was a continuous "click click" as we all dashed past, lifting the flap.' Anon

'My abiding memory is our total obsession with food. The basic fare was quite disgusting – oceans of yellow custard and loaves of grey National Bread on which one spread a nauseating mixture of chocolate spread (made at one's scrum table from cocoa, sugar and milk) . . . The fear of being tongue-tied when sitting up to Minnie Ha Ha, who in any event did not wish to listen to chatter whilst she tackled her kipper; the complicated procedure of selecting tables; the difficult art of staring at the girl opposite until she remembered to ask if you would like some water, bread or whatever. I recall how I cajoled dear Dr Mills into prescribing yummy Radio Malt for me (not that horrid Cod Liver Oil and Malt) and persuaded him that Marmite was essential for my well-being.' Anon

'It was amazing how we all adapted to the new way of life, and I remember vividly that first autumn we were here, the freedom of movement, the beautiful surroundings and the discovery that hill walking was the most exhilarating activity ever.

'Derwentwater froze over that first winter and we skated on the lake and the snow was thick enough to make an igloo on the front lawn of the hotel.

'Our education continued as before – there was no drop in standards, only a change of conditions. I shall always appreciate the way Miss Monk and Miss Lucchesi came up from Brighton by rail to give us our music lessons; their description of their wartime journeys was quite horrific, but they never missed, and the orchestra continued as before.

'We made our contribution to the war effort, gardening and knitting (sweaters for the Argyll and Sutherland Highlanders, thick mittens with trigger fingers for the Russian front soldiers).' Anon

'The windswept Downs of Sussex gave way to beautiful, wooded, welcoming mountains. At the same time the rigid discipline of the Brighton days was replaced by a far less formal way of life . . . The freedom must have gone to my head. On the way to the Chapel one morning I discarded my hat — unthinkable. My punishment was that I had to play games in my hat — a fate worse than death at that self-conscious age. Anyway, at the last minute the heavens opened and it poured with rain. No games!'
Maureen Eastwood (Miller 1935-41)

'My recollections of Keswick school days include being taught bridge by dear Lloydy Bill at the house prefects' weekly get-togethers; going down the long corridor to quell the noise of some exuberant youngsters in their bedroom, to hear the lookout say, when I reached the door, "It's all right, it's only Squance"; a picnic on one of the islands in the lake with Miss Fyleman and spitting cherry stones into a bottle.' Anon

'I was one of the few members of the Francis Holland School to go with Roedean to Keswick. I remember particularly the great friendliness and feeling of togetherness I met on every side. Never for a moment did I feel out of things or lonely, and being an outdoor girl the wonderful challenge of climbing with Miss Spearing thrilled me and provided me with an interest that I've never lost.' Patty Maxwell (Scott 1940-41)

'I think my first memory of Roedean at Keswick was of Miss Tanner – large and impressive, but not at all formidable. I had arrived from a boarding school on the south coast which had closed because of the war, my mother had just died, and I must have been immersed in grief and lack of confidence. However I felt reassured and supported by her kindness and understanding, as well as amazed by her prodigious memory of the names and circumstances of every girl in the school.' Jane Spicer (Mackinnon 1940-44)

'My memories include lines of pixie hoods bobbing through Fitz Park; the occasion of Pastor Niemuller's visit when we in the congregation were singing *A Safe Stronghold Our God Is Still* while he sang the hymn in German – a great moment; the queue for hair washing by the team from a Keswick salon, followed by a session by the fire, or using the dryer in the maid's room; the Music Club singing Gilbert and Sullivan to a "pressed" audience of the local servicemen – we hope they enjoyed it; how the garage was transformed into a studio with murals, printed curtains, but cold, very cold in the winter. We sat muffled in scarves, cloaks, extra socks and mittens while, I swear, the paint froze on our tin palettes.' Anon

'Aircraft used to fly low over the lake; later we learned that they were practising for the Dam Busters' Raid. Watching them from my bedroom window one day, I saw a plane coming low out of the jaws of Borrowdale. It disappeared from sight over the lake, there was a bang and it did not reappear. For three days we were not allowed near the lake while the wreckage was located and lifted, and the bodies recovered.

'I remember taking all my clothes, apart from tunic and shoes, into bed with me on winter nights and dressing under the blankets next morning. I remember being hungry and buying rum butter in the town to be eaten after lights out with the handle of my toothbrush.' Vivien Allen (Hallet 1937-43)

'I faked a tummy pain to avoid a maths lesson, was put into sick bay and from there, in spite of protestations, was taken to the cottage hospital. There I had my appendix removed – the first Roedean girl to be operated upon. I had two lovely weeks of recuperation at a guest house on the other side of Fitz Park.

'An abiding memory of envy of Hilary Garstin, who fell over the handlebars of her bike descending a mountain path. She suffered temporary concussion, as a result of which she was excused from taking any exams that term, and sat, wreathed in happy smiles, reading books of her choice from the fiction library, while her unfortunate friends continued on the unremitting path of sweat and swot.' Pamela Gilbast (Seager 1937-40)

'At the end of term we would bag our seats on the train the night before we left. The carriages had all been shunted on to a side line at the station and we were up at 4am for breakfast before being shooed on to the train for home.

'I remember Hilary Garstin falling off her bike half way up a mountain. She was concussed and I stayed with her, stripping off as much as I dared to keep her warm (it was sleeting). The others cycled off to alert a doctor, who had to reverse his car up the track as there was no turning point.

'Hilary, Daphne Dawkes and I got lost on an expedition above Rydal Water. We were meant to aim for Grasmere. Eventually we were picked up in the dark in pouring rain by a couple driving home to Ambleside, who telephoned the school. Mrs Wivell, The Tanner and Lloydy drove over to collect us. The sixteen or so miles back to Keswick were passed in stony silence. I don't remember any punishment, but I do remember Lloydy suggesting that we should be chained to responsible girls, also that no one should go on an expedition again without twopence to telephone if we got lost.

'I remember picking soft fruit in the vicar's garden and picking hips and haws; the salmon leaping in the Greta as we walked through Fitz Park; the cedar wood shop in town and its lovely smell; the cockatoo in the aviary in the hotel gardens. I remember Daphne stuffing books and a pencil box up her knickers coming from the station classroom to the school bedroom to swot (illegal). A train had just unloaded hundreds of commandos, who had come to train in the hills. Daph's elastic gave way on the platform, showering pencils and papers everywhere, much to her embarrassment and confusion. But the soldiers loved it.' Margaret Hill (Davies 1940-44)

90

'I remember trying to persuade the hotel cat to stay just a little longer on my knees, to keep out the cold; laying pennies along the pavement in Station Road for the Wings for Victory Week mile of pennies; sitting hunched against the driving rain and eating a sodden picnic lunch; bathing in Derwentwater with the novelty of fresh water waves; the odd and unpredictable movement of the suspension bridge over the Greta.

'Best of all I remember standing in the space between the carriages on the 5am train for home, and watching the sparks fly and the undertinge of reddish gold on the steam cloud as the engine raced down Shap to Oxenholme.' Rachel Nugee (Makaver 1939-44)

'At one House Fancy Dress Elizabeth Hale, Susan Lloyd Williams and I dressed up effectively as Hitler Youth. Late that Saturday evening we went on to the station platform to fetch something from the form, and passengers were alarmed to see a line of goose-stepping, saluting brown shirts advancing on them.' Gillian Cotgrove (Grindley 1941-44)

'I remember the awful head colds we had. We never had enough handkerchiefs so we had to wash them out ourselves and flatten them on the bedroom walls to dry. My blazer sleeves often had to catch the drips. I also remember darning and re-darning stockings and navy blue knickers until they were covered in darns.

'I loved the surroundings – seeing the hills and mountains on waking up and going to sleep. We learned Wordsworth's poetry my first year for School Certificate and living in the Lake District made it so relevant.' Sheila Oberdieck (Miller 1935-43)

'It seemed a real adventure – coming to Keswick in September 1940. I had never seen mountains before, and found them at first quite frightening.

'I remember the warmth of Mr and Mrs Wivell, the cockatoos and other birds in the garden aviary, the fun of having lessons in a station waiting room and a hotel conservatory. I remember the countryside around the hotel – the beauty of Derwentwater and Friars Crag, the pigs rooting wild in the woods and the excellent bacon they provided for breakfast.' Nancy Pirie (Crow 1933-40)

HMS VERNON

*'On dark summer nights, out of the deep purple across the Channel,
the V1s first appeared like fireflies until the glow of their tails
became fierce back-burner flames.'*

BELOW a bell push above every student's bed at Roedean was an ivorine label engraved with the legend 'Press the button if you need a mistress for any reason during the night'. The young sailors who moved into the school when it was requisitioned by the Admiralty during World War Two needed no second invitation but, instead of 'the blonde brass of Betty Grable or the deep dark charm of Vivien Leigh', of whom trainee Thomas Gurney dreamed, the restless sailor was more likely to be visited by an irate CPO who threatened unspeakable punishment 'if ever he pressed that ....ing button again'.

No sooner had the school closed in the summer of 1940 to prepare for the evacuation to Keswick, than a contingent of Argyll and Sutherland Highlanders arrived for training, occupying Number Three. Then came the Queen's Royal Regiment, followed by four Canadian regiments and the London Scottish.

On April 7, 1941, the Royal Navy took over the school, and Roedean became HMS Vernon. The shore-based training establishment had been bombed out of its Portsmouth headquarters. On the next clifftop to the east, the newly built St Dunstan's Home for blinded service men was also requisitioned by the Navy. During the war, some 31,500 officers and men passed through the school on various courses.

An apocryphal story, repeated by many Roedean Old Boys, relates that there were still a few Sixth Formers remaining at the school when the Navy arrived. HMS Vernon's CO, the story went, insisted that they leave before the sailors moved in. 'My girls will be all right; they've got it up here,' said the mistress in charge, tapping her forehead. 'Madam, it matters not where your girls have got it, rest assured my sailors will find it,' said the CO. Sadly, for it is an excellent story, it cannot be true; the dates do not coincide.

HMS Vernon provided intensive training courses in torpedoes, mines, depth charges and shipboard electrics. Some courses lasted just two weeks, others took several months.

Their first sight of the imposing clifftop buildings made markedly different impressions on the sailors. Some saw Roedean as a grand stately home, others as a dark, grim prison. Thomas Gurney, who spent the summer of 1944 there, loved 'the stately building overlooking a green that sloped down to the Sussex cliffs'. Charles Farr, September 1943 to April 1944, considered the contrast between Roedean and Chatham Naval Dockyards 'very uplifting to a young sailor and good for morale'. James Hinton, July 1943 to February 1944, thought it looked drab and institutional, and Len Tindall was reminded of Alcatraz.

'I was very young,' Tindall recalled. 'In fact I was of an age where, with a gender change, the right connections and a gym slip, I could have been at Keswick, bellowing out the school song.' He had just completed a torpedo course in Portsmouth and was prepared 'to take on the might of the German Navy'. So it came as a surprise to be issued instead with a travel warrant to Brighton, and to fetch up in the dead of night, in a snow storm, at the gates of a girls' school in Sussex.

'Through the snow flurries it stood bleak against the sky and my mind went back to the films I had seen about Alcatraz. To make matters worse, as I entered the guard room, a voice barked: "Go art agin and knock that bleedin' snow orf yer".'

Many of the ROBs remarked on the unusually small rooms at Roedean, finding them cramped after the great barracks and dormitories they had come from, although all relished the relative privacy of a single, double or three bed 'cabin'. 'It was such a luxury after the smelly accommodation of sleeping quarters with hammocks slung from the ceiling, virtually touching,' said Farr.

'A sprung bunk, a cabin to myself and the invitation to ring for a mistress! One did dream!' was Gurney's comment.

P T Greenwood, then a green young officer, was with a group who were summoned to a classroom and shown a large box. 'We were told that if we ever mentioned anything about the inside of the box, or the lecture, we would be taken off for hanging or shooting – whichever was the easiest,' he said. 'Inside was the British version of the ENIGMA coding machine; if necessary we would be called upon to repair it. Just as the lecture started the alarm for a gas attack drill sounded so on went gas masks. We had been told to coat the inside of the eyepieces with a thin layer of wax to prevent them misting up, but nobody had, so whilst we could hear, we never saw very much.'

Hinton and three others shared a bedroom in Heaven where an enormous length of thick rope was coiled beneath one of the double bunks. 'We were told that it was our fire escape, and that in the event of fire we had to secure one end to the bunk and lower the other out of the window. Very difficult it proved to be on the one practice we had,' he said.

Not all the trainees lived in the school. Some were accommodated at St Dunstan's and others in private houses in Brighton. Unlucky Richard Kelsall, June to July 1943, suffered a dreadful billet in town where the food was poor and the bed was full of bugs. Peter Day fared better. He and twelve other sub-lieutenants were given a flat in Marine Gate at Black Rock. They had their meals at Roedean but slept in the flat. One evening all thirteen went to the Hippodrome to see Flanagan and Allen, and Zoe Gail, in *Black Vanities*, and afterwards they took the three stars back to their flat for a party.

Robert Foster rented a flat in Rottingdean so that his wife and son could join him in Sussex, and James Marigold, son of an OR (Joyce Mathey, 1900-09) took a house in Brighton to be with his wife. Another Vernon officer with Roedean links was M F B Ward, an instructor, who was married to OR Patricia (Sayers 1926-29), was the son-in-law of an OR, Lucile Sayers (Schiff), and the father-to-be of a future pupil, Mary (1952-58). This family, too, lived for a time in Rottingdean. Patricia said: 'It always came as a shock to see sailors instead of girls at Roedean.'

Jack Griffin, on a fortnight's course in 1944, had digs in Kemp Town and his recollection was of 'classes, lunch, classes, tea, classes, dinner, lorry, digs, lorry, breakfast'.

Like the girls of Roedean, the sailors were often hungry. 'The food always seemed to be supplied with plenty of beetroot and lettuce,' Gurney said. 'They masked the quality of the soya link sausages.' A favourite Navy sweet, he said, was a pastry tart spread with a large quantity of jam and finished with a layer of thick custard. 'Very good for morale.'

Hinton thought the food satisfactory – 'though it must be said that some of it found its way out of the school, in the possession of some of those responsible for serving it. In particular, eggs, butter, sugar and tea disappeared this way – presumably on to the black market. Customs and Excise officers sometimes positioned themselves at the gate and searched, selectively, those leaving the establishment. On such occasions the word would always get around and a large black ace of spades would appear on the noticeboard in the hall as a warning to would-be offenders.'

The White Ensign flew proudly from the flagstaff in front of the quadrangle – renamed the quarter deck. At the main gate a guard with fixed bayonet stood, and in the guard room were a petty officer and two ratings. A perimeter sentry, with rifle and bayonet, patrolled night and day. Sam Morley, in his book *99 Years of Navy* (Quiller Press, 1995) remembered the lurid thoughts and fears that crowded his mind when he was on duty watch during the long night hours. He had visions of a U Boat lurking below and of swarms of Germans scaling the cliffs and surging across the coast road to capture HMS Vernon.

The whole establishment was expected to attend Sunday Divisions on the quarter deck. Charles Farr remembered parades on brisk winter days with 'marvellous views of the sea, snow on the ground and clear skies'. The previous winter had been arctic and iron hard, with snow drifts well up the outside boundary walls, and to Frederick Barrett the parades were 'very bleak indeed'.

As well as Sunday Divisions there were services in Chapel and, for officers, drinks in the wardroom afterwards. Gurney liked the peace of the Chapel and remembered that there was always a full house, the service being taken by 'sky pilots' as the Fleet Air Arm padres were known. 'After Sunday Divisions some of us used to go to Neville House (a family hotel at Black Rock) for a cuppa, a biscuit and a quiet read of the Sunday papers, or we went ice skating in Brighton.' The Sunday services were always sea-oriented, Hinton recalled, with such hymns as *Eternal Father*.

While the young trainees came and went, the war raged on, and although Brighton suffered some of the worst attacks outside London and the industrial areas, few ROBs recalled them. Sam Morley remembered flashing lights and distant rumblings from across the Channel, like a massive thunderstorm, when the Germans cut down the ill-fated Commando raid on Dieppe in August 1942 – the so called 'rehearsal' for D-Day.

'My time at Roedean was doodlebug time,' Gurney wrote. 'The V1 flying bombs made regular visits throughout June. We rigged a Lewis gun on the plant room roof at St Dunstan's. If you could hit them in the gyro or master compass area you could send them back home.

'On dark summer nights, out of the deep purple across the Channel, the V1s first appeared like fireflies until the glow of their tails became fierce back-burner flames. My first sight was on one summer lunch time. We were enjoying a half pint at the bar at St Dunstan's and I remarked to a friend how ironic it was that such a lovely view through the windows could never be appreciated by the blind residents. As I spoke this unusual flying machine chuffed by the window. We thought it was a new type of aircraft in trouble, as flames were coming out of the end. I think that doodlebug dropped in on Croydon by way of Lewes.'

Ray Garrad, who considered Roedean the best billet he had in his four and a half years in the Navy, remembered the time he and his classmates were assembling for a course photograph 'when suddenly there was the roar of low flying aircraft and the sound of cannon shells being fired,' he said. 'It was amazing how quickly the quadrangle cleared. There were no casualties or damage. One of the German aircraft was shot down by a Canadian-manned

Ack Ack battery adjacent to Roedean. The plane crashed into the sea less than five hundred yards in front of the school. The pilot's body was washed up two weeks later.'

Edwin Chapman, August 1943 to March 1944, found that the great majority of the 'inmates' – recent civilians, many of them, who had experienced air raids in crowded industrial areas – were contemptuous of the possibility of harm in such a remote place as Roedean. 'Consequently they preferred to stay in bed when an air raid warning sounded. However, the Navy took this matter very seriously and those of us on duty were instructed to wake everyone and tell them to get into the shelters (very cold, damp, depressing places). I drew the short straw on one occasion and was allocated the Wrens' quarters. At eighteen years of age, having what I now regard as a sheltered upbringing, and without the civilising influence of sisters, I was completely unprepared for my task. Some Wrens were adorned with what appeared to be miniature Radar aerials. I can give no better description of the metalwork in their hair. In reply to my request that they should go to the shelters, some smiled sweetly and went back to sleep. Others, who had a more complete and coarser vocabulary than myself, told me in no uncertain terms to "go away".'

The trainees' courses were highly concentrated, with classes morning and afternoon, and compulsory revision in the evenings, so there was little time for leisure activities. As well as their training at Roedean and St Dunstan's, the sailors attended practical torpedo classes at the Dreadnought Garage in Brighton, and in the garage of the Grand Hotel.

Marching back from the Dreadnought on Saturday mornings, Hinton said, he occasionally slipped away from the back of the column at the Clock Tower and took off up Queens Road to the station for an unofficial weekend leave – although only when he had found a duty stand-in.

When they could, some of the sailors went to Brighton to see a film, or attend a dance at The Dome or the Regent Ballroom. Others preferred walking on the Downs or watching ice hockey.

Only the officers appear to have taken part in sport at Roedean. Captain Marigold played hockey and tennis, and Harry Howting played his first game of hockey at Roedean when his team was beaten by 'ruffian' Wrens. There were also, he said, a few games of cricket against local service sides, but on the whole organised sport was rather rare.

'I am proud to call myself a Roedean Old Boy,' said Tindall. 'It taught me the first lessons of survival in the service. What and what not to volunteer for. By logging the dials in the boiler room one would not only enjoy the warmth but could chat up the Wren cooks to one's advantage. By visiting various ammunition dumps on the Downs one could eventually arrive at a cottage

96

During the 1920s and early 1930s pictures of the school, painted by pupils, were used to illustrate the Roedean calendar.

Above is a picture of the school from the cricket field, painted by Margaret J Marshall, who was a pupil between 1922 and 1928.

On the right is a view of the Chapel interior, painted by J Pearman Smith.

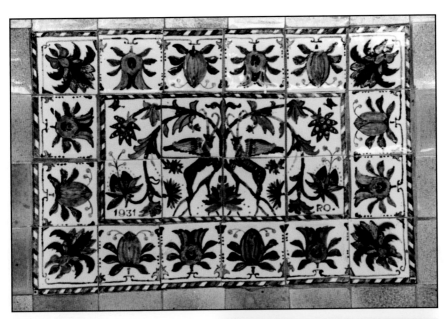

The tiles that line the Studio walls
were all made during the 1920s and
1930s by pupils under the charge of
Dorothy Martin, and are on various
themes of fantastic mythical foliage
and animals. They include the signs
of the zodiac, the months of the year
and a selection of the seven deadly
sins and the virtues.

The picture left, of VE Day celebrations at Keswick, was painted by Judith Rich (Willmore 1945-49) when she was in the Third Form. She said: 'It shows a huge bonfire on top of Latrigg, and girls climbing up in white sweaters and navy shorts. It was a magical experience as most of us could not remember the experience of a bonfire ever before. Keswick Station, in the picture, shared the forecourt with the hotel. Watching the scene are Number Three house staff – from the right, Miss D B Will in silk stockings and high heeled shoes, Miss Joan Spearing, housemistress, with a slight hunch as she always held her shoulders in a rather compact manner, Miss Thompson, who was our games mistress, an enthusiastic mountain climber and who wore trousers, and Miss Godfray, who wore blue often and had two hair buns at that time. I am not sure who the girls are.'

Evening Argus

Headmistress Ann Longley and students Emily Hodge, Victoria Scarlett, Flavia Taylor and Sophie Clarke celebrate the news that Roedean had come top of the class in 1994. Schools inspectors gave the school a glowing report, praising the high academic standards and the happy environment. The pupils were articulate, questioning and quick to pick up ideas, the inspectors said, and staff and pupils shared a mutual respect which encouraged learning.

Another of the calendar paintings from the early years is pictured left. This one is of School House. Artist unknown.

whose occupant made the best apple pie in the world. By volunteering for guard duty at the Dreadnought Garage I could not only get on friendly terms with the Hippodrome chorus line, but could get a free ticket.'

Two marriages were made at Roedean during the conflict. Jack Parsons, on an artificer course between December 1941 and August 1942, met a Wren called Vi and they married on June 5, 1943. Vi had arrived at the school in July 1941 and she remained there for the duration, serving with other Wrens on the administration side of HMS Vernon. Vi's strongest memories were of Princess Marina inspecting the Wrens, of the wave after wave of ships going down the Channel on D-Day and of the service of thanksgiving in the Chapel at the end of the war.

Leading Torpedo Man Felix McClusky and Wren Dorothy Hamlet, who married in 1942.

The second marriage was between Felix McClusky and Dorothy Hamlet. Their story was told by Dorothy's brother, Ronald, former Boy Telegraphist, RN. He said: 'My father was Chief Torpedo Gunner's Mate at Roedean and I visited the school just once, whilst on a seven day leave. Felix was qualifying for TGM in my father's class and helped carry my late sister, a Wren, to the sick bay when she fainted on the school premises. We used to say that Mac carried her off in '42 and he's been carrying her ever since. It was a marriage made in Heaven. Alas, they are now all gone to that great torpedo battery in the sky.'

IN 1994, half a century after his service at Roedean, Sam Morley called the school to enquire whether a group of septuagenarian sailors could pay a visit. Roedean was delighted to hear from him, and lunch and a conducted tour were arranged. On July 20 that year, fifty four old matelots were re-united, and the Roedean Old Boys' Association was formed.

SPECIAL OCCASIONS

Memories are strong of house plays, staff plays, school plays and colour plays over the decades, of recitals and poetry readings, of attending concerts, operas and plays in Brighton and London.

'EMPIRE Day used to be our great day,' said Phyllis Bower (Hopkin Morgan 1917-21). 'The whole school lined up in single file and saluted the flag; it made a lovely long snake. And then the rest of the day would be a holiday and something would be arranged for us.'

The day, May 24, began with prayers and then the girls were told where they were going for their outings. Each house had a different destination. But before they could run to the open charabancs, where huge picnic hampers had been loaded, there was the ceremony of the flag. 'One of us would beat on a drum while the school solemnly marched in single file down to the lower flat where there was a flagpole,' Eluned Macmillan (Carey Evans 1929-39) said. 'The Union Flag was raised, we saluted and marched back.' Then it was off to Ashdown Forest, perhaps, to Chanctonbury Ring, Arundel Park, a zoo or to

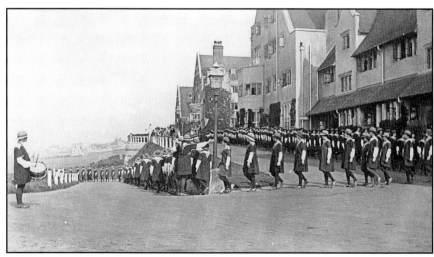

The march past to salute the flag on Empire Day, 1927.

Haslemere. 'It was wonderful to see forests, and bluebells, and to have our picnic out of doors,' Eluned said.

Her delight in nature was shared by many girls – sometimes to their own great surprise; few realised how much they missed woods and fields, flowers, trees and rivers. Roedean's treeless grounds on bare Downland, with nothing but the sea in front, were strange and alien. Other than the date on the calendar, there was little indication of changing seasons. Emmeline Tanner was conscious of this and each Michaelmas term she organised a bus trip for the whole school, so that girls could see the glorious colours of trees in autumn.

Efforts were made to improve Roedean's stark acres; few were successful. Queen Elizabeth the Queen Mother, when Duchess of York, attended the planting of 300 beech trees in the grounds. 'We all sang lustily at the small tree the

Latin teacher Miss MacSwiney and house matron Miss Ricards unpack hampers at the 1921 Empire Day picnic; in the background, one of the Southdown charabancs used to take the girls on their annual treat.

Duchess planted,' said Jean Borradaile (Gilmour 1932-38). 'It died. Only thirty survived, and they must have been cut down for the new dining room.'

Speech Day, which coincided with summer half term, was looked forward to almost as much as Empire Day. Pauline Norman (Davenport 1928-33) gave an account of the occasion in the Thirties. 'It began on Friday with the school concert. Many parents came, and there was an art exhibition in the studio. Our parents stayed in Brighton hotels. After supper there was a rehearsal of the Greek play. On Saturday our parents arrived during the morning and everyone went into the Hall for a speech by a visiting celebrity, who first gave out Sixth Form prizes and School Certificates. Parents then took girls out to lunch.

'Those concerned returned by 2pm for the Fathers' Match. Then there was tea in the Hall for the teams, mothers and daughters, and the parents departed for supper. Later the fathers' teams and the mothers returned and joined the whole school in the Hall where there were funny speeches by the captains, and

*The Ford and Aunt D (Dorothy Lawrence) at
the 1921 Empire Day picnic on the Downs*

*Girls make merry in a mud hut on
a country outing in 1927*

other fathers, alternating with semi-humorous school songs. PL was usually present and she embarrassed us by reciting *Little Bo Peep* in various childish intonations; we never knew why. After *Auld Lang Syne* and pump handles (all the school shaking hands with all the guests), parents left for their hotels.

'On Sunday parents came for Chapel service and then could take us out for the rest of the day. We had to be back for supper and Chapel. On Monday our parents came at 10.15am and again took us out until supper time, when we finally said goodbye. After supper there was dancing as on Saturday nights, but twelve dances instead of six. On the next Saturday we performed the Greek play in the Quad and all parents who were interested came down again.'

The Greek play was an annual institution, performed outdoors, in which the whole school took part. Greek dancing was another Roedean tradition and an OR who was at school in the Fifties remembered the local youth lining up along the perimeter fence to watch a display of 'Isadora Duncan style' Greek dancing before the Queen Mother. 'Girls were prancing about in bare feet, and short tunics, carrying great long spears,' she said. Another OR remembered the embarrasment of her father 'roaring with laughter at the spectacle'.

Among the visiting celebrities on Speech Day ORs remembered Lord Baden Powell, Princess Alice, Countess of Athlone, Freya Stark, the Duchess of York and Education Secretary R A Butler MP, whose wife was an OR.

Drama and music always played a large part in school life and memories are strong of house plays, staff plays, school plays and colour plays over the decades, of recitals and poetry readings, of attending concerts, operas and plays in Brighton and London. 'One great event was going up to the Old Vic to see John Gielgud in *Richard II*,' said Iris Ingram (Clark 1929-31). 'We were transported from Victoria Station in a Black Maria. Some experience!'

Roedean girls were exposed at a young age to many aspects of the arts.

Clifford Curzon, Leon Goossens, Myra Hess, Yehudi Menuhin and Jacqueline du Pre were among the musicians who played for them, and there were talks by people of the stature of G M Trevelyan, Lawrence Binyon, John Laurie and Dilys Powell.

'Cecil Day Lewis came to judge the Poetry Speaking competition one year,' said Vivien Allen (Hallett 1937-43). 'First prize went to Jill Balcon, who later married him. I was a proud second.' Vivien also remembered when OR Nancy Spain visited Roedean in her WRNS uniform. 'I was so impressed with her talk I volunteered for the Wrens when I left, but failed the medical. Her book, *Thank You, Nelson*, was devoured by many of us.'

Gillian Grenfell (Manley 1946-50) recalled the *Keswick Review* at the end of her first term in Number Four House. 'I took part in the acclaimed Kipper Ballet where we danced behind huge cardboard kippers. This was in honour of the Wednesday breakfast endured throughout the Keswick years.'

A Keswick highlight was Clifford Curzon's recital on December 3, 1941 – not, though for Eve Bysouth (Dowson 1939-46). In her diary Eve wrote: 'Before tea, instead of changing into djibbahs, we changed into "coats and skirts" for we are going to the piano recital by Clifford Curzon (he is a famous pianist). Those who were going to the recital, went and put on their big-coats and hats, then we had to be chequed in different parties. Roysia and I were in different parties. I went with Betty Dean, it was getting dusk when we started at 5.30pm. When we got there we sat in the large hall, I couldn't see, hardly anything, only occasionally I caught glimpses of Clifford Curzon. He really did make one laugh sometimes, for he sometimes played at arms lenght with his head flung back, or with his head bent down and tapping at the notes he looked like a monkey trying to find something, and turns everything upside down in a great flap; he was always wagling his head about and played the notes with a fine flourish of the hand.'

Dame Emmeline Tanner with Princess Alice of Athlone at a speech day in the 1930s.

A performance of *Noah's Ark*, staged by the staff, caused a sensation in the Forties. Said Diana Kay (Johnson

1945-51): 'All the girls laughed when they saw mistresses dressed up as giraffes or monkeys, and we were severely reprimanded. The play was not intended to be funny at all!'

In the Seventies Andrew Lloyd Webber and Tim Rice visited to see the girls perform *Joseph and His Amazing Technicolor Dreamcoat.* 'They said they had never thought it could be performed like that,' an OR reported somewhat ambiguously.

Famous parents always caused a stir and a visit remembered by pupils from the Thirties was the time when Gertrude Lawrence arrived, with Douglas Fairbanks Junior, to see her daughter Pamela play Lady Macbeth in the Number Three House production. 'All eyes were on them instead of on the play,' said Gwen Hollington (Paxton 1932-37). Years earlier there had been great excitement with 'heads hanging out of every window', according to Iris Phillips (1916-19), when Seymour Hicks and Ellaline Terris visited their daughter Betty.

Other VIP visitors remembered over the years were the Emir of Katsina; Suzanne Lenglen, who demonstrated her forehand drive; the Duchess of Gloucester, who inspected Guides and Brownies; Princess Margaret, who was there both for the school's fiftieth anniversary, and to open the new dining hall; Prince Charles, who opened the theatre in 1994, and astronaut Helen Sharman.

The annual display of Greek dancing, c1932.

LEISURE ACTIVITIES

'In the autumn term there was the Maids' Dance. They danced with the prefects, who acted as hostesses, the head girl leading off with the senior school house maid. No doubt the maids hated it as much as we did, but noblesse oblige. And it was almost worth it for the food.'

LEISURE activities used to be prescribed, and organised, almost always within school grounds, and overseen by mistress or prefect. Games were compulsory, but many girls also enjoyed playing in their own time. Dancing, play-acting and reading were approved leisure activities. Phyllis Bower (Hopkin Morgan 1917-21) remembered the Duty List – half a dozen classics of English literature that had to be read in leisure time – on which girls sat an exam at the end of the year. Attendance at winter Sunday concerts or lectures was also compulsory, as was the weekly letter home.

Early pupils were allowed two outings a term, with parents or guardians only. Those whose families lived abroad never left the grounds unless, by special concession, they were allowed to go out with a friend's parents. Rosemary Naegele (Hurst 1938-40) said that her father always invited 'a refugee girl' out to lunch and tea. 'There were many such in those years,' she explained.

On a day out with parents, girls gorged on sweets and ice cream, stuffed themselves with cream cakes in a Rottingdean tea shop, or one of the grander Brighton hotels (the Metropole was rumoured to be out of bounds – all those dubious couples named Smith in the dirty-weekend-in-Brighton days), spent a fortune on the piers and tried to cram in a visit to the cinema, too, before the supper curfew.

Girls were not allowed home at half term; instead, parents visited. Sometimes girls who had no visitors were taken by staff to the cinema or to the Palace Pier as a treat.

Other leisure activities included Guiding (Scouting in Roedean's early years), mending clothing or knitting (and gossiping), listening to gramophone records in the practice rooms of the music wing (no lyrics allowed), playing Monopoly, chess and cards, joining a club (history, geography, literature, music) or spending time on the current craze – one year it was yo-yos, another a complicated game called kick-a-can.

'We had no leisure time,' Ruth Conolly (1921-26) said. 'All our time was planned.' Betty Kent (Bidder 1925-30) agreed. 'There was little time left unoccupied during the week; from breakfast to supper we were ruled by the bell marking the end or start of a lesson, meal or other organised activity. Saturdays and Sundays were less rigid, though still well filled. There was sometimes a play and many odd moments were filled with walking, in close-knit groups, up and down the terrace, or on the Downs in small approved parties,' she said.

'Life was organised and disciplined, and we accepted it,' Frances Haselhurst (Spedding 1934-39) said: 'I'm sure it has had a strong and good effect on our lives. Certainly Roedean to WAAF was an easy step. We were taught to walk tall, to be proud of ourselves and to be independent.'

The ballroom dances every Saturday night (compulsory, some thought), when girls danced with each other, were a highlight for some, a cringingly embarrassing nightmare ('bust to bust') for others. Dances were booked ahead, and tall girls always took the men's part. 'Where were the boys?' Iris Ingram (Clark 1929-31) asked. Army life for a recruit was less rigorous than life at

Roedean, she said. Alison Adburgham (Haig 1925-29), writing in *Punch* in 1963, said: 'We danced with each other, to a piano played by one of us. We danced the foxtrot, the tango, the quick-step, the waltz and the Charleston, to the sounds of *Tea for Two, I Want to be Happy, Lady be Good* and *Yes, We Have no Bananas* . . . On the Saturday of half term there was extra long dancing . . . an occasional brother would be produced in a dinner jacket and he had to dance with his sister's friends in their black woollen stockings and afternoon djibbahs . . . In the autumn term there was the Maids' Dance. The groundsmen were not invited, nor did the maids bring partners. They danced with the prefects, who acted as hostesses, the head girl leading off with the senior school house maid. No doubt the maids hated it as much as we did, but *noblesse oblige*. And it was almost worth it for the food.'

Hallowe'en was another high point, especially in the years between the wars, as girls had the freedom, for one night, to make mayhem. Eluned Macmillan (Carey Evans 1933-39) said: 'We had ghost walks, dipping for apples and treats and we were allowed to have races down the main corridors and make as much noise as we wanted to. I still remember the exuberance and excitement of Hallowe'en.' Pauline Norman (Davenport 1928-33) said: 'Every year the sub-prefects organised a very jolly party for Hallowe'en. We (Number Four) had the Hall, other houses had other venues. Ours was improvised fancy dress, party games (blindfold, guessing smells, tastes and textures) ending with a skit by the prefects impersonating members of the staff.'

Patricia Altman (Rae 1955-60) won a prize for the most original costume of the year when she appeared as a tortoise. 'I made it out of a green eiderdown, and had brown paper bags for my legs and head, which I was able to retract at will,' Patricia said.

Keswick made dramatic changes possible – for the duration of the war. Instead of being on one site, behind high walls and fences, the living and school accommodation was widely spread and girls were able to roam the town, the fells and the lakeside on foot or bicycle. Wednesday afternoons were set aside for hobbies, Diana Poole (Wilson 1938-47) remembered. 'A few of us helped Miss Barron in the hotel vegetable garden. She was in charge of fruit picking and we found this a profitable means of obtaining extra additions to the provided food.' The usual job was tending gooseberry bushes, Diana said. 'Sometimes we were promoted to raspberries, strawberries and blackcurrants. It was a very good hobby!'

During the lonely years in far away Keswick housemistresses did their best to arrange opportunities for fun. 'We were told yesterday that we are to dress up representing a book, play or film title,' Eve Bysouth (Dowson 1939-46) wrote in her 1942 diary. 'All day we have been trying to fix up the costumes. At six o' clock we all went into the lounge all dressed up. Roysia dressed up as the "Snow Queen", I went as "Murder in the Cathedral", I had my two sheets draped over my body and a girdle to keep them in, on my head was a pillow case, I was meant to look like a monk. I had a gold cross (cardboard painted yellow) on my chest and in my heart was stuck a dagger, blood was dripping from the wound (a piece of rolled cardboard pinned to the sheet represented the handle of the dagger, the blood was pieces of red paper pinned on). First we played games then we paraded round the room. Clare won first prize, she was "The Great Dictator".'

Lack of space in the Keswick Hotel meant that practice pianos were in some of the bedrooms. This was fine by Jenifer Fairpo (Fowler 1941-48), whose room mate's cousin was an excellent pianist. 'She would come and play music from shows like *The Desert Song*, while we dressed in bedspreads (very Arabic-looking, with striped borders) and sang and danced about,' she said.

The down side of Keswick was that few girls were visited by parents during the war, both because it was so far north and because of difficult travelling conditions, although this, too, had its advantages; rules were relaxed and girls were allowed out with any other relatives who happened to be in the vicinity.

Back in Brighton, leisure activities were not quite so restricted as before, yet certainly girls felt the loss of their freedom keenly. Boys from local public schools attended occasional, heavily-chaperoned dances with senior girls, and there were some reciprocal visits to the boys' schools. Mary Browning (Feachem 1956-62) saw the events as sporting fixtures. 'We danced *against* Lancing and Christ's Hospital,' she said. Mary Lisa Owen (Davies 1956-63) was in a group of girls who attended a return dance at Brighton College. The dancers, she said, were locked in the school hall for the duration. Sarah Saunders-Davis (Osborn 1960-67) remembered the agony of dances with boys' schools 'if your frock was not groovy or you did not have a partner after the first five minutes'. The turn of speed at which the lights went out was the essence of a successful evening, Sarah said. The dances became more frequent over the following years, and partners were bussed in from a wider range of schools – Tonbridge, Hurstpierpoint, Wellington, Eastbourne. They were always disasters, according to Sona Shah (1988-1990). 'One time,' she said, 'we had three boys' schools that came and trashed two kitchens and bedrooms in Lawrence House.'

There were also 'socials' with girls and boys from Varndean School in Brighton. Ann Hulme (Prall 1945-50) remembered both the dances and the socials as 'awkward'. At the dances there were always more girls than there were boys, she said, and, at the socials, the Brighton girls not only had nicer dresses, but Varndean pupils had established friendships that excluded Roedean girls .

By the end of the Forties, sub-prefects were allowed to go to Rottingdean, alone, on Saturday afternoons (to 'pig out' on egg and chips or welsh rarebit), while full prefects were trusted to go unescorted to Brighton. The privilege was later extended to include Sunday. By now, girls could also go out with friends of the family (subject to written permission from parents), and the number of day outings was stepped up to three (or it may have been four; memories conflict) a term. A few ORs thought it was just once.

Private wirelesses, 'great big things', were allowed, but girls could tune in only at certain times. Sunday lectures and recitals continued – enjoyed by some, loathed by others, alternating with 'suitable' films shown in the Hall. Merry Rushton (Newth 1948-54) remembered the excitement of seeing *Buffalo Bill* 'masculine and daring', featuring a 'very grande lady in a hat who talked about Peroooo (Peru).' Delighted girls imitated her for weeks. Suitable films included *The Red Shoes, The Dambusters, Monsieur Hulot's Holiday, Reach For The Sky* and *I'm All Right Jack* ('all about villainous, layabout working class people'). It cost one shilling to see a film and girls paid with their school cheque books.

A more educational use of leisure time was when Roedean girls joined pupils of other schools on Franco British Society visits to the battle sites in France in the immediate post World War Two years.

Some girls occupied themselves by keeping gardens. Diana Kay (Johnson 1945-51) remembered little plots behind Junior House, 'where we attempted to grow things in the poor, rocky soil, but none too successfully'. The roller skating rink at the end of the lacrosse field was popular with some girls, the tennis courts with others. Jill Sheppard (Robbins 1948-53) taught herself table tennis in the school hut and subsequently became a university champion.

Saturday dances were still on the list of approved leisure activities, but the dancing was strictly ballroom and, said Rosemary Athay (1955-59), 'some people were never able to do anything but trad for the rest of their lives'. 'We wore our best house dresses to dance with each other!' said a bemused Merry. 'Two houses joined together for each session, alternating the following week. Sometimes a senior girl would ask a junior girl, which was a huge honour.'

Merry loved going to The Royal Crescent Hotel in Hove when her parents visited. 'We saw famous actors who were playing at the Theatre Royal,' she said. 'Alec Guinness once picked up my hankie which I dropped in front of him!!!'

Stephanie Chapman (Watson 1952-57) had memories of Saturday afternoon bus walks, usually wet. She said: 'Southdown coaches took us to various places, always involving steep ascents on the Downs. My wellingtons were always a size too big, I always had asthma and I wheezed all afternoon.' Bus walks, Kristin Hollis (Stephenson 1953-60) explained, were a particular Roedean thing. 'We took the bus to a destination somewhere on the Downs and then did a bit of a walk, and took the bus back. We were usually equipped with packed lunches and stopped for tea in the afternoon.'

Kristin was one of many ORs who welcomed the lectures and concerts in school, and the visits to theatres and concert halls locally and in London. Skipping the lecture or recital, said Jacqueline Rokotnitz Zhislin (Sawyer-Kammer 1953-57) – who was less keen on enforced culture – 'was almost punishable by death', but times changed and Mary Anderson (Moss 1958-63) said that during her time attendance was voluntary.

Jill Fraser (Fox 1953-58) had a more adventurous attitude to leisure and when she was not exploring the heating tunnels under the school (forbidden) she was trying to escape over the Downs for apple strudel in the Austrian Cafe at Ovingdean (also forbidden).

Jane Midgley (Lankester 1953-58) and her friends used to spend Sunday afternoons walking up and down the boundary fence 'scoring points for how many waves, smiles and rude signs we got'. Patricia Altman and her group went to a special place in the grounds that they called Yearning For Freedom. 'This was because the whole school was enclosed by a fence and there was the sense that we were unable to get out,' Patricia explained.

The Seventies brought greater liberation – more parental outings were allowed, payphones were installed for the girls' use, there were television sets to watch (in Junior House programmes were chosen by the housemistress; *Blue Peter* was considered safe) and Sixth Formers in Lawrence House lived independently of main school, coming and going as they wished, on trust to behave themselves and uphold the honour of the school. Senior girls went to the cinema in Brighton on Saturday afternoons, to Browns to socialise with friends – even to pubs. 'Asda was nearby, cheap and much visited, as was the cinema at the marina,' said Charlotte-Anne Nelson (1990-97). 'Much time was also spent on the 'phones (for which there were huge queues) and, in the latter years, on the e-mail.'

CHAPEL

'Matins gave us the chance to study the visiting parents sitting in the galleries and decide which of the mothers was wearing the most ghastly hat. The girls were allowed to sit with the parents, thus enduring the embarassment to the full!'

A SUM of seven thousand pounds was subscribed to build the Chapel and Cloister Garth and by the time of the dedication on May 6, 1906, there were sufficient additional funds to install a three-manual organ, the marble floor of the aisle and the arched ornamental ceiling of the Sanctuary. Architect Sir John Simpson's plan for the interior was detailed, and over the decades it was fulfilled as gifts were given in memory of Lawrence relatives, of Old Roedeanians, of happy schooldays.

At the outbreak of the World War One, the four senior houses presented White Ensigns to HMS *Hercules*, HMS *Canterbury*, HMS *Neptune* and HMS *Collingwood*, and when these ships were de-commissioned the flags returned to the Chapel where they were later joined by a fifth – that of HMS Vernon, which had flown from the Roedean flagpole during World War Two.

The Chapel pictured in the 1920s.

'When I was about sixteen, I remember going to Chapel before breakfast in the quiet of the early morning, when all the corridors were deserted, soon to be filled with bells summoning and dismissing, with people hurrying,' Sonia Bicanic (Wild 1932-38) wrote. 'In the summer the cloisters were planted with wall-flowers, brown flecked with terracotta, yellow flecked with orange, producing a still fragrance that filled all the arches.

'Only three or four other girls used to do this so early in the morning. We would slip in, not noticing each other, and take the place we were accustomed to, right at the back, near the aisle or the wall. What first took me there I can never recall, but the kind of contemplation that I discovered then has never deserted me.'

The Lawrence sisters stood firmly by their faith and, from the very first, attendance at Chapel on Sunday was compulsory – morning and/or evening (memories vary) – for all except nonconformists, Catholics and Jews. The 8am Communion was for those who had been confirmed. The other services were Matins and Evensong.

Nonconformists and Catholics went by taxi to their own churches in Brighton and Jewish girls received instruction in school, although the whole school was expected to attend Chapel for formal occasions, such as the Armistice Service, Remembrance Day, Empire Day, Harvest Festival and the Carol Service. Keturah Crawford (Robinson 1918-22) remembered Nora O'Kelly accompanying the Catholics to church and Miss Lowenstein taking Hebrew classes for the Jews. Girls who were not Church of England were known as The Heathen, Angela Pirie (Hunter 1922-30) said.

'When we were about sixteen we were all confirmed (I can't remember any who weren't),' said Betty Kent (Bidder 1925-30). 'After that we were expected to appear at Early Service a reasonable number of times, though it was never compulsory. We took our religion, as we took life in general, very lightly in those days.' By the time Beryl Barns (James 1932-38) was confirmed girls were no longer allowed to wear the customary white gowns because, Beryl explained, the ceremony had become something of a dress parade. Instead, girls wore their school coats and skirts, with a white veil. Confirmations were carried out by the Bishop of Chichester or the Bishop of Lewes.

Eluned Macmillan (Carey Evans 1929-39) sang in the choir, and loved it. 'We prepared every Tuesday for the descants, psalms and special hymns. The Christmas Carol service was wonderful; people from Brighton came streaming up the drive and the Chapel was packed,' she said.

Another enthusiastic chorister was Paula Haigh (Cannon 1934-38). 'I keenly enjoyed school worship, but I was not above joining in the common act of "fainting" in Communion,' she said. 'I don't know how many, like me, acted it, but I was not reproved.' Nancy Kueffner (Hurst-Brown 1937-40) went one better; instead of pretending to faint, she taught herself how to do the real thing, and was regularly removed from Chapel. A biscuit and a cup of tea for the early morning communicants was introduced to prevent the fainting – whether genuine or phoney – not that it had much effect, for the phenomenon was still happening twenty years later. Sarah Saunders-Davis (Osborn 1960-67) remembered occasional mass fainting in the summer term – 'viewed with much amusement by Mrs Fort!' The school chaplain (Chappy), Sarah said, was a total disaster: 'His long winded sermons gave no guidance to teenage girls, and the mass faintings were a welcome distraction at this point.'

Being in the choir had its advantages. Up in the gallery, no one could see if you read a book during the sermon, said Ruth Maclean (Gimson 1936-41). 'Life in the choir was a joy, as well as being a good introduction to some fine church music,' according to Ann Hulme (Prall 1945-50).

Gweneth Cannon (Feather 1931-36) remembered that she and the other Jewish girls used the library on Friday evenings to observe the Sabbath, and on Sundays, in the Thirties, Mr Halevy from Brighton College taught aspects of Judaism in one of the classrooms. By the Seventies, religious instruction for Jewish girls had moved to Saturday morning, in the main hall. Jillian Gordon (Albury 1939-48) said that although Jewish, she enjoyed attending Chapel because she found it a sanctuary, and an escape during her school years.

Post Keswick, the two dozen or so Jewish girls had prayers each morning, taken by a senior prefect, and they received religious instruction on Sundays from a visiting minister. Ann Portnoy (Levy 1944-47) said Roedean was liberal, allowing girls to leave for the Jewish High Holy Days, and Gillian Van Gelder (Solomon 1946-51) thought the school enlightened and tolerant on the subject of religion. She admitted, though, that she was not as appreciative as she should have been of the religious instruction provided for Jews.

A contemporary of Gillian's felt differently. The school was bigoted, she said, and she cited Norah Horobin's ban on Jewish girls at a memorial service for King George VI. 'She said our attendance would be a blasphemy. We were most upset.' Another Jewish OR recalled the time when her sister went with other prefects to help serve at a Confirmation Tea. 'The housemistress called her back and told her off for going. The phrase used was, "What if the Bishop had spoken to you!"'

'Looking back,' Felicity Russell Heuter (Russell 1968-75) wrote, 'I have the feeling that those of us who were not Church of England (Jews, Catholics, Muslims, nonconformists) were, in a very subtle way, looked at askance by other girls – not by staff though.'

Being excluded from the Chapel because she was a Catholic was a sore point with Mary Sgarlat (1974-75), a Sixth Form student from the USA. She explained: 'Having been educated at an Anglican school in the States, and grown up on all the English hymns, I was really annoyed to find I could not attend Chapel every morning. I could go on Sunday but could only do a reading on Saturday, when the service was not in the Chapel. I adore English choral music and singing, and to this day I attend Anglican services as well as Catholic ones.'

Between the wars there was strong emphasis on religion, with house prayers each day, and a daily assembly as well as the compulsory Chapel attendance. 'The religious framework did, I think, exert a beneficial effect on the ethos of the school,' said Jean Marwood (Sharp 1937-42). Rosemary Watts (Stephens 1933-37) said: 'The whole essence of the school was non-denominational – I hope it still is, so we were reasonably unprejudiced about race or creed.'

'Some houses had prayers before supper each evening, but in Number Three we went along individually to Chapel after prep,' Mary Marriott (Thompson 1937-40) said. 'It was very pleasant at the end of the day to wander along with a friend or on one's own and spend a few minutes quietly in private prayer.'

Rosamund Huebener (Benson 1937-42) wrote: 'I liked Evensong and will never forget singing "Oh hear us when we cry to Thee/For those in peril on the sea", with the wind howling round the Chapel on autumn and winter evenings.'

A solemn occasion remembered by many ORs was the announcement in Chapel, by Miss Tanner, of the abdication of Edward VIII. Margaret Jackson (Harris 1935-39) recalled the Headmistress stressing how important the role of women, for good or bad, could be.

The Forties emerged as a strange decade of opposing views on the part that religion played in school life. Gillian Summersgill (Field 1945-48) thought that there had been no particular emphasis on religion, while Diana Kay (Johnson 1945-51) believed it had played an important role. Rosemary Clark (Adcock 1945-51) said: 'The significance (of religion) was/is longstanding. We learnt a lot of what is now called right and wrong.' Joanna Burrows (Hamilton 1945-49), from Roedean South Africa, considered Brighton 'a little irreligious', while Janet Garwood (Ing-Simmons 1947-51) wrote: 'The Christian religion was taken very seriously and we were biblically taught. However, since becoming a committed Christian, I realise that the need for personal commitment to Christ was not stressed at school.'

Margaret Shimmin's (Greig 1946-50) best memory of Chapel was of the service taken by the newly appointed Bishop of Coventry, just after his bombed cathedral had been rebuilt. 'He started by saying, "I am a piece of gum stuck under the seat in the fourth row from the back of the Chapel",' Margaret said. 'After that everyone sat up and listened! Normally we played "cricket" during the sermons. "Ands" were runs, "buts" were wickets.'

'Our spiritual lives were taken seriously and, mostly, reverently,' said Ann Hulme. 'But a favourite naughty ploy was to wait until the senior/prefect had practised reading the lesson before a service, and then stick a page or two of the Bible together with soap. The poor victim would sometimes read several sentences before discovering it made no sense at all.'

Another popular distraction was described by Sarah Saunders-Davis.

'Matins gave us the chance to study the visiting parents sitting in the galleries and decide which of the mothers was wearing the most ghastly hat. The girls were allowed to sit with the parents, thus enduring the embarassment to the full!'

An organ student's leaving dare was remembered by Patricia Altman (Rae 1955-60). 'She had been assigned to play one morning and as the Headmistress (Miss Horobin) walked out down the aisle, this girl played the Dead March!'

'If I shut my eyes and say Roedean, it is always the Chapel I see,' Merry Rushton (Newth 1948-54) said. 'I was not deeply religious, but I loved it, especially the white marble, and the music.' Because of all that white marble, more irreverent girls dubbed the Chapel 'the bathroom'. Merry found herself, years after leaving school, sitting next to a fellow member of the choir at a wedding. 'We couldn't get over the *deja vu* of hearing the unchanged and unique timbre of each other's singing voices,' she said.

Josephine Breyfogle (King 1953-55), from Roedean South Africa, said that Chapel was at the heart of school life in her time. 'I often felt sorry for the people who did not go due to their religious affinities, because it was such a central part of life's routine.' Angela Jefferies (Blunt 1954-57) considered it a discipline that did the girls no harm. But the perceived, to some, emphasis on religion, had diametrically opposite effects. There are ORs who are eternally grateful for the grounding in Anglicanism given by the school, and others, like Sheila Vince (Martin 1954-59) who now attend church only for weddings, baptisms and funerals.

'Of course Chapel was compulsory,' Jacqueline Rokotnitz Zhislin (Sawyer-Kammer 1953-57) said. 'Everything was. Choice was not something that you were considered mature enough, or intelligent enough to be offered.'

For Sarah Saunders-Davis, high spots were the Carol Service, 'always a wonderful occasion', and the oratorios sung with Brighton College 'if only to chat up the boys'.

'The ritual learned at school has been valuable in later life. I did not come from a church-going family . . . and am very glad now that the Chapel was so central in our lives,' Carolyn Phillipo (Williamson 1961-69) said.

DISCIPLINE

'Sub-prefects made us stand on a table in the SPR and talk for two minutes, without faltering, on some obscure subject.'

INFRINGEMENT of school rules was punished by a discipline mark, Iris Phillips (1916-1919) recalled, while responsible behaviour was rewarded by being made a monitor, 'and being given jurisdiction over the behaviour of lesser mortals'. There were four order marks to a discipline mark and receiving one of these meant early bed on Saturday night, and no dancing. Seriously unruly girls were sent to the San for a day to mend sheets. It was the prefects who enforced school rules, and who gave order marks. One of their duties was to write the names of culprits in a black book for the housemistress to see. Winifred Hargreaves (Wade 1923-28) remembered conduct marks, called cons, while discipline marks were known as dish, she said.

Betty Kent (Bidder 1925-30) wrote: 'We were an easy going generation and had not learnt to be unco-operative and aggressive, so did not find discipline irksome, and hardly any punishments were needed. It was quite enough to be sent for by a prefect for a pi-jaw and then, if necessary, sent to the housemistress or the deputy housemistress. To be sent to Miss Tanner was appalling. The only punishment I remember being given by a prefect was to learn something by heart. I chose something from the Shakespeare play we were doing, which came in useful for School Certificate later on.'

'Discipline was strict, but cheerfully accepted,' said Betty's sister Ina Murray (Bidder 1927-33). Crimes of the time included running in the corridors, talking during prep, rudeness, reading under the blankets by torchlight and untidiness. Pauline Norman (Davenport 1928-33) said prefects could order girls to run once, or twice, round the cinder path for some misdemeanor. Ruth Johnstone (1933-36) received a harsher punishment for her crime. She climbed into the attic above the music wing, missed her footing on the beams and put a foot through the ceiling. Ruth, or her parents, had to pay for repairs.

It was through the system of prefects and sub-prefects, Lavinia Greenwood (Malim 1933-38) said, that girls learned to work with others. And when they became prefects themselves they learned to handle others and to use their authority wisely, under guidance.

The ultimate punishment, expulsion, was reserved for the ultimate crime, which usually had something to do with boys. Two ORs remembered a girl being expelled in the Thirties for 'an escapade behind the haystack with a boy'. Vivien Allen (Hallett 1937-43) remembered two girls being expelled; 'one for being pregnant, the other for being caught *in flagrante* with a Keswick High School boy behind a bush in Fitz Park'. And Diana Hinman (Hunter 1955-62) remembered a contemporary being expelled for smoking.

Thirties pupils called order marks 'ticks'. These went up on a list, and more than three in a week resulted in early bed on Saturday (which meant not only missing the dance but, worse, the two chocolate digestive biscuits after the dance); not being allowed to play in a match; being forced to watch a match; or writing out lines. Sylvia Perry (Denis-Smith 1936-40) thought detention preferable to standing on the sidelines on cold, wet, windy days. In detention, she remembered, she learned virtually the whole of *Macbeth*. Others mentioned learning pages from a dictionary, verses from the Bible, reports from *The Daily Telegraph* or *The Times* – all of which had subsequently to be recited to prefects in their studies. Merry Rushton (Newth 1948-54) remembered the humiliation of 'all the prefects gathered in condemning silence while one stumbled through some boring piece of journalism'. Ann Hulme (Prall 1945-50) said that a punishment favoured by Tiddles was learning the psalms. 'I know a remarkable number of them,' she admitted. 'Once learnt they were copied out from memory in her study. On one unsupervised such occasion, I wrote in Biro (then new, and frowned upon) on a single sheet of paper, leaving a rewarding copy indented on poor Tiddles' polished table.'

Missing the school play was considered the direst punishment, and in Jean Marwood's (Sharp 1937-42) house, a particularly hated punishment was being condemned to have the first bath – at 6.30am.

Ruth Maclean's (Gimson 1936-41) worst punishment was being banished to the San for a weekend of 'solitary'. What was Ruth's unspeakable crime? She said: 'One or two of us hid in a haystack in the grounds; searches were made on the assumption that we had run away!'

When she was in Junior House, Nancy Kueffner (Hurst-Brown 1937-40) did her best to steer clear of trouble because 'Miss Black's tongue was the most ferocious weapon I have ever known. She was vicious.' Miss Black was the then Junior House matron.

A mean punishment Angela Highmore (Edwards 1938-42) remembered was having just bread for supper one night a week for several weeks. Angela's crime was playing about during singing lessons.

Mistresses taught, and prefects ran the school. This was the impression many ORs received. Generally, the prefects were respected and approachable;

just a few were feared. Their role was to ensure the smooth ordering of their houses – making out table lists and bath lists, taking prep, supervising letter writing, looking after table manners at meals – and to set an example to younger girls. 'The prefects were up on Olympus as far as the we juniors were concerned,' said Vivien Allen.

At Keswick, talking after lights out could result in the culprit being sent to sleep in a sub's room for a week. 'Naturally,' said Dilys Jordan (Dunn 1939-44), 'the sub sent to the younger girl's room (usually four in a room) was not very pleased.' Weeding the hotel garden was another Keswick punishment.

Sarah Curtis (Myers 1945-53) remembered when, as Head of House, she unsuccessfuly tried to persuade Miss Middleton to make a naughty girl a sub-prefect 'to induce in her a sense of responsibility'. Sarah said: 'My idealistic (and I still think correct) theories of how you get people to change probably led me to become a youth and family court magistrate'.

Nicola Frith (1950-57) remembered having to clean prefects' studies, their shoes and cricket pads, for breaking some rule or other. The sub-prefects, she said, 'made us stand on a table in the SPR and talk for two minutes, without faltering, on some obscure subject such as the eye of a needle, the head of a pin, or the first two years of Queen Anne's reign. If you dried up they threw heavy books at you and you had to do it all again the following week.' Was a Roedean girl responsible for creating BBC Radio Four's *Just a Minute*? This particular punishment was stopped in the mid Fifties when, one OR said, the prefects' powers to punish were much reduced.

Punishments became impos – impositions – and these ranged from cleaning a prefect's study to composing a poem, Kristin Hollis (Stephenson 1953-60) explained. 'There were no real punishments, only psychological ones – and they worked,' Jacqueline Rokotnitz Zhislin (Sawyer-Kammer 1953-57) said. 'Being left in the JPR when all the rest of my form went to the SPR, that was a killer!'

Sarah Gibbins (Miller Logan 1956-58) remembered fines being imposed for lost property. Tidy bedrooms were compulsory, and Sarah was astonished by the untidiness of girls' rooms in the Eighties, when her daughter was at Roedean. Mary Browning (Feachem 1956-62) was 'excommunicated' for dancing on the GDR table. 'I was not allowed to speak to anyone and had to eat my meals separately,' she said.

Katharine Coleman (Mackenzie 1961-66) was once caught taking an extra bath. 'I was sent to the housemistress and as punishment had to sit in her draughty hall in my dressing gown, in silence, for four hours, being stared at by all and sundry,' she said.

Felicity Russell Heuter (Russell 1968-75) and Lindsey Gee-Turner

(1971-77) both said that, in the John Hunt era, there had been no real prefect system. 'Such duties were shared out amongst all sixth formers,' Felicity explained.

Seventies punishments, Felicity remembered, were to be gated, or made to stand with hands on head for a whole lesson. Bell duty was mentioned by Fiona Watson (1972-77); this required the miscreant to rise at the crack of dawn and ring a handbell on all floors, for a week, to wake up everyone.

A decade on, an extremely unpopular punishment was being forbidden to watch television, and Zoe Green (1988-95) recalled 'having to sit with the entire JH in hall one night, with bowed heads, to "repent" of greed for taking more sweets than deemed appropriate for a mf (midnight feast)'. 'Prefects,' Zoe said, 'did not impinge on your consciousness, apart from telling you to tuck your shirt in.'

Girls arrive for the Michaelmas term, 1949. 'Po-hatted' and carrying overnight bags and lacrosse sticks, they disembark from a fleet of Southdown buses.

THE SPECIAL

At the end of a girl's last term at school, it was traditional for her to throw her hat into the Thames from the school train.

THEY used to meet under the clock at Victoria, taken there by parents, by school staff or by Universal Aunts who had escorted them across London from other termini, and then make their way to Platform 18 for the School Special. There were happy, laughing girls, boisterously waving lacrosse sticks as they spotted friends, and sad, tearful girls, clinging to their mothers and dreading the return to school.

'Crossing London with a suitcase and a lacrosse stick was tricky – I always felt sorry for those with 'cellos,' Jenifer Fairpo (Fowler 1941- 48) said.

The Special was the 4pm scheduled train to which extra carriages were added for Roedean pupils. During the First World War, Iris Phillips (1916-19) said, when services were disrupted, the school carriages were sometimes attached to troop trains.

From Brighton Station girls were taken to school by horse-drawn cab, Antonia Joll (Ramsden 1917-27) said; later generations were met by a fleet of Southdown buses.

The school train from Victoria was a jolly affair, all agreed, with girls excitedly exchanging gossip about the hols. Merry Rushton (Newth 1948-54) remembered 'the dread as the taxi neared Victoria Station and the same family joke every single time, about De'ath, the nearby butcher's shop'.

Susan Elsey (Chamberlayne 1950-55), Jill Fraser (Fox 1953-58), Elizabeth Thomas (Cawdry 1953-57) and Jo Breyfogle (King 1953-55) all mentioned that at the end of a girl's last term at school, it was traditional for her to throw her hat into the Thames from the school train. Girls who did not travel home via Victoria sometimes threw their hats out of whatever other train, or car, they happened to be in – although tossing a hat from anywhere but the railway bridge over the Thames somehow lacked the cachet of the real thing.

The School Special was not mentioned after the mid-Seventies when the service must have ceased. Later pupils travelled independently by plane, train, coach and car – and today, in the late Nineties, some girls are still escorted by staff to and from Victoria Station at the beginning and end of term.

Friends gather at Victoria Station for the return to school. The girls pictured are: Laura and Venetia Fawcett, Elspeth Beard, Veronica Hankey and Sharon Jaque. The photograph dates from the early 1970s.

CAREERS GUIDANCE

'If you weren't Oxbridge material, you were on your own.'

CAREERS education and guidance at Roedean today is a continuous process. Students are encouraged to find out about themselves and, using the Careers Resource Centre, to learn to make decisions and develop personal action plans. Sixth Form students follow a structured career programme which includes a weekly briefing session and a fixed careers lecture programme. Guest speakers, conferences, courses and open days give access to detailed information about higher education, and a careers administrator arranges visits and vocational experience. From being what many ORs regarded as the school's weakest area, careers guidance has become one of its strongest.

The Memories Questionnaire revealed just a small minority of ORs – right up to the Seventies – who were satisfied with the help they were given to choose a career. In the school's early years the emphasis was very much on grooming ambitious, academically gifted girls for university, Girton and Newnham principally, and London medical schools, while little was wasted on non-academic students, and on girls destined for finishing schools, or whose only ambitions were the debutante season swiftly followed by marriage.

Angela Pirie (Hunter 1922-30) wanted to be a doctor. She said: 'I was advised that, although with hard work I should qualify, I would not be in any way outstanding, and would only get poor positions.'

'In my day,' said Pauline Filipowska (Crommelin-Brown 1935-38), 'careers guidance was negligible. When I said I wanted to be a secretary my housemistress became Lady Bracknell and uttered "a secretary!" to my mother in such a condemning tone that the subject was dropped'.

'There was no question of university in 1941,' Isobel Bernstein (Forsell 1935-41) said. 'Miss Martin advised art college, but it would not have been considered as essential to the war effort, so choice was limited by that.' Audrey Kenyon (Hinchliffe 1937-41) explained: 'Most people joined the forces or war work of some type'. A Keswick pupil who wanted to be an architect was told that it was unsuitable for a woman. 'All the servicemen were returning and needed university places, so we were told to go home and get married!' she said.

124

Pamela Thalben-Ball (1939-44) left to go to a French finishing school in Scotland. 'My housemistress, Miss Lloyd Williams, thought this pointless,' Pamela said. 'If you think you can give Pamela charm by this you are sadly mistaken,' Miss Lloyd Williams told Pamela's parents.

'If you weren't Oxbridge material, you were on your own,' Margaret Williamson (Blench 1944-46) said. 'University places were scarce because, properly, the few women's vacancies were offered to girls demobbed from the services.'

By all accounts the Fifties was a bleak period for careers counselling – when equality of the sexes in the workplace was at last beginning to happen and there were bright new prospects for women.

The parents of some girls stepped in when the school failed to advise. 'My father took matters in hand,' said Stephanie Chapman (Watson 1952-57), and Cherry Edgerton-Bird (1953-59) thought her mother of more help than the school. Susan Child (Locket 1955-61) said: 'There was a careers room with some boxes of leaflets, but I know full well that it was my father who did all the scouting round to try and find the sort of course I wished to follow'.

A surprisingly large number of ORs reported being told they were not good enough for a particular career, or would never achieve their aims. Sheila Vince (Martin 1954-59) said: 'I gave up the idea of studying medicine when my house mistress told me I would make a mediocre doctor.' Rosemary Athay (1955-59) was told she was not university material, so she left, took A and S Levels at a technical college, and subsequently read law at Nottingham University.

'I wanted to become a fabric designer, but the school felt that it would be a shame to have to spend another year studying art,' Katharine Coleman (Mackenzie 1961-66) said. 'They suggested teaching, or something secretarial. My parents allowed me a sporting go at Oxbridge, so I ended up there. However, now I am a full time engraver, maybe I should have followed my own instincts. During my university and research career I was invited back by the headmaster to talk to prospective university students and I was anxious then to encourage those who were uncertain to follow their instincts rather than simply go to university for its own sake.'

Gail Maughan (Dawe 1968-72) said that on leaving she was asked to sign a book saying that her future career was going to be physiotherapy 'as it looked better than secretary'.

And yet, despite this perceived failure on the school's part it had given its pupils an education equal to the best in the country and its alert, well educated, self-confident girls found their own way. Pupils who were not considered among the academic elite destined for Oxbridge, found other universities, academies, training colleges and polytechnics, and they became musicians and architects, scientists, doctors and dentists, accountants, administrators and lawyers.

Sona Shah (1988-90) said that guidance was given upon request – 'although I think methods of career counselling were fairly outdated and were too much oriented towards "jobs for women". There wasn't much variety.'

Unlucky Sona just missed out; within a year or two revolutionary change gave Roedean a careers department equipped for the millennium. 'Huge amounts of help were given,' Charlotte-Anne Nelson (1990-97) said. 'Dr Bailin, the careers adviser, was brilliant, all knowing and terrifying. It was largely due to her guidance that I secured a place at Cambridge.' Portia Da Gama Rose (1990-95) agreed. 'Once Dr Bailin was in charge of careers we all got a lot more information,' she said.

THE LIBRARIES

*'Cleaners had taken out all the books in the Ref for
dusting, and replaced them according to colour.'*

UNTIL the new wing was built in 1911, the school's library – comprising some two thousand books – was housed on shelves in the gallery of the Hall. It quickly became obvious that the gallery was too cramped, and that dancing, and other activities taking place in the hall below, were distracting to students attempting research.

The new wing contained staff accommodation, the art studio, and a long, panelled library having purpose built bookcases down one side and mullioned

*Designed to resemble a country house library, the magnificent
Ref was 'a place of refuge' – 'an oasis of peace and calm.'*

windows overlooking the sea on the other. It was designed by the school's architect, Sir John Simpson, to resemble the library of a country house. The books were removed from the gallery on a wet Saturday afternoon early in October by queues of girls passing volumes from hand to hand.

This was the Reference Library, the Ref, and it remains today very much as it was in 1911. There was a separate Fiction Library, the Fic, and each house had its own small library of suitable stories for girls.

In 1993 library services were reorganised and the main hall became the Central Resource Centre, containing reference materials, classic and modern fiction, non-fiction, periodicals, documents, video and audio tapes and CD Roms. Junior House has its own library of fiction, non-fiction and reference books and the Ref, now a study area for the Sixth Form, contains the school's heritage resources, reference material and a collection of books by Old Roedeanian authors.

From the outset the magnificent Ref was used only by Sixth Formers, more specifically only by academic Sixth Formers in the early days, according to ORs. Former pupils described it as 'a place of refuge', 'a lovely place where one could be peaceful and uninterrupted', 'awe inspiring' and 'an oasis of peace and calm'. Girls felt privileged and 'grown up' when they graduated to the Ref. They wrote of the warm panelling, the polished tables, the creaky chairs, the 'cosy' smell of the books and the wonderful seascapes from the windows.

The small house libraries were stocked with 'wholesome' books (Baroness Orczy, Georgette Heyer, Angela Brazil, Dickens and Bulldog Drummond), but circulating surreptitiously, 'in brown paper covers' said Lavinia Greenwood (Malim 1933-38), were Mazo de la Roche's *Jalna* and *Whiteoaks* books.

A later generation circulated racier 'black list' novels – *Lady Chatterley's Lover, Angelique, Katharine* and *Forever Amber*, Bridget Veitch (Evans 1957-63) disclosed. All books taken in to the school had to be vetted by the house mistress, and signed by her inside the cover, Bridget explained, adding: 'Books without a signature were confiscated; I can't think why we didn't forge signatures!'

A pupil from the Twenties remembered the librarian's shock when, at the beginning of a new term, she found that the cleaners had taken out all the books in the Ref for dusting, and replaced them according to colour; apparently it took two weeks to put everything back as it should have been.

Vivien Allen (Hallett 1937-43) used to gaze longingly through the glass of the swing doors to the Ref on her way to or from the Studio, 'eager for the time when I would be able to use it, but it was not to be; by then we were in Keswick. A few of the books came with us to be housed in what had been the

Keswick Hotel's Smoking Room. Missing out on the use of that beautiful library at Brighton was one thing I really held against Hitler.'

Vivien was shown around the school by an older girl during her first term in Junior House. 'She pointed out the Governor's Room and just inside the door was a small bookcase. I asked what that was and she said, "Oh, that's the ORA Bookcase. They're all books written by Old Girls." Heaven knows why, but from that moment I was determined that one day I, too, would have a book in that bookcase. It took a long time. I was eleven then and my first book, *Kruger's Pretoria*, was not published until I was forty five.'

Fiona Hodges (Ewart 1967-72) thought the old Fic one of the great under-rated resources of the school. 'I spent much time there and found things I'd never seen or heard of. It seemed woefully under-used. There were bound copies of *Punch* right up on the top shelves, lots of good children's literature, and quite a lot of twentieth century stuff, too. The room itself was poorly sited, dingy and unwelcoming, and prone to that great hazard of the timetable, being used as an extra classroom. But I thought it was a real resource and bastion of peace and quiet for uninterrupted reading.' Of the Ref, Fiona said: 'I only have to smell oil-fired central heating and I am back in the Ref, dozing in the slightly stuffy air, watching the others all apparently working'.

When library facilities were reorganised the Central Resource Centre was hailed as 'a fantastic improvement' by Sarah Watts (1986-94); 'excellent and comparable in comfort to my Cambridge college library,' by Zoe Green (1988-95) and 'an immense asset' by Portia Da Gama Rose (1990-95).

FORTY YEARS ON

Caroline's story

W HEN Caroline McDowall received her questionnaire so many clear, sharp memories of her Roedean schooldays came flooding back that the four-page form was, plainly, inadequate. Caroline embarked on a series of long essays, one to cover each question asked. The first arrived at Roedean in January, 1997, and the others followed over the next eleven months. Caroline's memories captured so perfectly the time and the place, the values, aspirations, joys and sorrows of school life on the cusp of change, before the new freedoms of the Swinging Sixties both swept away pre-war attitudes to the education of girls in single sex schools, and gave the girls new expectations, that it was decided to publish them as a book within a book.

Caroline McDowall (Gamlen, Number Two House) lives in Winnipeg, Canada

I was at Roedean for five years – 1955 to 1960 – and those five years are the most vivid and the longest and the most important in all my memory. School is still with me. Rarely a day goes by that I do not think of school – my friends, my teachers, things we did, things I was in trouble for and, just occasionally, things I actually learnt. Of all those, the ability to work extremely hard, to hold on long after there is nothing left but the Will which says 'hold on', has perhaps been the most valuable.

I miss the kind of friendships we made at school most dreadfully. They were a form of bonding and I did not know, when I left school, that that was not how future friendships would be. I have had friends since school, but none as strong, as deep, as all-encompassing as those.

My memories and experiences at Roedean were coloured by the fact that I was a very square peg in a very round hole – I did not fit in and in spite of everyone's efforts, I was often very unhappy. I came to the school with very little experience of anything other than of doing what I had been told to do; I had not been to dancing classes, I had not been encouraged to think for myself, I was unaware of music or fashion, I was very green in every way – I was not ready for Roedean.

THE DAILY ROUTINE: During the week breakfast was at 8am, so there was a bell (tinks) at 7am and at 7.30am, I think. There was another bell at 7.55am at which point you shot out of your bedroom to rush downstairs with everyone else. I often got up early to do work before breakfast, practising maths, writing character sketches of each person in the play/book we were doing in readiness for the essay that would surely be required, re-reading books/plays, making notes on this topic or that topic, just in case. Close to exam revision time I would clear the top drawer of my dresser and invert it to use as a desk top. If you shared a room, doing this early morning work without waking the other person was difficult. You had to muffle the alarm clock and not move about, so all the books that you needed had to be on the chair by the bed, ready. I spent many terms in single rooms so this was not too much of a problem.

Caroline Gamlen when she was in Lower V, July 1957

I was much involved in sports, and we had sports practices before breakfast. There were times, very brief, when a pre-practice snack of hot chocolate and a couple of biscuits was available in the dining room, but usually we played on an empty stomach.

We had to strip our beds before breakfast. Matron would check, and a list of offenders would be read out by Aunt M (Miss Stenning) during breakfast. I learned how to strip my bed very carefully so that re-making it was easy; effectively it was already made, but turned back.

There was a rota for baths – each bath was scheduled for one user in the morning. I hated morning baths (and still do). In the evening there was again a rota for the baths. Everyone was scheduled for three baths per week, one of which was a morning bath. It was important to leave the bathroom 'nice' for the next person. Discussion on verrucas often came up. I dried in the bath and stepped out into my slippers.

During breakfast Aunt M would read out the names of those who had mail and they could go up and collect it from her. How I longed for a letter. It gave me a sense of importance to be called up and to have people watch, and ask me who my letter was from. I was prone to writing long letters – my parents asked me to write less! How insensitive of them. Could they not see how unhappy and insecure and lonely I was simply from the fact that I wrote so much? My parents rarely visited me to take me out; much of the time they were abroad, and when they were home the journey was difficult. When they did come, we would go to a café near the front in Rottingdean and order a Knickerbocker Glory – a tall glass full of jelly, fruit, cream and ice cream. What a treat!

After breakfast we had to clean our rooms (mop under the beds, shake the mat, empty the Wackie-B, dust the dresser) and have them inspected by a prefect.

On Mondays Ma P (Matron) inspected bedrooms and put up a list of those that did not pass. You then had to do them properly and have her check them. She also checked that your drawers were tidy. It was tiresome if you shared with an untidy person. I was not naturally tidy or organised, but so afraid of trouble that I religiously set a rigid routine for myself to be sure I got all these things done. In senior years, if you had a good record with Matron she did not check you any more.

I don't remember the time for going to bed, but lights-out was taken seriously. The times were set by what form you were in. Some people had torches and read under the bedclothes, or listened to faint radios (Radio Lux) under the covers. Aunt M looked for lights on and listened for talking after hours. When four of us were sharing a room at one point, we set a trap as a warning of her approach (buttons in a tin can and some black thread). I found it very distressing when I couldn't sleep, having just to lie there in the dark. I think eventually Aunt M realised this and ignored my light being on. Sometimes she would come in to talk in a friendly way and wish me good-night. I liked that very much.

We were not allowed to wash our own hair. For those of us with greasy hair this was a problem. Shamp was scheduled once a fortnight with a rough, long finger-nailed lady on Monday afternoons. There were no hair dryers. With our wet hair wrapped turban-wise in a towel we went to kneel in front of Ma P's gas fire; it was very sociable and cosy. Eventually I was allowed to have my hair washed once a week. Sometimes I would creep to the bathrooom in the middle of the night to wash my hair. Drying it was difficult. When one friend and I shared a room on Heaven we caught rain water in our tooth mugs for washing our hair at night as we believed it would make our hair softer. Some people would put their hair in curlers at night. On Mondays we had to wash our hair brushes and combs and put them on our dressers for inspection.

We were not allowed to wash our clothes. I was very conscious of the laundry bill and only ever gave in enough to meet minimum requirements, but I found that I could wash a few things and screw them tightly in a towel to get them close to dry, and then surruptiously hang them somewhere, or put them under the bottom sheet of the bed at night to dry.

If you did not have a lesson you were expected to be in the JPR or SPR doing prep. There was a scheduled prep at the end of the day also, supervised (often with difficulty) by a prefect in the JPR. It must have been an awful job! The desks in the JPR and SPR were forerunners of the workstations of today. At the back of the desk was a book rack and shelf unit. The desks were dark and shiny from years of use. Desks had to be tidy and were inspected; offenders were publicly listed.

Lessons started promptly at 9am. There were two lessons, then mid-morning break, three lessons then lunch at 1pm. In the afternoon there were games, except on Wednesdays when there were house practices for those on teams, and time off for others. I think we were supposed to pursue hobbies. I used to enjoy going to the dressmaking room and working alone on my latest project. Tea was at 3pm, then there were lessons, and often prep periods, until supper at 7pm.

We also had lessons on Saturday mornings and these always had a more relaxed atmosphere than those during the week. Saturday afternoons were 'off', except for those of us playing sports. Many people were able to go out when their parents arrived to pick them up. After supper on Saturdays there were house dances where we could wear either a school dress or a dress from home.

We had no access to telephones at all, and did not receive calls except for desperate family emergencies. These would be taken in the house mistress's study under her supervision, without any thoughts about invasion of privacy.

MEAL TIMES: There were, I think, twelve tables in the dining hall, five down each side and two joined end to end down the middle. Aunt M sat at the clock end of the double table and Smelzer (Miss Cameron) at the other end. At lunch time assigned staff members sat at the ends of most of the other tables. These included Ma P by the SPR door, Stonehenge (Miss O'Callaghan), Miss Denham, Cucumber (Miss Cumberland) and Stooge (Miss Sturgis).

Each table had seven people, one or two from each form. The whole table group moved from table to table (I think it must have been daily) to progress round the dining hall – except for tea when you could sit where you liked. At the same time we rotated round the table so that different pairs of people would have to sit up to the various members of staff and make polite conversation with them. I was very nervous when it was my turn to sit up and I am sure it must have been a trial for the staff, too. I remember how hard Miss O'Callaghan would help, and how Miss Denham was apparently happy not to bother to talk at all. Miss Sturgis was the most terrifying.

While I was still new I was informed that I would have to sit up to The Lady Gardener the next day. I was very afraid; how could I make conversation for a whole meal to such an auspicious being? Would my manners let me down? I worried and worried and inevitably lunch time arrived and I had to do it. The Lady Gardener turned out to be just that – a lady gardener as opposed to a gentleman gardener. I don't remember what we talked about, but even I could see how silly I had been!

Eventually, having rotated round the tables, you came to scrum table. This was the table that served the meals, with people carrying two or three plates at a time from the serving table in the little kitchen (the meals were made downstairs and brought up on a huge hoist). If there was any food left, and there usually was, scrum table would serve seconds to those with their hands up. The great thing about scrum table was that there was no-one to sit up to, and having served everyone else, you could eat as much as one wanted. It was wonderful to be on scrum table on Sundays because for lunch there were the most delicious puff pastry squares I have ever tasted, with slightly burnt sugar on top.

The most difficult lunch item for me was the caper sauce that came with lamb. How to get rid of those little black balls? And junket – so slithery and those artificial neon colours.

For breakfast during the week there was cereal or porridge, a cooked item and toast and marmalade. I actually liked porridge, but many did not. With plenty of butter, salt, sugar and milk on top it looked revolting. The cooked item might be bacon, sausage, grilled real tomatoes or hot tinned tomatoes on toast (very sloppy), baked beans or – oh! horrors! – scrambled egg. How did they make it? Did they start with eggs? Presumably they were powdered eggs reconstituted. The end result came in a variety of textures from junket to loose lumps, a range of colours from sickly pale to sunshine, and accompanied by differing amounts of strange liquid. It was awful but you could get it down with butter and plenty of pepper.

Tea always looked so nice with the red gingham table runners and the food out ready to eat. You could sit where you liked and bag places for friends by tipping up the chairs. I think there was more or less unlimited bread. The first job was to mark the pat of butter into equal portions before taking your own. Would I have it all on one slice of bread, or apportion it so that there was some for each slice? There was a cupboard under the window where people kept their jam from home (tuck). Some people, notably Caroline Druiff, were very kind and would share their jam. Black cherry jam makes me think of Druiff. The school provided jam and other spreads; I think Fry's Chocolate Spread was the most popular.

Saturday teas were barely supervised and in the winter, when the gas fire was on in the JPR or JCR, we would sneak out with bread and toast it by the fire – wonderful smell, dreadfully wicked! And very difficult without a toasting fork.

Saturday suppers were the times when jokes were shared. There was a time when I wrote them down and put them in my writing case, which I still have – a gift from my father that first birthday in Upper Fifth, a small brown leather attaché case, fitted with correspondence compartments, which I used all through school as my overnight case. 'Two peas in a pod – why didn't they marry?' 'Because they were Batchelors!' 'Do you know the story of the illegitimate Rice Krispie?' 'It had plenty of snap and crackle but no pop!' Pretty pathetic, but it was all very funny then.

Sunday breakfast, called Starvation, was actually very nice. There was no cooked breafast or cereal/porridge, just rolls, butter and marmalade – lovely. Towards the end of breakfast a Six One would read a short appeal she had prepared on behalf of the deserving cause for which the day's Chapel collection would be taken. The least you could give was 2d, on little cheques from the school cheque book. Each house had cheques of a different colour. We could use cheques, too, for laundry bills and a few miscellaneous purchases Ma P might make for us in Brighton. The amounts were added to our parents' invoices at the end of term.

If Aunt M did not attend meals, the Head of House would sit in her place, say

Grace, supervise and make announcements. The Head of House (I remember Biffo) was usually a very popular person and so she did not have many problems, apart from noise. Jokes were often told at supper amid gales of raucous laughter.

There were two important things about birthdays – the number of cards you got and The Tea. The number of cards was significant because it was a measure of your popularity; the more cards you got the more people liked you. At least, that was how I interpreted it. Since there was no school shop and no way in which to buy birthday cards once at school, we had to remember to purchase and pack a stock of cards (and gifts) before leaving home. This proved useful early training in advance organisation.

After my first disastrous birthday tea I never had another. My end-of-September birthday happened just after the beginning of term, while I was still very homesick. For tea you could put three tables together in the dining room and invite friends (even people from other houses). The fare was the same as the regular tea but you could have a birthday cake from home, and candles that would be blown out to a chorus of *Happy Birthday* and *For She's a Jolly Good Fellow*.

For my tea I asked my grandmother to send me a cake (my parents were abroad); this she did, but the calamity was that she did not send any candles. What was I to do? How could I have a birthday cake without candles? I was distraught. The shame of it. My ingenious and creative friend Squashy thought of a wonderful solution. We would go out towards the roller skating rink and pick scarlet pimpernel flowers to go on the cake instead. She had seen some just the other day. They would be so pretty and would blow off, rather than out, just splendidly.

That afternoon (cold, wet and windy) we trudged out, me very sad and upset, Squashy confident and supportive, to pick our scarlet pimpernels. There were not many, but we found enough eventually. I had my tea, with my saviour Squashy right beside me, and the time came – I blew off the flowers and everyone sang. The kitchen staff were furious and I was in Deep Trouble for my Thoughtlessness.

UNIFORM: I was not at all fashion conscious and so, as long as the clothes we had to wear were warm and comfortable, that was all right. In very cold weather, and during out-of-school hours, we could wear our cloaks indoors and underneath we could carry a hot water bottle. I was very fond of my cloak – an extra blanket at night, an easy thing to throw over the top of whatever else I happened to be wearing to keep out the wind and cold, a Batman sail for windpower on the roller skating rink, something to snuggle into on bad days.

My problem was shoes. The regulation school shoes were Physical Culture, available from Dickens and Jones and a few other suppliers. They were not stocked in Southampton where my family lived. They were quite expensive brown leather slip-on style shoes which had to fit properly in order to stay on. My mother believed that looser shoes with straps or laces were better for your feet. When I was a new girl my mother would not buy Physical Culture shoes. Instead she purchased two pairs of brown leather shoes with straps; I remember one pair being particularly pretty, as I thought, with little flowers punched out around the top. When I got to school, completely new and completely lost and completely homesick, I was in Dire Trouble because of these shoes.

We went to London, to Dickens and Jones, to buy the whole school uniform before my first term. What an amazing amount of clothes, and so many of each thing! All that trying-on! As laundry was sent out once a week and took a week to come back, I can now see that I needed two weeks' worth of clothes. I was quite small at that time and so my mother bought the uniform very much on the large side and took up huge hems and double hems. Everything, even the handkerchiefs, had to be marked with Cash's name tapes.

During the week we wore loose, almost straight navy tunics with our circular house badge sewn on the front. Under these we wore short sleeved white shirts and a house tie (unless you had won your colours, in which case you proudly wore a special tie). A navy V-necked sweater or cardigan was allowed and a blazer was optional. Eventually I managed to buy a secondhand blazer from someone leaving and was so pleased to have it. There were still a few of the old style, long sleeved, round necked Viyella shirts around. People liked to wear them if they had them. Prefects wore suits and later on, I think, when we were in the Sixth Form, we wore our own skirts and blouses.

For games we wore a white cotton shirt with a collar that folded back to leave a V opening, pleated navy shorts and a heavy white sweater with a fold down collar.

For tea we changed into house dresses – woven woollen dresses that buttoned down the pleated bodice front to the waist, with self-fabric buttoned belts. House dresses were very comfortable and came in quite a few colours – cherry red, light blue, royal blue, sage green, brown. A few people had djibbahs passed on to them from previous generations of Roedeanians – Highly Desirable Garments! They were loose velvet tunics in beautiful colours; some with embroidery on them.

I think we wore stockings with our dresses once we were in Lower Fifth. They were held up with Sassy-Bs – elastic, lace and nylon creations tied around the middle like twisted rope, with four dangling tentacles to clutch the thickened tops of the tiresome, wrinkling, ladder-prone stockings with seams that slid around your legs.

On Sundays we wore navy suits for Chapel along with shirt and tie and stockings (except for the Middle and Upper Fourth). The suits were tailored jackets and straight skirts with two pleats at front and back. The skirt seemed very tight and constricting. Later, the Sixth Formers could wear their own navy suits.

If you went out (only with parents, of course, or with a friend's parents if you had permission) you wore the suit and hat. Hats, navy blue, with a house hat band, were worn only for going out and for travelling to and from school at the beginning and end of each term. You would be In Trouble if you were seen leaving or arriving at school, or out in Brighton or Rottingdean, without your hat on. In winter you also had a navy overcoat, but this was not of regulation style.

On Saturday nights, when we had house dances (two houses met in the hall for dancing to non-vocal music, under the watchful eyes of staff and prefects) we could wear our house dresses or a dress from home and court shoes. I remember some people being very interested in what people's home dresses were like. I remember the importance of the very stiff petticoat with layers of stiff and pretty lace and net to make the skirt stick out as far as possible. People like me stood around the hall, or sat (wallflowers) on the not-too-numerous chairs, and waited for someone to ask us to dance. Braver and more confident people did the asking. Older students were often kind and asked younger students to dance. Those who had a crush on someone were on tenterhooks, hoping equally that that person would, and would not ask them to dance.

In summer we had simple square necked cotton dresses with pastel vertical stripes on a white background. I've an idea we wore those instead of our tunics in hot weather, for Chapel and for going out, too.

All these clothes were transported to and from school in a trunk of regulation size. On arrival, younger students' trunks were unpacked under the supervision of an older student who checked that they had the right numbers of everything, that everything was named, that everything was put tidily away in the drawers and that they didn't have anything that was not allowed – sweets, jam, 'improper' books (my mother gave me a Nevil Shute, *The Rainbow and The Rose*, that was deemed 'not suitable'). Trunks disappeared at the beginning of term and reappeared a day or two before the end of term for repacking.

Sweets and jam were put in the tuck cupboard in a tuck box or large biscuit tin. The tuck cupboard was located on the large landing area between the SPR and Aunt M's bedroom; it would be opened by a pre for fifteen minutes after lunch. When we went out we would restock our supplies. If you were lucky, a parcel with more tuck might arrive from home. Jam was kept in a jam tuck cupboard .

GAMES: I loved sports. I loved being outside, being free and able to run around. We played games every afternoon except Saturdays (unless you were on a team and playing matches), Sundays and Wednesdays (when there might be practices).In winter we played lacrosse on Seesaws (so called because it sloped; the seagulls used to collect on Seesaws before breakfast, squawking in raucous chorus to encourage curious worms to poke their noses out), Jubilee and Pitches One, Two, Three and Four, with Aunt M and Miss Robertson as coaches. I think Miss Isherwood was sometimes a goalie coach. We wore bibs which indicated what position we were playing. It seems to me that we played in almost all weathers. Periodically we greased the leather thongs of our lacrosse sticks with Vaseline.

I thoroughly enjoyed lacrosse and would have loved to win my colours, although I never did. My friend Dido (Diana Townsend) won hers. As I had already played lacrosse in junior school I did not arrive as a beginner, and always played on school and house teams. I can still see, and hear, Aunt M running up and down the side of the field, caught up in the excitement of the game, urging us on when it looked good, and utterly disappointed when we made a mistake. At half time someone would bring sliced sections of oranges still in their skins for us. We travelled to matches in buses. Benenden was a great rival. I remember, too, The Downs School, which seemed small and friendly.

In summer we played cricket and tennis. As you got older you could choose which to play. Unfortunately I chose cricket, because my brother was good at it. I was not a really good player and only occasionally made the team – but the grass was warm, the sun shone, the daisies grew, the breeze was kind and carried away the smell of the sea. Another summer game was stoolball, a cross between rounders and cricket. Some years we did a little track and field in the summer. I remember sprints and a few other races, but little else.

I particularly hated swimming. The school had its own outdoor pool, with a springboard and diving board, changing area and bleachers for spectators. It was located behind high hedges just beyond Number Four House. Again Aunt M was the instructor. We did not have regulation costumes, but they had to be one piece and 'acceptable'. We did the bronze life saving training and I still have my medal. Again there was inter-house competition, which was very exciting. I swam breast stroke for Number Two.

Indoors we had gymnastics and dancing. I loved gym. We worked on apparatus – beams, horse, box, ropes, wall bars etc, rather more than on the floor and on mats. One term we did creative gymnastics, using chairs; great fun!

Herky B (Miss Baron) taught dancing – Scottish, Greek, sword, ballroom – but I was no good at dancing. Miss Baron would be amazed to learn that I am now a member of an English Country Dance demonstration group. In the Upper Fourth we learned the Highland fling. I was all arms and legs, totally unrhythmical, utterly ungraceful. But I was determined. During the Christmas holidays I practised my Highland fling over and over and when we returned to school in January I hurried to find Miss Baron. 'Miss Baron! Look! I can do the Highland fling!' And there in the corridor I raised my left arm, stood tall and turned out my feet ready to begin. Miss Baron cut me short. 'Caroline,' she said, 'we're doing Greek this term.'

HOUSE LIFE: Houses had little to do with each other. Some people did have friends in other houses and there was healthy competition in sports, but you certainly felt a stranger in another house. Things were done very differently in each house.

We had very close ties to people in the same form and in the same house. House loyalty and identity were very strong and so you felt a sense of belonging with older and younger people in the same house – more with the older people, I think. I have to say, ashamedly now, that I think I largely ignored people younger than myself. You greatly respected people older than yourself; the older they were, the more aloof they seemed, and the more respect you accorded them. You were expected to attend if an older student spoke to you, rather as if a staff member had spoken to you. Disrespect would have consequences.

We did not have fagging, but younger people were expected to have a crush on an older student – someone two or three years older. I did not understand this and didn't get involved in it, but someone with a crush on someone would perhaps try to do secret favours for that person occasionally, or would be embarrassed if that person took notice of her. I remember quite a lot of pressure when I was new to encourage me to have a crush on someone. As I didn't know anyone and didn't want to be so silly, as it seemed to me, I just avoided the whole thing.

When I went to Roedean in 1955 I had never heard of Valentine's Day or St Valentine. Someone had to explain it all to me. We celebrated the day in a very secret way. At the beginning of February (in Number Two House anyway, I don't know about the other houses), we wrote the names of fourteen boys (supposedly boys we knew, but if, like me, you didn't know fourteen boys, you just picked names) on tiny pieces of paper and folded them up and put them in one of your shoes and walked around with them safely compressing. Each morning we took one out and threw it away without looking at it, so that on the morning of February 14 we could take out the last name and see whom we would marry, or love.

This reminds me that, with Aunt M's encouragement, we sometimes celebrated the first day of the new month by saying 'rabbits' (or was it 'hares'?) last thing the night before, and not speaking to anyone in the morning until we had walked down the stairs backwards and said 'hares' (or was it 'rabbits'?) to the first person we met at the bottom.

We did not really get to know people in other houses until the Sixth Form, even though we attended classes with those of the same year as ourselves. There were some friendships between people in different houses – perhaps they knew each other from home, or perhaps they travelled to or from school together; there were also friendships between people in different years, but there would probably have been a reason why, such as being introduced through siblings.

The only member of house staff whom I remember at all was Flo, the friendly cleaner on Heaven. She would go into Brighton on her afternoons off and buy Harlequin-type romance books, or comics. These she was not supposed to show us. Occasionally she would buy some sweets and share them with us. I think she was perhaps afraid of being over-familiar with us. She was very friendly and looked comfortably motherly in her brightly coloured cotton dresses, in contrast to our navy uniform and the suits and tweeds and sensible clothing of the teaching staff.

Many staff members had nicknames. As we did not use their names when speaking directly to them (we addressed them as Madam), I found it difficult when I was new to find out what their names were. It was very easy to offend and therefore to be In Trouble quite unintentionally. I clearly remember in the Upper Fourth being asked by Cucumber to give a message to another teacher. I remembered the message, but how was I to say whom it was from? I did not know her name, only her nickname. It was a most dreadful problem. The teacher to whom I was trying to deliver the message became very impatient. I think in the end I tried to describe her – tall, glasses, but would it be rude to say she had white hair? Up near the staff room were the staff mail boxes, where we put our homework in open wooden lockers ready for marking, and these had names on them – one way to find out, once I realised.

DISCIPLINE: I was very afraid of being In Trouble, and rarely was, certainly not intentionally. However, fear of trouble can be very troubling also, sometimes even worse, perhaps, than the trouble itself.

I don't think we were allowed any make-up. Perhaps Sixth Formers were allowed lipstick when going out? Lack of education and experience with such things was a handicap upon leaving school. No jewellery was allowed except watches, presumably studs for pierced ears and possibly a cross on a neck chain.

Hairstyles were the bane of my life! Short hair was supposed to reach only as far as the collar. Longer hair was to be tied in a ponytail or plaited. In any case it had to be tidy. Mine was thin, lank, greasy and rarely tidy. I longed for my hair to be attractive like everyone else's. I tried rollers, curlers and Kirbygrips and everything I could think of. At the end of one holiday, in order to solve my perennially worrying what-about-my-hair problem, my mother arranged for me to have my hair cut short and permed. What a mortifying disaster. My hair went to a frizz. I wore my hat on the train to Brighton, in the taxi from the station to school, and for as long as possible in our bedroom (a three room) upon arrival. I had to take the hat off eventually and there was a stunned, shocked silence from my room mates. At last the silence was broken by a huge guffaw: 'Bubbles!' If I could have willed myself to evaporate in that instant I would have.

Punishments fell into two main groups – those inflicted by staff and those inflicted by prefects, but I can't actually recall exactly what the punishments were. Teachers could be pretty scathing verbally, and for many people this was shaming enough. Teachers could send you out of class but quite what happened then I don't know as I was never sent out. I think people stood outside the classroom door in the coridor to be 'found' by another staff member, even The Robin.

Just what punishments were inflicted for house infringements, I can't remember either. Certainly lists of those whose rooms did not pass inspection were posted on the house bulletin board. Aunt M would announce at breakfast the names of people she would like to see. I suspect a talking to, appealing to one's sense of honour, shame and/or duty, was probably often punishment enough.

Prefects maintained discipline during preps in the JPR (silence, no moving from one's desk, no doing anything but school work), in the corridor outside their studies (where we lined up for Chapel, open lectures etc) and in the school hallways ('no running'. I learned to walk extremely fast, a sort of glide, rolling the foot and pushing forward from the toes).

I had just one impo from a prefect. I had to learn by heart a certain column cut from a newspaper and then recite it on a certain day at a certain time to a group of prefects who were, I think, seated like an interview panel at the far end of the Fiction Library – terrifying.

THE SAN: A quiet place of care and retreat – and Bluey, everyone spoke so fondly of Bluey. I spent several sessions in the San. It had large simple bedrooms, full of space and light and air. There was a radio speaker on the wall, and you could listen to pop songs even during the day (at certain times). You were not pampered, but felt cared for. Meals, the taking of temperatures and Bluey's and Matron's visits were scheduled to a clockwork routine, giving a sense of quiet order and security.

The only treatment I remember was Gargle-and-Swallow, a white concoction of aspirin and warm water which we had to gargle with, and then swallow. Ugh!

I remember how we all went over to the San for our BCG vaccinations. We lined up and were 'done' at the door to the common room. The common room had a library, a big window looking south near which was a big armchair, and a large table where we could do schoolwork, jigsaw puzzles, play patience, or write letters, and listen to the radio.

People looked forward to being sent to the San. There was a belief that someone in our house managed to develop a rash before a certain test by scrubbing her back with a brush. She was taken over to the San, brush and all, for a couple of days!

I particularly enjoyed being in the San for a few days when I wasn't actually ill. I had an unsightly black eye from stopping a shot in lacrosse and was sent there to await improvement of my appearance.

Bluey and Matron did not spend much time with us as I remember. I wonder what they did all day when there were few inmates in the San? And where did they live? And where was the kitchen? It is surprising, looking back, how little we knew.

At the beginning of each term a list of appointment times would go up on the house noticeboard for Hearts-and-Lungs, Backs-and-Feet and Bugs-and-Fleas. We would take a comb and wait, feeling rather nervous, chilly and naked in our dressing gowns, slippers and pants, outside Aunt M's bedroom. One by one we went in to her bedroom (large, tidy and deep rose pink). She looked us over in a very general way, took our pulse, tapped our chest area, checked the undersides of our feet and watched our backbone curve and straighten as we touched our toes and then came up again. Then she parted our hair to check for a clean scalp.

For the first three weeks of term everyone would have her temperature taken before breakfast by Ma P. She set a large table just inside her sitting room door and we slowly filed round the table with thermometers under our tongues so that she could read them at the other end and record the temperatures in her book. Ma P also had a book in which she recorded periods. If there were an epidemic, like Asian 'flu, the taking of everyone's temperature on a regular basis was reinstated. For the Asian 'flu epidemic, the second floor of bedrooms was taken over as a sick bay because the San was already full. I shared a room with Mary Pepper, who was in the same year, and we became good friends. During this time we found it very helpful to test each other as a way of doing revision, and we went on testing each other and helping each other for the rest of our school days.

When we were in the Sixth Form it was decided that two sixth formers from each house should spend a term 'living' in the San rather than in their own houses. I don't know why this was decided, or why Jennyrose and I were chosen, but it was such a happy term. We were on the second floor of the east wing. We realised people were trusting us and made sure we did not do anything wrong. I think Bluey brought us a hot drink of chocolate around lights-out time.

We all got on so well. I particularly remember Rehana Naim of Number Four House and the night we turned the lights off in her pretty bedroom and sat around 'willing' a jar in the centre of our 'thought circle' to move – and, do you know, it did! I was so scared.

I liked living away on my own, and I liked the walk outside in the air and the wind to go to school. It seemed to me that that was how almost everyone in the world went to school and so it must be normal, and therefore proper.

THE LIBRARIES: Strangely enough my strongest memory of the imposing, silent, revered and beautiful Reference Library is of walking through it, from one end to the other, to get to Miss Horobin's drawing room, to take tea (about once a year) with Mrs McKinnon. I was at the school on a charter entry, which must have been some sort of scholarship for students with overseas connections. My family never mentioned it to me. Money and finance were taboo subjects. But Miss Horobin explained to me delicately that Mrs McKinnon paid part of my fees and that I should therefore be Grateful.

I am sorry to say that libraries did not play a significant role in my life at Roedean at all. I think one of the reasons I more or less ignored the Ref was that I had no idea how it was organised, how to find out something. Why didn't someone show me how to consider the essay question, use the catalogues, find three books, use the indexes, decide what was relevant, make notes and put it all together as an essay? I believe there are times when totally direct and directed demonstrated instruction is required.

The atmosphere in the library was not conducive to relieving the bumbling beginner. The library was beautiful, obviously a prize possession. Big windows all along the south side, large long tables of beautiful wood all down the middle and beautiful wood panelling housing bays of books along the north side. I remember a huge dictionary; I was fascinated by the size of it, and discovered that words came from something called Old English, as well as Latin and French. I began to follow words and their roots through the different definitions – until I felt that people might think it odd that I spent so long hunting around for a word in a dictionary.

You did not talk, whisper, drop anything. You sat at a table, head down, writing. It was perfectly obvious that everyone else knew what the library was for and how to use it. Today one can be brazen and express ignorance and ask questions and not lose face. Back then ignorance was shame. And anyway, who was there to ask? A teacher? Possibly, in private, if she just happened to be in the vicinity at the right time – but you couldn't talk in the library. Double the shame to ask a fellow student.

The fiction library was on the second floor next to the staff common room. It had tables in the middle and shelves of books all round, arranged in alphabetical order by author. So easy and logical. I suspect we signed out on the honour system and as most of us took honour very seriously, this was probably a satisfactory and economical organisational system.

I enjoyed reading and tended to get caught up in the lives of the people in the books. I was excited, and moved to tears by sadnesses. I read *Cry The Beloved Country* and another book with a black cover about a man who escaped from a camp in Siberia and walked through the Gobi Desert to escape. When I found books I liked, I read them again and again.

There was also a library, I assume a fiction library, on very dark stained wooden shelves in the JPR in Number Two House along the dining room wall. These books seemed to be well worn and comfortable in their much thumbed covers. I don't think we signed these out.

SPIDERS: Do people still wander off to Spiders to get away and look across the fields to Brighton peeping over the far hilltop? It is a hill in my memory – any bump in the landscape to a Winnipegger is a hill. Spiders was an untended copse-like area of rough terrain, left after construction of the Chapel or some other building project, perhaps. It was located at the top of the drive, just before it turned right to lead across the front of the school. But I never thought of Spiders in connection with the drive. I used to walk out of school near the science wing northwards up the slopes and through the long grass to the encircling mound just before the wires of the boundary fence. We were not supposed to go right up to the boundary fence – there was an inner invisible boundary. I would turn left along the top of the mound inside the boundary, and look down at the roofs and windows of the school below. There were little shrubs and wild flowers growing among the grasses, and little hollows where you could sit in the warm sun and read a book. Beyond the Chapel you reached the sprawling branches of real (but rather small) trees and the rough ups and downs and mounds of Spiders, this special, unregulated, out-of-school place, where you could sit and not even see the school. To the left, the sea shimmered; ahead, open freedom spread uninterrupted and out of bounds.

CHAPEL: For me, Chapel grew in importance, significance and affection over the years. It was something I missed for a very long time after I left school.

It took time to get to Chapel. You could sense 'going somewhere else'. You passed through the quiet stone cloisters where open arches framed the almost-never-walked-on lawn, round stone corners and up stone steps. Chapel was unique because it was silent, unsupervised, available at any time and beautiful – beautiful because of the marble, the panelling, the stained glass windows; beautiful because of the common voice yearning for goodness; beautiful because the windows coloured the air that filtered in; beautiful because of the poetry of the hymns of Songs of Praise and the old wording of the collects, prayers, epistles and gospels; beautiful because of all the hints and symbols a dreamy mind could find in the dusty flags shot through with bullet holes. There was the brass eagle lectern taking off like an aeroplane and taking all the wise words and ancient stories with him – or was he leaving them behind?

We went to Chapel before school every day but Wednesday (when we had an assembly in the hall) and Saturday. On Sundays there was optional early service before breakfast for those who had been confirmed. If you went to Early, you did not have to go to Evensong. After breakfast there was Matins, which was usually taken by the chaplain, but occasionally by The Robin. Parents and daughters sat in the gallery; the choir sat in front of the organ (where we could never see them).

We used the brown Oxford psalter with the phrasing marks; once I had figured out what the vertical lines were for, I found singing psalms very interesting and was sorry to find in church later that psalters were not used. I took my Oxford psalter with me to a service at St Paul's Cathedral while I was a student at Roehampton, and much regretted that I left it there.

After supper there was Evensong (or Compline during summer months). I found this the most beautiful service and looked forward to it. The evening hymns were gentle and nostalgic; at the final Evensong of the school year, with the sun glowing

144

through the jewelled windows, we sang (and wept) our parting hymn of praise.

Although it took some time to learn to like it, I did eventually enjoy the verses and responses of said Compline; I've since met very few people who know what it is.

During the week we could go to Chapel for peace and reflection at any time. I found this very helpful and felt a spiritual kinship with the other people I saw there in the evenings, although we never talked about it. Chapel was noticeably busier before exams!

We loved singing the Benedicite during Lent – what a rousing, all-encompassing exhortation! And *St Patrick's Breastplate*, with its wonderful verse of different tune, pattern and rhythm. Always on Remembrance Day (on my own) I find and silently sing *O Valiant Hearts* (to the 'proper' tune; over here quite a few hymns are sung to 'wrong' tunes as far as I am concerned). During the last part of the final term, leaving girls could each choose a hymn to be sung at morning Chapel.

Confirmation was one of the few occasions that my parents came to the school. This was very embarrassing because I was now taking religion very seriously, and considered confirmation very important – but religion, God, beliefs, were not family discussion topics. What was I to say to them about it all? Of course, nothing to do with such topics was discussed, we resorted to banalities, and I felt very awkward about the whole thing. A shame, because I believe my father had at some time been a religious man; he did care very much about people and the world. My parents gave me a beautiful gold fob watch which I wore and treasured. To my distress it was stolen during a break-in in 1991. Dear Aunt M gave me an illustrated bookmark of the prayer *Go Forth into the World in Peace*, which seemed (still seems) to me the essence of all we strive to be. It was a prayer we often prayed in Chapel. The Robin also gave me an illuminated bookmark: *God Be in My Head*. I was especially fond of this hymn and it seemed (still seems) to me so complete and yet so simple.

LEISURE ACTIVITIES: On Sunday afternoons there were frequent open lectures or concerts. These I considered deadly. The agony of trying to sit still. The agony of putting myself in the place of the person who was going to give the Vote of Thanks at the end. I'm quite sure we had excellent speakers and excellent musicians. All my memories are of the earlier years, of sitting near the back on a hard chair, with my writhing insides twisted and mangled in ever-tightening convolutions; a fear would come over me that I might not be able to last any longer – what would happen then? The Lawrences looked at me reprovingly from the portraits behind the speaker or musician, their eyes boring into me.

Sometimes on these occasions we played finger games, communicating in 'deaf and dumb', dancing an imaginary flea, or mime sewing our fingers together with an invisible needle and thread. Some people had a button on a thread to spin, but this made a whirring sound and was rather obvious.

When we were in the Sixth Form we went out of school to attend a number of lectures with other local sixth formers. Presumably this was some sort of Sussex Sixth Form Conference. After a while I began to listen and to see how arguments were formulated and how we were going to have a role, if we sought it, in shaping our world.

While we were in Six Two a dance was arranged for our year and the parallel year from Lancing College. I remember having one dance with one boy; he and I had lots to talk about and agreed that we could not dance and so we would spend the evening eating. 'Eats' were set up in the staff room. I did not know what his name was, but I remember thinking he was very nice.

By the time we were in Six Two I think we were allowed out of the grounds in small groups on our own. Any groups going out would have been very conspicuous with their uniforms, hats and gloves.

When we were in the Upper (Lower?) Fifth, three teachers took a group of about thirty of us to Italy during the Easter holidays. The weather was wonderful. I shared a top couchette and blanket with Jennyrose on the way to Basle; it was just freezing that night in that train compartment, and an awful long way from London to Rome. A couchette was very narrow for one person, let alone two! Jennyrose and I put our heads at opposite ends and hugged each other's feet to keep them warm. When the train stopped at stations along the way, people on the platforms tried to sell us things through the windows.

Before we left we had had classes in Italian to prepare us (*Uno timbro por Angleterra per favore. Prego.*). I know we visited many of the classic tourist venues, and had guides to explain it all to us. We stayed in comfortable accommodation and often had bus transportation, although sometimes we used the local, very crowded buses, with people hanging on the outside.

The young Italian men pestered and pursued us relentlessly. I was scared stiff. This spoiled a super and memorable trip. My friend Druiff was reprimanded by Miss O'Callaghan for accepting a red flower from one of these youths; she said it was a 'cheap' thing to do. I remember taking the local bus to get to the catacombs, only to have all these young men get on the bus along with us and try to break up our group into smaller and smaller groups. It was frightening for me – what must it have been like for the staff in charge?

The lemon ice cream and capuccino were wonderful. I drank chianti, brought a bottle home and made a (very unstable) bedside table lamp with it.

Most people had sensible and attractive clothes for the trip. I had garments my mother lent me, and I felt very much like some poor relation.

One of the happiest weeks of my life was my A Level geography field trip to Malham Tarn in Yorkshire. Annabel Robinson and I went in the Easter holiday of 1960. We had field excursions by day and lectures and homework in the evening. I loved everything about it – the hiking, the countryside, the people (we were boys and girls), the food, the work, sleeping in a dormitory, not worrying about clothes or hair or what one looked like. Somehow, one day, I long to go back to Malham Tarn.

We climbed a dry waterfall, traipsed through fog, splashed along becks (my new trousers, my first trousers, shrank), carried picnics and drinks and notebooks in a backpack, followed trails on the one inch OS map . . . what can I say? It was just wonderful.

The older I got, the more time I spent working in what I would call my leisure time. I did want to do well. In winter we would take our metal-wheeled roller skates and school cloaks to the roller rink at the far end of the pitches. I usually had some embroidery on the go, and knitted a white jacket for my toddler goddaughter. I spent many hours in the dressmaking room making clothes for myself or my little sister. Miss Corscaden, the dressmaking teacher, would buy the fabric and patterns for us in Brighton; we described it and she purchased. I would then work ahead on these projects in my free time. We would play jacks in our bedrooms or in the JPR and we played Scree and Racing Demon. Aunt M taught us Chicken Feed, another card game – very detrimental to the cards.

When we were in Upper Fourth Aunt M read to us. This was something I really enjoyed. It was so cosy; she was so welcoming. We would sit in her spacious, sunny sitting room, on the carpeted floor or on her attractive chairs and couches (even beside a fire in mid-winter) with our embroidery etc, and she sat in a large wing chair, with her feet on a pouffé, to read to us from a classic – *The Robe* and *The Woman in White* are two I remember. I was so sorry to find this did not continue in Lower Fifth.

MAJOR SCHOOL EVENTS: At the summer End of Term Assembly do the girls still sing the school songs? We sang them with terrific gusto, all except for that new rather wafty one. There was something suddenly fun and informal about the way Miss Horobin would introduce the songs. We sang them sitting down on metal chairs rather than on the floor, as the assembly was a formal occasion. Copies had been distributed so we each had a booklet which we had been trying to peep in and enjoy all through assembly, and she would appear to choose which one to sing in a very unrehearsed and unplanned manner: 'Let's see now, let's sing – how about . . . ' and it would be *The Cricket First Eleven, Forty Years On* or one of the others. We sang, and stamped and loved it.

The only school play I remember was *Antony and Cleopatra*. I recall lying in bed talking to Squashy (Sarah Rashleigh Belcher – we shared a room at the north end of Heaven that term) about how to make the sphinx, as she was involved with props. She was full of ideas and we spent quite a lot of time in the art room with wire, glue, newspaper and water making papier mâché and the sphinx. She did most of the making – props, plays and papier mâché were all new to me.

One year, Number Two House put on the play *Lady Precious Stream*, directed by Aunt M. I think I helped a little with props, after the success of Squashy's sphinx. My parents came to one performance, and 'don't stand on ceremony' became one of our favourite family sayings.

The Middle and Upper Fourth and Lower Fifth of Number Two House wrote and put on a scum panto in the gym in the winter. The purpose was to be hilariously funny and to incorporate as much school slang and as many teachers' nicknames as possible without being 'too obvious'. I have found the script for ours – I think Caroline Druiff was the moving force behind it, with Anna Dudley Page, Marian Hill and Theresa Wilkinson. It is no masterpiece, but is interesting because it revolves around Sputnik, Russian scientists and spies, Elvis Presley and a skiffle group, and a love element complete with a kiss. How daring!

THE SCHOOL BUILDINGS: I don't think we questioned or took much notice of the condition of the building and furnishings. That it was cold and draughty was sort of accepted and frequently the topic of jokes.

Each bedroom had a silver painted radiator under the window, and I guess it was cold. I've always liked a lot of bedclothes; I remember wondering whether putting newspapers beneath the under-blanket would make the bed warmer. My father, who rarely visited, gave me a radiator key with which I could carefully open the valve at the top of the radiator just a little to bleed off any air which had accumulated at the top. In winter we sometimes wrapped our cloaks around us to work or go about the building out of lesson time; we had hot water bottles, too.

Beside each bed there was a mat, to be kept clean and inspected on Mondays by Ma P. Bedroom hallways were carpeted; other floors were wood planks, very shiny after so much wear. The front stairs, which we students were not allowed to use, were carpeted in green; the stairway to the bedrooms and JPR, JCR etc, was dark stained wood. Classroom hallways had a lino-type floor covering; this lifted to give a strange cushioned feeling on very windy days.

We were not allowed to put things up on the walls of our bedrooms and we would have been in trouble had we marked or damaged our bedrooms in any way. The room was painted a bland cream colour; the bedside chair and dresser were painted white, and I seem to remember some cupboards being of stained wood. Bedrooms did not have locks.

There were curtains at the window, and bedspreads. It was exciting on the first day back to open the door and see what colour the bedspread was. We took our own linen and the school provided blankets and pillows.

Washing, bathing and toilet facilities were at the end of each bedroom hallway. There were about ten washbasins, separated by partitions to form open cubicles,

148

each with a towel rack on the wall. On Heaven there were just two basins and no dividers; it was much more relaxed and sociable and we chatted while waiting our turn.

The big iron baths were noisy contraptions, but large so that you could lie right down in the water (or was I smaller then?) Usually the water was hot, especially if you were one of the earlier people to bath. There was a cork foot mat and a towel rack. The bathrooms were large and steamy, dark green painted and sort of warm and friendly. There was Vim and a cloth so that you could leave the bath clean. Absolutely no-one was allowed with you in a bathroom, so you had to whisper very quietly. The doors did have locks on them, so it was somewhere to lock yourself away. Occasionally a group of us would lock ourselves in the Heaven bathroom to play banned records on someone's record player. This was also a good place to wash your hair at night.

Under the stairs leading up to the hall there was a little cubbyhole in which an older lady sat surrounded by a wonderful tangle of fat wires and single plugs to operate the telephone exchange. The panelling and the wood of the stairs was a warm, soft brown, and there was light in her cubbyhole. She seemed so technical, operating this complicated array of connections. She did not seem very interested in us, but I did manage once to get her to explain to me what she was doing.

Classrooms were very functional, with ample blackboard area at the front. The teacher had a very high desk and a very high chair on a raised platform from which to conduct the class. The most interesting classroom was Room 7. This was a small, narrow, bright yellow room, engulfed in chalkdust. It had a tiny recessed window, a teacher's desk, a small blackboard and two rows of tables for about a dozen students at the most. It was the one room I did not want to go into.

The art room was in the same wing as the reference library and quite different in every way from other areas of the school. The art and pottery sections were large and spacious with both windows and skylights. They were not set up in a structured way; there were lots of pictures on the walls, still lifes set up in corners, plants both living and dried, brushes standing up in jars, samples of this and that, pots and plenty of art-in-progress lying around. It was untidy in a very healthy and relaxed way.

There were two steamy, dark, warm, rather cramped temporary classrooms in the huts, in the space to the north of the gym and east of the Cloisters. These had cosy gas fires, long tables rather than desks, and I liked them. In the further hut I took O Level Maths with Miss Boyd (she made me believe I could 'do' maths – it was simply a puzzle to explore and work out rather than a set of arbitrary routines to follow, if you could remember what they were; but I never did get vectors!).

In the quite new science wing I think there were four labs on two floors. There was a small glassed addition where geraniums in pots grew for photosynthesis demonstrations in bell jars. Now that I grow my own geraniums from cuttings and seeds, and struggle with them through the long winter, the effects of light on the leaves, which I remember Smelzer explaining and me not being remotely interested in, understanding, or believing at all, reminds me of her every year. When the hot sun comes through in spring, the leaves develop dark crescents and then, if they get too much sun, they all go red and wither eventually. Yes, Smelzer, you were right!

A few people would make chemical concoctions in the back row. Labs had long black benches with sinks and water taps every few feet, bunsen burner outlets and a wide tray the length of the bench in which carefully labelled chemicals were arrayed in brown and clear glass bottles with corks or glass stoppers. I remember Smelzer kept the magnesium in her own locked storage cupboard. The big excitement was her demonstration, at the end of class occasionally, of dropping a small cube of sodium on a vessel of water and watching it fizz and race and hiss and dart about.

We sat on stools in our green science lab coats. We did physics, chemistry and biology (plant and human – safe topics like digestion and blood circulation). There were posters on the wall of anatomical humans, illustrating systems or naming body parts, etc. Sometimes Smelzer would do an experiment (I remember all the glass tubes and vessels set up in a complicated arrangement for distilled water) at the front and we would all crowd around to watch and for homework write it up with scientific drawings, following strict rules on what was scientific drawing and what was not, and write up Apparatus, Method, Results and Conclusion. Sometimes we experimented ourselves at the benches (soap and scum and soft and hard water).

Smelzer had the task of teaching us that An Acid + A Base = A Salt + Water, and she came up with dancing partners as a way of demonstrating this. She was full of energy and would go flying around in front of the equation and her stick man/woman pictures on the blackboard demonstrating how this dancing boy changed partners with this dancing girl in the other couple. I could never see how from the original equation you could tell which was the boy and which the girl.

Jennyrose went on to Do Science through Upper Fifth and Sixth Forms, and had pages and pages of equation computations. I thought she was incredibly clever. Almost everyone who was clever seemed to Do Science; it seemed to me that it must therefore follow that anyone who Did Not Do Science (like me) was not clever. When we were in Upper Fifth Mr Behrens joined the science staff. The first male teacher – what an innovation! How we eagerly awaited his arrival . . . and were rather disappointed; he was older and wore well worn, baggy brown suits.

The Gym was located between Number Two House mouse hole (the dark and narrow brown-lino'd corridor by the prefects' studies, where we lined up under the watchful eyes of pres – single file, no talking, stand still . . . often impossible), the new sunken geography room that looked on to the courtyard on the far side of which were the One and Two kitchens, and the huts to the north. The south side of the gym was a corridor area between the double swing doors at each end for people moving from the geography/Number One area to the rest of the school.

At the east end was the raised stage where we performed our scum panto. The gym itself was very light and bright with a light coloured narrow plank flooring and windows between sets of wall bars on the north and south walls. There were two sets of ceiling ropes, two sets of double horizontal bars, lots of mats (heavy, of rough coconut husk fibre, not these soft foam and plastic gym mats students use today), a horse, a box and a buck (a small and very high horse). This was my overall favourite. We did not use it until about Upper Fifth, presumably most of us were too short to spring that high, but with the springboard and a good leap you went up, up, up and the push – and you were flying in space. What a thrill!

We did many different vaults similar to those seen on the TV during the Olympics, and others – waterfall, scissors, handspring – it seems to me a shame that the wider variety of vaults that we did has been narrowed down to just a few these days to conform to the Olympic list. One Christmas term a small group of us were formed into a gynmastics club (I thought we were going to perform somewhere, but we never did) and we did some really novel and interesting acrobatic stunts with chairs. It was terrific fun and very clever.

During the last class of the term we often played shipwreck in gym class. I didn't like this, and preferred the control and quiet of working on apparatus under class structure; I was afraid of getting caught and ditched in the sea, and it seemed to me that being good at gym didn't make you a winner in this game. But other people liked it. All the apparatus was set up in the gym, several people were appointed 'it' and a game of tag ensued. The rule was that you could not put any part of your body on the floor (except in a few necessary stepping areas designated by hoops). Chasing and escaping had to be done over, through, along and via the apparatus.

I don't think that people of my generation here (especially the women) ever had any physical training to compare with ours (and I think it shows) and the physical education in schools here is pathetic compared to what ours was, in spite of all the talk and emphasis on participation.

An area that ordinary students never went into was the main foyer inside the front doors under the clock. I think perhaps it was out of bounds to all but staff, visitors and possibly the head girl and a group of about six pres that formed up to march into the quad in hats, navy blue suits and stockings to hoist the Union Flag on the terrace following strict rites and rituals. This area was down a wide and short flight of stairs from the main corridor, so we passed by it, and Miss Horobin's office right beside it, several times a day. Marble? Wood panelling? A door off it to the area under Miss Horobin's office? A square of carpet, I think, and possibly a portrait or two and a desk in the corner. It probably is now as it was then. I just remember a big, impressive and attractive space that we would not have dreamed of invading, although I think we came in that way when I arrived for the interview.

Another room was the book room or was it book cupboard? Small, anyway. Located at the west end of the second floor classroom corridor, between the dark north classroom where we did maths and the light and bright south room where we did catechism before Confirmation and history in Upper Fifth with Miss MacIntosh. The door to this room was usually locked, but we went there to get and hand in text books over lunch on a certain day of the week. I still have my *Palgrave's Golden Treasury* because I liked it so much I wanted to keep it. Unfortunately I rubbed out the pencilled names on the frontpiece, but the penned names are still there: 'Gillian McCullagh, No 3 House, Lower V A, 1947; Susan May, No 3 House; Penny Ashton, No 3; Maureen Taylor, No 3 House, Upper IVB, Lower VB.' A carefully looked after and well thumbed anthology, stuffed with bookmarks for my favourite poems and a few helpful notes from previous owners. I think we were allowed to buy some of the books if we wanted to.

Not only did we get some of our textbooks from here, this was also where we got our exercise books and rough books (fatter exercise books on softer, cheaper paper) to do our work in. These had ROEDEAN SCHOOL printed on the cover. I still have my Malham Tarn notes and a couple of exercise books of French literature notes. You took up your filled-up book, showed the teacher that indeed all pages had been used and that no space was wasted, and she gave you another.

Notes for tests and exams took up a lot of rough book pages and Jane Chandler showed me how she managed to write everything out time and time and time again by writing in her rough book the first time through in pencil and then turning it around and writing in it again from the other end in pen. This was the ultimate in conservation. Try telling that to a student – or an adult – today! Of course we had to write on both sides of the page in all these books before asking for another.

Speaking of writing, in Upper Fifth, in my first term, school complained very much about my appalling handwriting and set up remedial handwriting classes (before breakfast) with Miss Gee. We were only a small class, and the intention was to teach us italic. How I wish I had really tried and mastered this, for I can see how attractive it is to look at a page of beautiful handwriting, most especially italic, but I don't think I really tried or cared then. I did, however, realise the efficiency and speed of making a single flowing and continuous movement for each word, and experimented with ways to shape letters so they could all join up efficiently. My writing was never very even, attractive or consistent, but by the time I left school I could write at talking speed and when, many years later, I learned shorthand, I couldn't really see why it was necessary if you could write at talking speed.

Another room that I got to know well was the sick room. This was located behind the tuck cupboard, between the SPR and Aunt M's bedroom. It had a window that looked across Seesaws and straight out to sea. The bed was close to the window and you could be in bed and look at the sea, the stars, the seagulls and the weather across that wide horizon. I remember watching storms over the sea with great excitement as the lightning developed, leapt from cloud to cloud, and lit the world for an instant with a brilliant monochrome electric glare.

I watched the big cumulous clouds grow and change from shape to evolving shape – faces and lions and mythical creatures. I saw the faintest streaks of cloud gather more moisture, blow in the wind, pile up in rows and mark out fronts. I saw the moon over the sea in all her forms, sparkling on the sea on calm, clear starry nights, playing hide and seek with scudding coulds, and peeping as a crescent to join the party of the millions of stars.

From the sick room there was a locked door that led into the SPR. I used to listen very quietly to see if I could hear what the Very Senior People were saying in there, and who was talking – but I don't know that I ever heard much.

TRAVEL: I travelled to and from school by train and taxi, almost always to or from home in Southampton. Usually I had a through train ticket, but occasionally I had to change trains between Southampton and Brighton.

In those days, my family saw the journey from Southampton to Brighton as a long way. For the first couple of times my mother came with me on the train and then in the taxi up to school, but after that I did it on my own. If my father were home he drove me to the station, if not, until my mother learned to drive, I took a taxi from home to Southampton Central Station.

The most surprising thing to me now is that I have no memories at all of Brighton Station, but I have clear memories of sitting on the hard bench, appallingly conspicuous in my hat and suit and stockings, in the grey draught of Southampton Central, waiting, waiting, waiting for the dreaded train.

It was a monstrous steam train that zoomed around the bend from Bournemouth and the New Forest and huffed and puffed and roared and hissed with clouds of smoke and steam and smuts, and finally ground to a temporary stop at the platform. Would it stop long enough for me to get on? It went on huffing and puffing and churning out power and smoke, a living, breathing, impatient angry dragon come to get me . . . whistles and flags and men shouting; engine driver, ticket collector and guard in dark uniforms with flat peaked caps; the guard loading and unloading the van; people getting on and off; all hurry and noise, noise and hurry all mixed up.

I think my later journeys were by electric train, but it is the steam train noise and size and power and impatience I remember for going back to school. The open countryside and woods, fields of green and yellow, cows and horses, silent towns with people shopping, playing fields beside those huge inert factories with well known names like Johnson and Johnson close to Havant – all were sliced through by the digger-dig-dig speeding train. My mother would encourage me to take tea like a sensible lady traveller, but I was not any sensible lady traveller, I was a sad and nervous homesick girl going back to school.

Getting to the station was nerve-wracking if Father was taking me in the car. He was a seasoned traveller, understood the travel arrangements and timetables and systems and synchronisations, but I didn't. If my train was due to leave at 10am he saw no point in arriving before 9.55am. I imagined all sorts of scenarios by which I might miss the train and be in trouble. What if the train left early? What if the driver forgot to stop at Southampton? What if the train was already full and I couldn't get on? What if I got on the wrong one? What about a puncture, an accident, a traffic jam? Father must have been so disappointed to see how poorly I handled this very simple and ordinary routine – my tenseness, my total lack of communication and my inability to say goodbye sensibly and fondly must have been very painful for him, and I am sure he did not understand at all what was going on in my head, and so found it very frustrating and disheartening.

Actually, getting to school all began a week or ten days before the real date and so the journey seemed unnecessarily slow and long. One day, the Clothes List and my trunk would be at the far end of the living room or a corner of the games room, waiting. My mother would begin reminding me to start collecting and packing.

My parents must have informed the school ahead of arrival time at Brighton because a taxi would meet the train and drive me up to the house front door. A coach met the trains from London and brought bus loads of chattering people up to school. On arrival, with hat on and badge centred, the left glove on, and the right glove off, I would greet and shake hands with Aunt M politely, assure her I had had a lovely holiday, pass through the front hall, up the green carpeted stairs, and join the excited groups of those who had already returned – a sea of laughing, jolly, happy, navy blue girls who had all had wonderful holidays and were all obviously wonderfully thrilled to be back.

I think we reported to Ma P to find out which bedroom we were in, or maybe it was posted on the house noticeboard. We collected our bed linen from Ma P, made our beds and eventually it was supper time. This ended with Aunt M's favourite line: 'And now please go quickly and quietly to bed'.

I had my overnight things in the small attaché case, and eagerly awaited the arrival of my trunk so that I could arrange my drawers, and the ornaments and photos (five ornaments, three photos) on the dresser. The trunk was of regulation size with my name printed in white in capital letters on the top, as was required. Caroline Druiff had a trunk two inches longer. She said it was because she was so tall that she needed the extra length, but the men who came to take trunks away into storage explained that the regulation size was because of the way the trunks were stored all through the term.

I remember preparing for my very first term, at my grandmother's house. My tunic and dresses – one cherry red, one bright royal blue – hung from the picture rail in my tiny bedroom and I was so excited at the prospect of all these new clothes. Sewing on all those name tapes was quite a job for my mother and grandmother. I did some on the hankies; I think the list called for eighteen handkerchiefs.

As well as names, the tapes also had to have our numbers, for laundry purposes. Mine was 56. This number was the same as my number in the boot locker where I put my lacrosse boots under the wooden bench and hung my sports gear on a peg. I consider 56 my lucky number; it has stayed with me for all sorts of uses since I left school. Our first house when we were married was 56 Balcombe Road and my employee number now is 56036.

THE HEADMISTRESS: We had no informal contact with Miss Horobin that I can think of. I have no recollection of ever seeing her in Number Two House or out in the grounds in a casual way at all, and I can remember only two incidents of formal contact with her. The first was at the end of Lower Fifth when I went up on the stage to receive my gym colours; she pinned the badge on and shook my hand. The second was at the end of my last term when I went to her office to be presented with my Leaving Certificate. She spoke complimentarily about my achievements and what I had done for the school, asked about my future plans, gave me her good wishes and once more shook my hand. Presumably she had contact only with the Very Bad or those who had achieved Glory.

Miss Horobin was an imposing figure, sweeping through the halls in her billowing black academic gown, over tweed suits and sensible shoes.

She took Chapel and presided over assemblies with total authority. She did not intervene to impose discipline – no discipline problems would develop within her sphere. She did not appear to be involved in such aspects of school life; she was the head, the public figure. She did not look fierce or domineering, just commanding, in control and utterly confident.

The only inkling we ever had that she had any connection with discipline and students, apart from her Speaking To students standing out in the corridor (sent out) was when, one morning at assembly, she informed us that a certain student (who was notoriously Bad) had been expelled and that she expected to hear no more about her.

In Chapel she took daily assembly; sometimes she took Sunday Matins instead of the chaplain, and she usually took Evensong or Compline. Did she take Communion? I'm not sure now. She led sung responses and gave sermons; I assumed that she had been ordained. My father said she was just like a man, except that she was a woman.

I also met Miss Horobin briefly when I went to her sitting room for afternoon tea with Mrs McKinnon, my generous Charter Entry sponsor. It was just a fleeting glimpse on these occasions to usher me in when I arrived.

I remember Miss Horobin best from my interview before coming to the school. We arrived, my parents and I, one bright day in the summer term of 1955 at the big front door under the clock. I think we must have driven there. My father in his best dark suit, with his hair carefully combed and parted, determined to do The Right Thing, and determined too that I, and my mother, should do The Right Thing also. I was wearing a pale blue wool suit, a hat, white ankle socks and white gloves. We waited silently in a small dark room beside Room 7, across the corridor from Miss Horobin's study. Did I have a test to write? Yes, I think perhaps I did.

My parents went in for the interview first, and seemed to be gone for a very long time. Then it was my turn. I knew I had to be Very Polite. I went through the door into the light and brightness of her south-facing office and there she was, halfway between me and the window, with her hand outstretched for the handshake. I stepped forward bravely and put out my hand to take hers – but I had not removed my glove; no-one had told me that a lady removes her glove to shake hands.

Miss Horobin took back her hand, told me I should take off my glove before shaking hands. I removed it with great difficulty as I was shaking all over. Once again she put out her hand, I shook it and she smiled. I don't remember anything else about the interview; it probably was not long at all. An experienced head would have been able to sum up all she ever needed to know about me simply from that glove episode, I'm sure. My father wanted to know all about it. What had she asked? What had I said? How could I tell him about the glove incident?

THE STAFF: Those who mattered, the ones I remember, the ones (a select list) whom I got to know for whatever reason – they were all characters.

In front of me is the four foot black and white panoramic school photograph from July 1959. I have not looked at this picture for years. Mesdames, in this picture you all look so *young*! So much younger than ever you are in the picture of my memory! And I am terribly sorry to see that there are some of you I don't remember and one or two whose faces and subjects I remember, but not whose name.

This picture shows 373 girls, including Junior House, and seventy five staff, including teachers, matrons and San staff and, I assume, the admin staff (Mr McLeod, the accountant, is the lone man at the end of the row). Domestic staff (am I wrong – who is the lady with the big bow on her dress at the far left?), custodians and groundsmen are not in the picture, although everyone else must have depended on them greatly for their contributions to keep the place going.

Many staff, especially the older ones, had nicknames, but newer staff did not necessarily get nicknames. I suspect the practice was dying out in the Fifties. My father was fascinated by school talk scattered with these outrageous names when I regaled the family with exaggerations of goings-on at school; he would tease me and egg me on to talk more (or imitate Stooge) just to enjoy the school slang, the names, the fun of it all. My mother thought it very disrespectful.

Teachers always wore their academic black gowns when in the classroom and about the school on school days. Some gowns were in much better condition than others. We would look out for a teacher who had sat on the chalk and so had a white patch on her gown – we might even put chalk dust on her chair . . .

We rarely saw school (as opposed to house) staff in the main school area out of school class time. I remember once, one evening, encountering Dwu near the staff room (there was staff accommodation above the staff room level; we *never* went up there and barely knew where the staircase was). Dwu was dressed in a green wool suit and had *no gown*. Was she still Madam? Safest to assume so! Of all the school staff, she was the one most likely to be about, to stop and chat, and we liked finding her and talking about out-of-school things we had read about in the paper. She taught us Current Events in the evenings at one point – an excellent idea.

After we had done exams, such as O Levels, it was considered proper for us to write to the teachers of the various subjects, once we received our marks in the mail in August, to thank them for having taught us.

It was a pretty impressive sight at Speech Day or the end of term to see all the staff on the hall stage, all in gowns. We noticed who sat next to whom and had ideas about who would not want to sit next to whom!

In this photograph, Aunt M is close to the centre, just a couple of chairs from The Robin. Aunt M was fair and caring and must have been 'on the job' for very long hours all term long. If one of us received a parcel we went to her office to collect it; we might even have to open it in her presence to let her see what was inside (tuck to go in tuck cupboard; no 'improper' books).

Aunt M had a rose pink carpeted bedroom on the first floor above her office, a room away from the SPR and beside the narrow corridor that led to the small group of bedrooms above the kitchens. That group was called Colony; Mary and Steph Cole, Shovel and Jane Chandler had rooms there several terms. Aunt M had a large office and an attractive sitting room with a huge fireplace. Usually we met Aunt M in her office, but for social groupings she invited us into her sitting room.

Aunt M had a loud and commanding voice on the games pitch, and really cared that you ran for the ball, caught the ball, could pick it up cleanly. She would run and catch and throw in lacrosse to demonstrate to us how it should be done. In summer she was more involved with tennis than cricket; she cared for the style with which we played; she also taught swimming and bronze life saving. She was interested in house tournaments and was an anxious as anyone that Number Two should do well.

In this picture she is wearing her string of pearls, a floral summer dress, pearl earrings and a kind smile. Typical. Her skin is well tanned from all the outdoor activity. She looks just as I remember – but younger!

Beside The Robin is Miss Kettering. Is there any significance in this seating arrangement? Miss Kettering and Miss Gasston taught art. You would never have known, unless you saw them in their art coats in the art room. There were no beatnik, outlandish, tell tale signs. They were middle aged and just like all the other teachers in tweed suits, sensible shoes and stockings.

Miss Kettering taught painting, Miss Gasston taught pottery and lettering and was deputy head of Number One. I did black-letter and tenth century, and still have some of the pieces I did. Tenth century lettering was very useful for posters. In the pottery class I made and glazed a Father Christmas figure.

I did embroidery as one of my A Level art subjects with Miss Kettering. We sat in her large and rather muddly studio behind the art room for this. It was slow progress, designing and embroidering a bedspread. I was bored long before it was finished, but I did finish it after I left school and still have it. I also designed and made a very successful black, white and red felt cushion incorporating buttons in the design.

Miss Ratcliffe and Miss Pickering are to the right of Aunt M. Miss Pickering joined the staff while I was at the school and taught Latin. An excellent teacher, and a soft and gentle lady. She was physically a little larger and wore soft colours, pink, pale blue; she had a pale complexion and slightly gingery hair. She took me aside one day and told me I was quite good at Latin and could consider going on with it in a serious way. A revelation to me – it gave me a terrific lift. You could even go to her out of school time and ask for help and she would help you and go on to discuss other matters if you wanted to. She spent a lot of time with me as I tried to work out which subjects to drop, which to do for A Level and what to do when I left school. This was particularly kind of her as I was not in her house – I think she was attached to Number Three.

Next to Miss Pickering is Miss Boyd, another kind and very important teacher for me, although I had her for only a couple of terms, for maths, in the huts. I had been going to do maths in the summer of 1958 along with my other O Levels but I was ill during the spring mock maths exam and so it was decided I should not write the O until December that year. Thus I was moved to Miss Boyd's class. She was motherly and gave me confidence. She was good at explaining, but firm. I arrived for one geometry exam without my protractor and compasses and she would not let me go and get them. I did my best using the protractor marked out on the back of my ruler and dividing distances rather than bisecting with compasses as I should have done, and she marked the exam and accepted it.

Next to Miss Boyd is Dwu (Miss Butcher). She looks very pale and a little ill even in this picture. Perhaps it was just her very fair complexion, but we always thought of her as ill. Hence her name – Dwu, death warmed up. Dwu was a well liked history teacher, but I did not have her for history. The only classes I ever had with her were current events for a brief period when we had to read newspapers and discuss issues in the paper. I was absolutely no good at history. The only exams I ever failed were history in Upper Fourth and Lower Fifth with Miss MacIntosh. I could not wait to drop history.

Miss MacIntosh was a younger teacher and had difficulty keeping order in the classroom. We were in the south classroom at the west end of the second floor of classrooms, rather out of the way, at the end of the corridor.

Next to Dwu is Sister from the San, dressed in her nurse's uniform, cape and badge and white hat, and next to Sister is Stonehenge (Miss O'Callaghan). You look *so much younger* than I remember you!

In the picture her very high forehead and strong smile show clearly and you can sense the grim determination that characterised her. She was an excellent teacher, who knew exactly what had to be imparted and used every force she had to try to get it into you. She was completely organised and systematic. She could not have tried harder to make us absorb more vocabulary. She made French learning as like Latin learning as she could, with rules to follow and conjugations to learn. She could get angry eventually, and would turn red. She was very intense, and would smile widely to try to soften the way she came across. This was when her teeth showed, hence her nickname. I admired and respected her greatly. She was attached to Number Two for lunch, and I liked sitting up to her because I admired her, although I don't know that that made conversation any easier. But she knew you were sitting up and tried to converse, and while the results may have been a little forced, you appreciated her efforts.

Now that I see her picture and see that she was not 'old', I realise that probably she could relate to us and what we were trying, or not trying to do, very well.

Next to Stonehenge is Miss Denham; she taught geography to Annabel Robinson and me in Six One and Six Two in the sunken geography room, and arranged for us to go to Malham Tarn for our field trip. She was also in Number Two for lunch, at the table in the corner, and did not seem to need to talk much during lunch. She was quiet and thorough and I liked and respected her.

Further along is Ma P (Mrs Peters), the Number Two House Matron. Another very special lady. Kind and cosy and apple-dolly grandmotherly, Ma Pa must have been very busy. She wore a white coat over her clothes, and had a nursing badge. Her office-cum-living room, with a bedroom adjacent, was on the middle floor of bedrooms, a couple of floors up from Aunt M's bedroom. For meals, she had a table in the dining room, the one beside the door that led from the dining room to the front stairs. She cared for us when we were ill, took our temperatures when we reported not feeling well, bought a few things for us in Brighton on her afternoon off and organised and kept records of mass temperature takings through the first three weeks of every term. Ma P organised the weekly laundry and maintained the linen cupboard where school blankets and pillows were stored. We dried our hair in front of her gas fire on shampoo days, or she dried it for us with her electric hair dryer. She checked that we had washed our brushes and combs and had set them out on our dressers on Mondays.

Just by her door was a large closet for thermometers and medications. She had a writing desk with a fold-down writing area on the far wall and a chaise longue behind a screen. She tactfully introduced me to deodorants and other 'necessaries'.

Tiddles (Miss Middleton) is sitting on The Robin's left. Tiddles was the powerful head of Number Four and a geography teacher. Annabel and I studied North America with her, sitting at the highly polished and very solid table in the middle of her office which was somewhat Victorian and oppressive with large, dark furniture, not like Aunt M's. Tiddles was small in stature, but one sensed she was great in power. Number Four House was sort of different and a little aloof from the others because of her, it seemed. All the houses were different; each girl thought her own house the best – but Number Four was more different than the others. Tiddles was ambitious for Number Four and wanted to excel.

I think Miss Patterson is sitting next to Tiddles. She taught classics and was the head of Number One. I had her for Greek, for a week or two. After O Levels there were still several weeks before the end of term. The school had an excellent way of filling these weeks for post-O people. The teachers offered classes in other subjects for this short time and we could sign up for anything we liked, whether we had done it before or not. And so I enjoyed a brief introduction to Greek.

I don't recognise the staff member next to Miss Patterson, but the second is Peahen, Miss Woodcock. She was one of the mainstay English staff, quiet, serious, a little sad. She is sitting next to Smelzer, squinting in the bright light of the sun, having taken her glasses off.

Smelzer was the deputy head of Number Two and we all had the idea that she did not really get on with Aunt M. We did not see them together much. She had a small grey poodle dog which I simply didn't like, and I think she smoked. I remember going to her once, something to do with a cheque; it must have been to get actual money for something and she asked me to endorse the cheque. I had no idea what that meant and she was surprised to find that I did not know about cheques at all.

Further along again, looking very lively and Francaise, is the popular, lively and highly respected Mlle Lavauden. We were divided into divisions by ability and achievement for academic subjects such as Latin, French, maths etc, and the best teachers taught the highest divisions. Thus I did not have Mlle Lavauden until near the end of my time. She was utterly French in every way and taught French in French. I remember her teaching us about Rousseau's ideas, and Emile, and being converted to this new, to me, way of bringing up children; what an eye-opener!

And so I come to write about TCC, Miss Creyke-Clarke, her friend. Interesting – she is not in the picture. What can I write? I was terrified of her. In Upper Fourth we, the small bottom French division, had TCC in the bright yellow and chalk filled Room 7. We got off to a bad start, TCC and I. I had spent three weeks in France one Easter not many years before, and my paternal grandmother had been brought up in France, so perhaps my spoken French belied an understanding of the language which I did not have on paper. She wanted me to speak still better and worked on my accent every time I spoke; perhaps she sensed that I could do French, but it was my written work that was our ultimate disaster.

As she saw it, I was very careless. TCC was determined to cure my carelessness. She made learning French a misery for me. I went on being careless and she went on devising new ways to cure it. Even if I rewrote and rewrote things after she had corrected them, I could not get them written without careless mistakes. Eventually she began to halve my marks for every mistake she considered careless. Imagine what this did to my marks, to my averages.

On good days she would take out the large watch she carried on a chain around her person, and demonstrate its various chimes and tones and bells, and tell us how it had saved her in the darkness and dangers of Paris during the war. Perhaps she was a sad person, burdened with tragedies beyond anything I would ever know.

Many years later my mother saw the announcement of her death in the newspaper and sent it to me. I am ashamed to say I felt a great sense of relief.

About halfway along this side is a tall lady with a very long neck, Maggie B, Miss Braund. We took speech (elocution) with her for only a term or two – '*Do you remember an inn, Miranda, Do you remember an inn?*'

Next to her, looking rather masculine with her short haircut, is Miss Robertson. Along with several other staff, Miss Robertson taught games and gym. I think she was on the England lacrosse team – and was Miss Isherwood goalie for England? Miss Robertson taught cricket too, and looked really at home on the pitch. We played and competed keenly under her direction. I never got to know her or found her a character. I think of her in brown.

Next to Miss Robertson is Stooge. Now there is a character for you! Even for the photograph Stooge is taking a typical pose. She is pushed back and up in her chair, her eyes are shut, and she is wearing a very formal suit with dark trim. At any moment she will raise her left hand and gently scratch the side of her nose with her little finger.

Stooge taught English – literature, poetry, précis and comprehension. Woe betide you if you did not do your homework or answered a question incorrectly. She was small and fiery and would get angry with little provocation. Red would rise from her collar and slowly spread up her face. She would get stiffer and stiffer and push further and further back in the chair. You had advance warning – she would push back, raise her left hand and scratch the side of her nose with her little fingernail. She had no time for fools. Sitting up to her for meals was frightening, too, as you could easily offend her. Stooge was feared and respected; she was one of many excellent teachers.

Although I was afraid of her, I came to like Stooge. I dreaded reciting Shakespeare in class in case I got stuck, even though I had learned the work; nerves can dry up the voice and brain regardless of the advance preparation.

Further on down the row, in double row of pearls and a suit, is Miss Corscaden. She did not wear a gown but was very proper and saw to it that we were proper too. She taught us dressmaking in the large and well equipped room on the second floor beyond the teachers' mail boxes. There were five or six hand-operated Singer sewing machines at a huge central table, and one or two treadles. There may have been an electric machine too, and there were two irons.

The dressmaking room was open on Wednesday afternoons and weekends, so I made lots and lots of things, but I rarely wore them. The fun and success for me was in the making. I remember quite a few of the garments I made; a grey/white herringbone check circular skirt, a yellow sleeveless summer dress with a pattern of coloured pins, pyjamas for my sister, nightdresses, a green and yellow multi-pleated skirt from a pattern which I still have, and still use.

Miss Corscaden once casually mentioned to me that I might consider sewing and dressmaking as a career after school. It was not a long discussion. I could not see how making dresses or children's pyjamas would ever earn me enough to live on. If only I had asked, had found out more, had known about, for instance, the London School of Needlework, or that there was a whole fashion industry dependent on people to design and make up clothes.

Now I have a rather odd hobby. Although I like making things from new, I don't really have the time, patience, need or funds to do this, so what I do instead, and thoroughly enjoy because it is quick and cheap and, as I see it, conservationist, is to take an old garment or secondhand garment and alter it, making it into something else, something new.

Miss Corscaden's teaching skills pay off – Caroline wears one of the costumes she designed and made for her English historic dancing demonstrations.

The teacher I cannot find in this picture is Herky B, Miss Baron, who taught dancing. She did not wear a gown and wore a dress rather than a suit as a rule. Someone else not in the picture is Miss Gee. I think she had left by then.

Miss Gee taught Latin when we were in Upper Fourth and Lower Fifth. Like Miss MacIntosh, she could not keep the class in order and we were very surprised to hear that she was to be a house mistress at Benenden.

EXAMS: Exams were incredibly important, the very purpose of what we were doing in the classroom and for prep, and the driving force for the extra learning and studying we did outside class. I have taken exams with various institutions since leaving Roedean. Few have ever been as formal and with such strict codes of 'exam behaviour'.

For a given subject, such as maths or English, there were several papers – trig, algebra, geometry, grammar, comprehension, précis, literature. Here in Canada, even the most senior students do only one exam for each subject! And if it is of two hours' duration they complain that it is too long! I'm sure at Roedean we regularly took exams of two hours and even more.

School exams were written in classrooms, in utter silence and under the strictest rules and supervision, on larger-than-usual paper which had lines, a pre-printed red margin on the left and a hole at the top left through which a length of string was tied to keep the pages together. Start and end times were written in large characters on the board. Papers were distributed face down; the teacher watched the clock until the hands reached the start time, and then she instructed us to turn the papers over. A warning would be given ten minutes before the end. There was no disturbance. No-one spoke. No-one left early. At the end of the exam the teacher said 'Stop', we put down our pens, tied the string and the teacher came round to collect the papers.

University of Cambridge O and A Level exams were written in the hall. Long tables were set up and people were seated well away from each other. It was very formal, very strict and utterly silent and serious – like university exams.

CAREERS GUIDANCE: My contribution on this topic is not a fair representation of career guidance, counselling and direction provided by Roedean to those of us who left the school that sunny July in 1960.

I was not coping well with school by late Lower Fifth and into Upper Fifth, the years in which our future education path tended to be set. The focus for me shifted from what would I do to what could I do. I am sure all staff quietly had a hand in this, although I did not know it. Aunt M was the one I recognised as helping me and Miss Pickering also listened to me, talked and was very supportive and helpful.

I don't know what the formal structure for post-school planning was. Who had responsibility for meeting students to discuss possibilities, to show them what a huge range of avenues was open to them, to explain that while you may not be top-of-the-class at Roedean, even the most average student at Roedean was way ahead of lots of others in the outside world? Was it the role of the house mistress and her deputy? Was it considered a parental responsibility and not the school's direct responsibility at all? I have no idea.

I suspect this was all a grey area. I suspect that most students were expected to go on to university and so the need was rather more to decide which were their strong subjects so that they could pursue a sensible combination of subjects in school to be sure of getting the right place at university without being too concerned about what they were actually going to be.

Certainly Oxford and Cambridge were the universities that everyone wanted everyone to get into; they were very superior to all the others, most of which I had never heard of. A few students would have bypassed this step in school life because their future was mapped out for them by very definitive plans their parents had for them; those going on to finishing schools or into family businesses, for instance.

I also suspect that the school could see this shortcoming, knew that Lower Fifth was too early for a girl to decide what she was going to be, given the narrow range of experience and knowledge of most girls then, particularly those sheltered by the confines of privileged homes and restricted boarding school life.

Part of the reasoning behind the outside lectures and events that we went to in the Sixth forms would have been to get us out, to show us what was available, to broaden our horizons, but it did not really take us very far. That being said, this is how I remember it and how it was for me.

What we were going to take at university defined what we were going to take for A Levels and the combination of what we were going to take for A Levels along with what we were going to take at university defined what we were going to take for O Levels. Thus, in an oversimplification, it appeared that we needed to know by the end of Lower Fifth what we were going to be.

What was I going to be? I remember talking to friends, certainly, family, certainly, probably staff too. Eventually I said firmly one day 'I'm going to be a teacher'.

Long before, in West Africa, when I was about eight, I had privately decided I would be a missionary and would come back to Africa and help people. I told Dowda, our steward, but I never told my parents. I knew, even then, that they would not approve. So, later on, at school, when they asked what I wanted to be, I had already decided. I wanted to be a missionary. But I knew this was not acceptable. I thought Aunt M would approve, although I doubted that she would have thought me suitable. I thought, but with less conviction, that the school would also probably approve, since so much that happened at school revolved around Chapel, being good, helping others, being thoughtful. But my parents – they would not approve. I would have to be something else.

Someone suggested that I be a physiotherapist. I went to see the doctor who lived next door to us at home to ask her what they do and how you become one. 'Oh, my goodness,' was her reaction. 'You have to learn the names of all the bones and nerves and muscles in the body. They are all in Latin. It takes *years*. You could never do that!' So I couldn't be a physiotherapist.

About this time, school, parents and the doctor gently informed me that whatever I was going to be, I should think of something that did not need me to go to university, as the stress of going to university and doing all that work and all those exams would not be a good idea.

What was I going to be? I knew of so few choices; it was quite pathetic. I didn't know how to find out about choices. I just sat and worried. There must have been information somewhere; I didn't know how to find it and did not want to show my ignorance in asking. We did sometimes talk about it at home, but those discussions were not very helpful, wide ranging, all encompassing or even always amicable.

Someone – my mother I think, suggested Norland nursing. This seemed fine – looking after babies and little children. It met the criteria, no university, and yet I would become something. For a while I was going to do this, but then it turned into being a Norland nanny and I sensed that school and some of my friends did not really approve of this. The servile aspect, and having learned all that Latin and French and maths, and for what?

From Norland nursing I was gently inched up the ladder to infant and junior school teaching. 'I'm going to be a teacher.' It all seemed settled. A big relief.

But then I had to be trained to be a teacher at this institution, or that one, or another, and the worry all began again. I had pamphlets from Froebel and a couple of other respectable training colleges, and did not grasp that they each had different underlying philosophies. That it mattered which you chose. I dutifully applied to three, got called for interviews and the first I went to was Froebel, on Roehampton Lane. They offered me a place, and I accepted. Froebel was not really a good choice for me. I really missed the straight academic challenge and was amazed (appalled) at what standards were considered acceptable.

One of my friends left to go to secretarial school and we stayed in touch. She enjoyed secretarial school and could see the possibilities of getting really good and interesting jobs. I very seriously considered doing the same thing, but the dread of telling my parents, and the concern for them having to pay back the grant aid that the government provided for me to attend college prevented me. How very, very silly of me.

And the final irony is that when we emigrated to Canada in 1975 I could not get a job here as a teacher as I did not have a university degree. A University of London Teaching Certificate (with Distinction) and several years' teaching experience was not adequate accreditation, although my wild friend who had a drama degree from

Bristol University and had no teaching experience at all, got a teaching job. So what did I do? A private secretary diploma course!

With my education background and secretarial qualification I became a school secretary. From there, I moved on to being an admin assistant in a high school, then a district business administrator with the school division. I completed my B Ed, majoring in French, in 1988 and have taken all sorts of courses in all sorts of things over the years. In 1995 I got my Business Administration Certificate from the local community college, and now what I'd like to do is brush up my Latin and take up part time Latin instruction, along with creative sewing of some sort, when I retire.

THE WEATHER: There is something ironic about a Winnipeger writing about the weather. If North Americans know nothing else about Winnipeg, they know about its weather! Very cold in winter, often very hot in summer (with giant mosquitos), wind, wind, wind all year round – blizzards of ice and snow that close the schools and shut down transportation, windchill forecasts that specify how long it will take your skin to freeze, fine granular snow that gets shovelled out only to blow in again and get shovelled out again several times between November and March; ferocious summer storms that darken the day, turning street lamps on, while inches of rain slosh down in record time; twisters that come from nowhere demolishing rural barns and seed bins; and, this year, floods. The hub of Winnipeg is Portage and Main – the windiest corner in Canada, so they say.

So what about Roedean weather? Well, wind is certainly the first thought that comes to mind. There were no big trees, only grass and wind-sculpted scrubby bushes and copses. There were lots of seagulls wheeling and screaming overhead, after their early morning Seesaws worming breakfast parties.

The wind was enough to propel you on the roller skating rink if you held your cloak out like a *Kon-tiki* sail. Perhaps acknowledgement of the wind was indicated right there on the clothes list, for not only did we have hats, we had headscarves, too, in school colours – brown on navy or navy on brown for One and Two, red on navy or navy on red for Three and Four.

I remember one winter making snowballs and a snowman on Seesaws with Jennyrose. I remember the excitement of watching summer storms over the sea from the sick room window. The clouds seemed alive as they advanced and grew and battled, lightning glimmering a warning, flaring to frighten the enemy, and firing bolts of brilliance from cloud to cloud or down into the sea abyss.

In summer there were always beautiful sunny days, perfect for sunbathing, and sitting outside, and playing tennis and strolling on the terrace. There were other lovely days, too, when you could sit on wooden benches along the raised walkway overlooking Jubilee, or play deep on the cricket pitch and feel the sun tanning you through the white cotton games shirt. Then, back in your room and changing to the next set of clothes, you looked in the mirror to see whether your BB line showed still more – a sure sign of health and beauty! Some people got such well tanned legs they could leave their stockings off (seamless stockings were just coming in) and, with luck, not get caught.

BRIEF ENCOUNTER: The main hall, where the huge and imposing portraits of the Lawrences were hung, and where assemblies, house dances, concerts, speech day and open lectures were held, had been used for drill practice by the Canadian soldiers stationed at Roedean during the war. The floor, in the late fifties, still had a very splintery surface and during assemblies, when we sat cross-legged on it, we would often get splinters in our bottoms.

About two years ago I visited Kelvin High School here in Winnipeg and met the head custodian to ask him the way to a certain room. Hearing my English accent he asked if I knew Brighton. Yes, I said, I went to school near Brighton. He was very excited to meet me – he had been stationed at Roedean during the war, and we talked about the buildings and the grounds – and about the splinters in the hall. He described how they used to march in their heavy boots up and down, up and down the hall for drill practice. He also remembered how cold and windy and draughty they found it, up there on the cliffs; a Winnipegger remembering the cold and wind? Winnipeggers are used to winters of -30°C and a howling north wind with snow and ice that freezes exposed skin in less than a minute!

APPENDIX A
School Slang and Sayings

Aunt	Lavatory
Backs and Feet	Medical examination
BB	Bust bodice (later used to mean bra)
Bilge	Biology
Bish	Faux pas
Bobbing	Saying goodnight and shaking hands with the prefect or member of staff on duty
Bog	Lavatory (from Seventies)
Boiled baby's arm	Roly poly
Boot Hole	Cloakroom
BUFF	Best United Friends Forever
Bugs and Fleas	Medical examination
Bunny run	Covered passage connecting different parts of the school
Cardboards	Lisle stockings
Carthaginian brick	A peculiarly hard pudding
Chit-chat	Informal meeting of prefects or sub-prefects with housemistress to discuss day's events
Chucked	Banished from a 'set'
Cockroaches	Area under floor by Bunny run
Continental shelf	Where girls sunbathed or watched matches
Crow's nest	Front room of Heaven
Cubie	Cubicle
Dead baby's arm	Roly poly
Ears and Eyes	Medical examination
Festooned hair	Hair falling over the face
Fic	Fiction library
Forties	Lessons (forty minutes)
Frogspawn	Tapioca pudding
Ganges River Muck	Caramel pudding
Garbage pudding	Pudding made from leftovers
GDR	Girls' drawing room
Going up the house	Blushing
Guillotine list	Names of girls housemistress wished to see after lunch
Hearse	The San cart
Hearts and Lungs	Medical examination
Heaven	The top floor
Home	A girl's house; the rest was school
Hotties	Hot water bottles
Jaw	Reprimand from a housemistress or prefect
JPR	Junior Prep Room
KCYS	Kindly Consider Yourself Squashed
Keen on	Having a crush on a senior girl (KO in the Seventies)
Keenite	A younger girl with a crush on a senior

KV	Watch out
Lax	Lacrosse ('crosse in very early years)
MF	Midnight Feast
MWF	Bath
Muck	Chocolate blancmange
MYOB	Mind Your Own Business
Old flats	Superior lax pitch
Pi-jaw	A talking to by a prefect
Pill	Lacrosse ball
PL	Piano lesson
Pre	Prefect
Prison	Roedean
Pump handles	Shaking hands with every member of staff on the first and last days of term
Ref	Reference library
Sack	Hold-all to carry books from lesson to lesson
Sassie-B	Suspender belt
Scrum tables	Free assembly at tea time
Scum	New arrivals, or those who had not made their mark
Sent to the Fic	Dealt with for talking in Chapel (no connection with Fic — fiction library)
Set	Group of friends in the same house
Sitting up to	Sitting next to a member of staff at lunch time and making amiable conversation
Special	Alternative to set meal for religious reasons and for vegetarians
Spiders	Copse of tamarisk trees
SPR	Senior Prep Room
Stave (the Staves)	Member(s) of staff
Stodge	Tea time sponge cake
Study P	Passage connecting each house to school corridor
Sucking- up to	Currying favour with staff
Tate and Lyle	Number One House matron and her assistant (in the Fifties), so called because of their thick lisle stockings
Ticks	Marks on a list; three in a week meant early bed on Saturday
Tights	Navy knickers
Tigs	I want
Tinks	Bell for getting up, Chapel, lessons, meals
Thames Mud	Chocolate blancmange
The Special	School train
TTS	Bath
You are smiling	Your underwear is showing
Veins	I don't want
Wackie-B	Wastepaper basket
Wash Hole	Wash Room
Weights and Measures	Medical examination
Worms on toast	Tinned spaghetti

APPENDIX B
The Contributors

OLD ROEDEANIANS

Abidian (Gregory, Madeleine 1955-60)
Adams (Nock, Mary 1956-61)
Adams (Kershaw, Rosemary 1964-69)
Adburgham (Haig, Alison 1925-29)
Allen (Day-Winter, Pamela 1936-42)
Allen (Drysdale, Joan 1936-39)
Allen (Jacobson, Hermione 1949-53)
Allen (Hallett, Vivien 1937-43)
Allsop, Carole (1972-78)
Altman (Rae, Patricia 1955-60)
Anderson (Moss, Mary 1958-63)
Arnell, Beatrice (1990-95)
Athay, Rosemary (1955-59)
Auerbach (Kohn-Speyer, Alice 1915-21)
Aylmer (Miller, Marelyn 1950-56)
Bailey (Ross, Janet 1942-47)
Bale, Nicola (1981-87)
Bale, Sarah (1984-92)
Barbour (West, Jennifer 1945-51)
Barns (James, Beryl 1932-36)
Bartlett (Rutherford, Elspeth [Eppie]1927-32)
Bashford (Kay, Margaret 1940-43)
Beaver (Spedding, Joan 1930-35)
Beretvas, Michelle (1985-88)
Bernstein (Forsell, Isobel June 1935-41)
Bicanic (Wild, Sonia 1932-38)
Borradaile (Gilmour, Jean 1932-38)
Bostock (Hall, Josephine 1935-41)
Bower (Morgan, Phyllis 1917-21)
Bowman (Read Smith, Joan 1921-26)
Breyfogle (King, Josephine 1953-55)
Bromley (Hunter, Beatrice 1930-35)
Browning (Feachem, Mary-Grace 1956-62)
Buckmaster (Mark, Elizabeth 1962-69)
Bull (Schwarz, Eva 1955-61)
Burges Watson, Eleanor M (1978-86)
Burrows (Hamilton, Joanna 1945-49)
Bysouth (Dowson, Eve 1939-46)
Cannon (Feather, Gweneth 1931-36)
Carlyle (Blatch, Susan 1951-54)
Carroll (Hollington, Alison 1933-37)
Chadwick (Burke, June 1961-69)
Chan, Michelle (1992-96)
Chapman, Elizabeth (1963-69)
Chapman, Clemency (1933-37)
Chapman (Watson, Stephanie 1952-57)
Chaundler (Phoenix, F Irene T 1929-35)
Child (Locket, Elizabeth Susan 1955-61)
Clark (Adcock, Rosemary 1945-51)
Clark (Bishop, Diana 1954-59)

Clothier (Rothwell, Barbara 1932-34)
Cobbett (Smith, Betty 1933-37)
Cochrane (Wallace, Mary 1926-30)
Cohen (Doniger, Myra 1922-28)
Coleman (Mackenzie, Katharine 1961-66)
Colston, Jean (1945-49)
Condy (Finch, Evelyn 1918-23)
Conolly (Warren, Ruth 1921-26)
Copeland (Goldstone, Rosalind 1958-63)
Cossons, Sylvia (1972-75)
Cotgrove (Grindley, Gillian 1941-44)
Cousins (Gauntlett, Ruth 1935-42)
Crawford (Robinson, Keturah 1918-22)
Cripps (Squires, Joan 1935-40)
Crosfield (Martin, Susan 1945-50)
Curtis (Myers, Sarah 1945-53)
Da Gama Rose, Portia (1990-95)
de Moller (Silverton, June 1960-63)
Davis (McCombie, Gillian 1935-39)
Dick (Marriott, Julie 1948-54)
Dodsworth Knowles (Underwood, Pamela 1934-37)
Doveton (Scutt, Lorna 1932-37)
Driver, Mary (1939-45)
Dunbar (Scutt, Sheila 1930-34)
Eastwood (Miller, Maureen 1935-41)
Edelstein (Briscoe, Grace 1918-25)
Edgerton-Bird, Cherry (1953-59)
Edward, Mathilde (1944-50)
Edwards (James, Phillipa 1949-56)
Ellis-White (Cattley, Janis 1947-52)
Elsey (Chamberlayne, Susan 1950-55)
Emmett (O'Connor,Doreen 1935-39)
Erskine (McLelland, Catherine 1940-46)
Fairpo (Fowler, Jenifer 1941-48)
Fawcett (Ireland, Valerie 1951-56)
Fenley (Trumpler, Pauline 1930-35)
Ferguson (Lowe, Helen 1935-41)
Fernandez (Barnes, Ann 1957-65)
Filipowska (Crommelin-Brown, Pauline 1935-38)
Folland (Baylis, Joy 1956-60)
Fox (Stuart, Hazel 1941-46)
Fraser (Fox, Jill 1953-58)
Freeman (Lee, Nancy 1921-27)
Frith, Nicola (1950-57)
Furneaux (Malden, Bridget 1939-43)
Garwood (Ing-Simmons, Janet 1947-51)
Gatti (Booth, Susan 1940-45)
Gatzke (Vickerman, Nancy 1946-48)
Gee-Turner, Lindsey (1971-77)
Gibbons (Miller Logan, Sarah 1956-58)
Gilbert (Seager, Pamela 1937-43)
Glyn (Weksler, Lynn 1965-71)

Gold (Maythan, Elizabeth 1937-40)
Goldsmith (Polecoff, Shirley 1948-54)
Gordon (Albury, Jillian 1939-48)
Graham, Frances (1982-89)
Green, Zoe (1988-95)
Greene (Burdett, Susan 1946-54)
Greenwood (Malim, Lavinia 1933-38)
Grenfell (Manley, Gillian 1946-50)
Griffin (Blyth, Elizabeth 1944-49)
Hadfield (Timpson, Ruth 1917-23)
Hafenrichter (Burbeck, Edith 1931-37)
Hagger (Gough, Mary 1963-67)
Haigh (Cannon, Paula [Pauline] 1934-38)
Halford, Jane (1927-31)
Hall (Bunn, Sharon 1971-78)
Handler (Cohen, Caroline 1970-76)
Hardie (Cameron, Elaine 1944-51)
Hargreaves (Wade, Winifred 1923-28)
Harvey (Woods, Barbara 1929-35)
Harvey (Frison, Elizabeth 1974-77)
Haselhurst (Spedding, F Patricia 1934-39)
Hatfield (Herford, Sylvia 1926-30)
Haworth (Arkwright, Eleanor 1913-21)
Haxworth (Silver, Erica 1924-30)
Head (Gardiner, Jessica 1971-78)
Heathcote (Seigel, Jane 1961-63)
Henley, Ann (1970-78)
Henry (Ball, Rosalie 1942-48)
Hess, Emmie (1916-20).
Highmore (Edwards, Angela 1938-42)
Hill (Davies, Margaret 1940-44)
Hinman (Hunter, Diana 1955-62)
Hobbs (Hutchings, Sally 1967-69)
Hodges (Ewart, Fiona 1967-72)
Holdsworth (Newnham, Clare 1956-61)
Hollington (Paxton, Gwen 1932-37)
Hollis (Stephenson, Kristin 1953-60)
Holmes (Carpenter, Joan 1930-34)
Hones, Julia (1956-62)
Hornby (Aston, Elizabeth 1950-56)
Houlston, Victoria 1984-90)
Howe (Lawes, Gwen 1949-52)
Howe (Bartlett, Isabel 1962-69)
Huebener (Benson, Rosamund 1937-42)
Hughes (Harris, Joan 1935-40)
Hulme (Prall, Rosemary Ann 1945-50)
Hulsen (Madsen, Yvonne 1953-56)
Hunt (Herbert, Margaret 1949-54)
Hutchings (Carter, Ann Marie 1938-40)
Ingram (Clark, Iris 1929-31)
Jackson, (Harris, Margaret 1935-39)
Jefferies (Blunt, Angela 1954-57)
Jefferies (Reynolds, Helen 1969-77)
Jepson (Oliver, Mary Patricia 1941-46)
Jennings (Lubbock, Pamela 1944-48)
Jervoise (Newnham, Jane 1953-57)

Joel (Tyler, Jennifer 1947-51)
Johnstone, Ruth (1933-36)
Joll (Ramsden, Antonia 1917-27)
Jordan (Dunn, Dilys 1939-44)
Kay (Johnson, Diana 1945-51)
Kaye (Angel, Kate 1968-74)
Kent (Bidder, Betty 1925-30)
Kenyon (Hinchliffe, Audrey 1937-41)
Kleanthous (Caplan, Valerie 1953-58)
King-Salter (Bailey, Rachel 1939-44)
Kueffner (Hurst-Brown, Nancy 1937-40)
Lankester (Shann, E Janet [Jinty] 1933-37)
Leakey (Holmes, Margaret [Alison] 1932-36)
Leanse (Fletcher, Joy 1941-45)
Lebus (Harvey, Jennifer 1960-68)
Leslie (Allam, Averil 1948-55)
Lindsay (Desborough, Mary 1952-54)
Macaire (Miller, Tatiana 1944-51)
Macdonald (Bennett, Carol 1945-48)
Mackendrick (Pelton, Tessa 1953-58)
MacLaren, Stephanie (Hall, Daphne 1927-32)
Maclean (Gimson, Ruth 1936-41)
Macmillan (Carey Evans, Eluned 1929-39)
Mainwaring (Watson, Pamela 1956-63
Makower, Frances (1942-47)
Marchant, Katie (1995-97)
Marriott (Thompson, Mary 1937-40)
Marsh (Moodie, Cynthia 1934-37)
Marshall, Barbara (1935-38)
Marwood (Sharp, Jean 1937-42)
Maughan (Dawe, Gail 1968-72)
Maxwell (Scott, Patricia 1940-41)
McDowall (Gamlen, Caroline 1955-60)
McKinlay (Hewitt, Deborah 1968-77)
McKinnel (Bleckly, Belinda [Lindy] 1940-49)
Melnick (Ezra, Yvonne 1936-40)
Melrose (Harper, Ann 1935-39)
Messer (Sworder, Rosemary 1933-37)
Miall (Leith, Sally 1935-36)
Midgley (Lankester, Jane 1953-58)
Miller (Ruddock, Ann 1947-52)
Miller (Horne, Joan 1932-36)
Misa (Spielman, Ruth 1945-49)
Moate (Heymanson, Joanna 1950-57)
Morris (Goodyear, Herta 1969-75)
Murdoch (Woods, Maureen 1932-39)
Murray (Bidder, Ina Petronella 1927-33)
Naegele (Hurst, Rosemary 1938-40)
Nash (Allen, Joscelyne 1928-31)
Nelson, Charlotte-Anne (1990-1997)
Nind, Joan (1933-37)
Norman (Davenport, Pauline 1928-33)
Nugee (Makower, Rachel 1939-44)
Nwandu, Adaora (1988-96)
Oakley (Harding, Julia 1946-50)
Oberdieck (Miller, Sheila 1935-43)

Orlebar (Ford, Nicola 1961-63)
Owen (Davies, Mary Lisa 1956-63)
Pain (Packham, Angela 1954-58)
Palmer (Francis, Marie 1924-26)
Peacey (Thirlby, Jean 1937-45)
Pearce (McDonald, Elspeth 1958-64)
Pemberton (Cameron, Gillian 1944-48)
Perry (Denis-Smith, Sylvia 1936-40)
Peters, Rebecca (1977-82)
Petrie (Illingworth, Pat 1948-51)
Phillippo (Williamson, Carolyn 1961-69)
Phillips, Iris (1916-19)
Pirie (Hunter, Angela [Ann] 1922-30)
Pirie (Crow, Nancy 1933-40)
Poole (Wilson, Diana 1938-47)
Portnoy (Levy, Ann 1944-47)
Quentin (Druiff, Caroline 1954-60)
Rance (White, Carol 1946-52)
Read (Brett, Jane Rosemary 1943-51)
Reeves (Stranack, Jeanne 1940-44)
Reid (Chamberlayne, Gillian 1954-57)
Reitlinger (Brach, Lily-Claire 1943-51)
Rich (Willmore, Judith 1945-49)
Robertson, Dassia (1989-90)
Rodriguez (Patuck, Roshun 1932-36)
Rokotnitz (Sawyer-Kammer, Jacqueline 1953-57)
Ruddock (Watson, Sandra 1979-84)
Rushton (Newth, Meriel 1948-54)
Russell Heuter (Russell, Felicity 1968-75)
Ryan (Plummer, Susan 1954-57)
Saunders-Davis (Osborn, Sarah 1960-67)
Sgarlat, Mary Anne (1974-75)
Shamash, Kim (1970-76)
Sharma (Bahal, Seema 1983-85)
Sharpe (Clarke, Gay 1952-59)
Sharrock (Heaney, Wendy 1977-82)
Schrager von Altishofen (Lovett-Standing,
   Nicola 1971-78)
Shah, Sona (1988-90)
Shelmerdine (Harris, Judy 1943-50)
Sheppard (Robbins, Jill 1948-53)
Sherburn (Lowe, Frances 1954-61)
Shimmin (Greig, Margaret 1946-50)
Shuttleworth (Olliver, Michelle 1962-67)
Sinclair-Stevenson (Walker-Smith, Deborah 1954-57)
Smith (Forsyth, Sarah 1958-64)
Sorby (Eastcott, Sheila 1964-72)
Spicer (Mackinnon, Jane 1940-41)
Steel (Simpson, Gillian 1955-62)
Steel (Day, Rosemary 1945-50)
Stevenson (Dixon, Sally 1953-60)
Stewart, Rachel (1991-97)
Stokes-Roberts, Amanda (1967-73)
Sudheesh, Anitha (1993-95)
Summersgill (Field, Gillian 1945-48)
Syer (Vallat, Judith 1954-58)

Taylor (Gordon-Smith, Frances 1958-62)
Taylor (Spathis, Penny 1958-62)
Thalben-Ball, Pamela (1939-44)
Thomas (Cawdry, Elizabeth 1953-57)
Thomson (Hood, Virginia 1961-65)
Tolfree (Kelly, Susan 1937-41)
Tolliday (Lycett, Vanessa 1949-54)
Tucker (Pinney, Janet 1946-53)
Turner (Myers, Naomi 1942-46)
Turner Jones (Bazeley, Gillian 1950-54)
Tyndall (Arkwright, Patricia 1934-38)
Van Gelder (Solomon, Gillian 1946-51)
Veitch (Evans, Bridget 1957-63)
Vince (Martin, Sheila 1954-59)
Walters (Challis, Margaret 1947-51)
Walters, Sylvia (1928-33)
Ward (Sayers, Patricia 1926-29)
Warrington (Porter, Bernadette 1950-55)
Waterhouse (Thomas, Helen 1926-31)
Watson, Fiona (1972-77)
Watson (Aubrey, Judith 1958-63)
Watson (Wheatley, Margaret Grace 1924-27)
Watts (Stephens, Rosemary 1933-37)
Watts, Sarah (1986-94)
Wegerdt (Dare, Angela 1949-56)
Weiss (Travis, Hilary 1949-56)
Wheeler (Lempriere, Renee 1935-40)
White (Dimond, Vivien 1936-39)
Whitham (Butler, Winsome 1930-36)
Williams (Taylor, Jennifer 1951-56)
Williamson (Blench, Margaret 1944-46)
Wood, Armorel (1975-80)
Wood (Jones, Elizabeth 1949-52)
Zepik (Messer, Kay 1963-67)

ROEDEAN OLD BOYS

Barrett, Frederick J
Chapman, Edwin A
Day, Peter A C
Farr, Charles
Foster, Robert A D
Garrad, Ray J
Greenwood P T
Griffin, Jack
Griffiths, Albert E
Gronhaug, Arnold C
Gurney, Thomas H
Hamlet, Ronald L
Hinton, James R B
Howting, Harry E
Kelsall, Richard H
Marigold, James R
Morley, Sam
Parsons, John and Vi
Tindall, Len

Ward Aubrey
Watts, Stanley A
Willett, Frank W

172

APPENDIX C
The Questionnaire

DAILY ROUTINE: What time did you get up/go to bed? Prep time, length of school day.

MEAL TIMES: Where did you eat/with staff/did you like the food/how much variety/how formal/social aspects – moving around?

UNIFORM: What did you wear for school/for leisure/for sport? How different was your uniform from that of today?

SPORT: What sports did you play/how often/where did you swim? Competitive matches?

HOUSE LIFE: Memories/formalities/informalities/how much contact with other year groups/relationships with house staff/school slang.

DISCIPLINE: How strict (make-up, jewellery, hairstyles)? What were punishments/incentives/role of prefects?

THE SAN: Routines/memories/infectious diseases/treatments.

LIBRARIES: Memories/facilities/organisational procedures.

CHAPEL How many services/what was compulsory/celebrations and festivals/significance of religion in life of school.

LEISURE: How was leisure time spent (lectures, dances, outings)? Parental contact during the terms.

MAJOR SCHOOL EVENTS: Speech day/plays/concerts etc. Memories of VIP/Royal visits.

FABRIC OF THE SCHOOL: Central heating/carpets/condition of bedrooms/study bedrooms/bathrooms. Condition after WW II.

TRANSPORT: Method of travel – beginning and end of term/weekend outings.

MEMORIES OF HEAD: Who was your head? Did you have much formal/informal contact?

TEACHING STAFF: Any characters?

CAREERS: How much guidance was given? Emphasis on Oxbridge/university/college places.

WEATHER CONDITIONS: Views of the sea/windy days/summer days/freak weather conditions.

KESWICK: Memories of evacuation/accommodation.

ANECDOTES

APPENDIX D
School Songs

The First Eleven

You may field perhaps at long-leg or at point,
Or perhaps your talent lies in fielding deep,
Or like to put your fingers out of joint
When bowling's swift – by being wicket-keep.
It doesn't matter where your place may be,
Or if batting or if bowling be your forte,
If in the Eleven you are playing,
Then of you we will be saying –
    'Well stopped! Well hit! Well bowled!
    Well tried! Well caught!'

Chorus: Oh! The Cricket First Eleven,
          We admire on every hand,
          'Tis the one above all others,
          We love best in all the land.
          May your scores be never failing,
          And your bowling ever true!
          Oh! Noble First Eleven,
          Here's the best of health to you.

And sometimes when your foes are rather good,
And each person somehow fails to break her duck,
The Captain thinks that on the whole it would
Be just as well some from the team to chuck;
When with frequent wides your bowling
    you disgrace,
And you miss what was a very easy catch,
Then we gave upon you sadly,
And all say you're playing badly,
We're much afraid that we shall lose the match.

Chorus:

But when the picture has another side,
When the score consists of hundreds still not out,
Then oh! We gaze on you with glowing pride,
And wild hurrahs and cheers we madly shout;
When it seems as if the ball you cannot miss,
And each bowler does the trick that's called the hat;
And the colours round are flying
And we are all denying
That other teams can play as well as that.

Chorus:

The School

Praise we now all to whom praises belong,
All who are worthy include in our song.
Slow-moving many and pioneer few –
Honour to those to whom honour is due!
Be you athlete or scholar, or naught but a fool,
Lift up your voices and honour the School!
Honour the worthy and honour the keen,
Honour her daughters and honour Roedean!

Praise to the scholar whom nothing perturbs,
Be it history, riders, irregular verbs.
Honour to those who by Isis and Cam
Thrill ancient dons with a brilliant exam!
Honour the wretched, whom yearly we see
Toiling their way to the goal of S.C.
Honour the worthy and honour the keen,
Honour her daughters and honour Roedean!

Honour to those who in tropical suns
Add to our laurels with runs upon runs;
Also to those who in wind and in rain
Shoot goals, and save goals, and shoot them again!
Honour to those who play tennis or swim,
To the stars of our dancing, the stars of our gym.
Honour the worthy and honour the keen,
Honour her daughters and honour Roedean!

What of the Staff, who with infinite pains
Stir to activity turnip-like brains?
Oh, when we look back on the ages of ink,
We know them for people who taught us to think.
Honour the mentors, sarcastic or kind,
Who pricked us and spurred us and gave us a mind.
Honour the worthy and honour the keen,
Honour her daughters and honour Roedean!

Whether at school you were brilliant or dud,
Ev'n if you left in the days of the Flood,
If you achieve an iota of fame,
We all will remember and honour your name.
Honour the present and honour the past,
That the future may honour the present at last!
Honour the worthy and honour the keen,
Honour her daughters and honour Roedean!

Giants

They say, who were here long years ago,
In those wonderful days of old,
That life was loftier, time less slow,
Than now can be seen or told.
All of them were tall and slim,
And fleeter of foot and stronger of limb,
Glorious afield and bold to swim!
But we, compared to those figures dim,
Are cast in a pygmy mould.

Chorus: For all of we, whoever we be,
        Come short of those heroins old you see!

They were splendid cricketers then, they say,
And they love to repeat the names
Of Marjorie for Captain, Druce for play,
And others who won their games.
No one now can with Maggie compare,
Batters like Mead and Scott are rare.
And Brunner and Brown were a dauntless pair.
But now we are craven and nothing dare,
And fall short of their noble aims.

Chorus:

They were scholars of marvellous might, they say.
Yes! Scholars of marvellous force,
They all studied Latin and Greek, for play,
And the circle they squared, of course.
Euclid of some was the special bent,
And on six books much time was spent,
'Til with honours they to Newnham went!
But we in the first book rest content,
And ever grow duller and worse.

Chorus:

But I think this is all a lie, you know,
I think this is all a lie!
For the hero race may come and go,
But it doesn't exactly die.
For matches, we win them, and will again,
And a first class comes to us now and then,
And if we are feebler in body and brain,
Less ready in bearing or risking pain,
We'll have yet another try.

Chorus:

Forty Years On

Forty years on, when afar and asunder
Parted are those who are singing today,
When you look back, and forgetfully wonder
What you were like in your work and your play,
Then it may be, there will often come o'er you,
Glimpses of notes like the catch of a song –
Visions of schooldays shall float them before you,
Echoes of dreamland shall bear them along.

Chorus: Follow up! Follow up! Follow up!
        'Til the field ring again and again,
        With the tramp of the twenty two men.
        Follow up! Follow up! Follow up!

Routs and discomfitures, rushes and rallies,
Bases attempted and rescued and won,
Strife without anger, and art without malice,
How will it seem to you, forty years on?
Then, you will say, not a feverish minute
Strained the weak heart and the wavering knee,
Never the battle raged hottest, but in it,
Neither the last nor the faintest were we!

Chorus:

O the great days, in the distance enchanted,
Days of fresh air, in the rain and the sun,
How we rejoiced as we struggled and panted –
Hardly believable, forty years on!
How we discoursed of them, one with another,
Augering triumph, or balancing fate,
Loved the ally with the heart of a brother,
Hated the foe with a playing at hate!

Chorus:

Forty years on, growing older and older,
Shorter in wind, as in memory long,
Feeble of foot, and rheumatic of shoulder,
What will it help you that once you were strong?
God gives us bases to guard or beleaguer,
Cames to play out, whether earnest or fun;
Fights for the fearless, and goals for the eager,
Twenty, and thirty, and forty years on!

Chorus:

ARMS OF ROEDEAN SCHOOL

The Blazon: Per Fesse under Arg. and Az on a Mounte Vert a Hinde at gaze proper collared and chained Or to an open Boke and charged upon the Shoulder with a Grid-Yron of the last.

The Motto: Honneur aulx Dignes.

The Interpretation: Thys Mounte upon a field of Silver and Blewe parted by a waving line signifieth the Dene whereon sitteth the Schoole aspected southerlie to the sea and skye. And the Hinde is for the young gerles therein for they weare the Collare of wholesome Rule and are bound to the Boke of Lernynge by a golden Chaine of Kindnesse. Yet they are free to move about the Mounte soe they forsake not their Boke. And whereas the Hinde is charged upon her shoulder with the golden Griddiron of the blessed Saint Lawrence the Founder's Patron soe shall the gerles carry always thro' their lyves the mark of their Mistress' teachynge. Admire now the bidding of the motto to give honour to those who be worthy and Honour Roedean.